D0758668

Goin' Back to Sweet Memphis

Feels like Second and Beale

Goin' Back to Sweet Memphis

Conversations with the Blues

Transcribed, Edited, and Annotated by

Fred J. Hay

Illustrated by George D. Davidson

The University of Georgia Press   Athens and London

© 2001 by the University of Georgia Press

Athens, Georgia 30602

Interview text © 2001 by Fred J. Hay

Illustrations © 2001 by George D. Davidson

Designed by Kathi Dailey Morgan

Set in Minion and Vendome by G&S Typesetters

Printed and bound by Maple-Vail

The paper in this book meets the guidelines for

permanence and durability of the Committee on

Production Guidelines for Book Longevity of the

Council on Library Resources.

Printed in the United States of America

05 04 03 02 01 C 5 4 3 2 1

Library of Congress Cataloging-in-Publication Data

Hay, Frederick J., 1953 –

    Goin' back to sweet Memphis : conversations with the

    blues / transcribed, edited, and annotated by Fred. J. Hay ;

    illustrated by George D. Davidson.

       p.   cm.

    Discography: p.

    Includes bibliographical references (p.) and index.

    ISBN 0-8203-2301-2 (alk. paper)

       1. Blues musicians—Tennessee—Memphis—

Interviews.   2. Blues (Music)—Tennessee—Memphis

—History and criticism.   I. Title: Going back to sweet

Memphis.   II. Davidson, George D., 1952 – ill   III. Title.

ML394 .H42 2001

781.643'09768'19—dc21   2001027287

British Library Cataloging-in-Publication Data available

Dedicated in loving memory of Joe Willie and Carrie Wilkins

Sooner or later we shall have to get down to the humble task of exploring the depths of our consciousness and dragging to the light what sincere bits of reflected experience we can find. These bits will not always be beautiful, they will not always be pleasing, but they will be genuine. And then we can build. In time, in plenty of time—for we must have patience—a genuine culture—better yet, a series of linked autonomous cultures—will grace our lives.

—Edward Sapir

I think this Beale Street music we call the blues could in time constitute a rough foundation of a new American culture.

—George W. Lee

Contents

Illustrations

Between Dark and Break of Day

Preface

Feels like Second and Beale

More than twenty years have passed since I left Memphis, but the mark it left on me may as well have been a full-body tattoo, one with designs that have taken me decades to divine. When Fred suggested that I write a brief preface about how Memphis affected me, I begged off. After all, Fred was "the man." It was he who was a confirmed bluesnik before he even arrived on the campus of what was then known as Southwestern at Memphis (now Rhodes College). Unlike me, he went to Memphis with aspirations other than just getting a college degree. Fred went to Memphis because it was the preeminent capital of Delta blues, a wellspring of funkiness, and home to a clutch of full-bore blues legends.

My own knowledge of blues at the time was almost nil, and in 1970 the world as we knew it was rapidly becoming unhinged. Blues was the furthest thing from my exploding consciousness. I knew absolutely nothing about Memphis except that it was almost one thousand miles from my North Carolina home, and by the time I graduated from high school I was eager to test my wings in a place where I was a total stranger. But in 1970, if you were a young person in Memphis and had even the remotest interest in music, blues was just about impossible to ignore. In what would come to be called the second blues renaissance, or the second blues revival (the first being appended to the early '60s folk music scene), Memphis was reeling with an amazing array of performers, a veritable funkucopia. Bukka White, Furry Lewis, Memphis Piano Red, and others played frequently in clubs and beer joints—Hot Mama's on Lamar, Peanuts Bar in Midtown, and Celebration Space in Overton Square. Periodically, hot local blues acts performed at the Overton Park Shell.

In the fall of 1972, I answered a call for ushers at the Second Annual River City Blues Festival held in the old Ellis Auditorium downtown, where Rufus Thomas emceed the classic WDIA R&B shows. The performers that evening spanned Memphis's rich stylistic spectrum of blues, from string-band era to hard, electric, postwar Delta. I was quite impressed, but in many respects, I just didn't get it. I had grown up on soul music, or "beach music," and was unfamiliar with this more primitive, tougher, and rawer predecessor.

Nevertheless, by the time I became friends with Fred, I was eager to learn more from him about these powerful, percolating rhythms called blues. Fred tutored me, much as if I were his student. He patiently played me songs in various styles and guided me slowly from the obvious to the obscure. I'll never forget driving with Fred from Memphis to Dallas one year; I swear we must have listened to Blind Mamie Forehand's "I Wouldn't Mind Dying If Dying Was All" for a full five hundred miles. Fred was a true blues hound and scoured the thrift stores and junk stores for rare bird 78s and 45s. He also sniffed out and lured back into playing one of the most gifted and highly influential guitarists ever to play the instrument—Joe Willie Wilkins.

Joe and his wife, Carrie, effectively adopted Fred, even giving him a new handle, Gene. (Lord knows why. Fred always said they just thought he looked like a Gene.) And from 1972 to 1976 he practically lived with them, getting to know kith and kin, which in the blues vernacular meant he was *kin'*, as in the line from Chester Burnett, a.k.a. Howlin' Wolf, "you my color and you my kin'." Fred chalked up numerous "whammies," multiday parties where barbecue vied with tricksters, suds, and song.

Though I was never part of that scene, I did visit Joe and Carrie with Fred on several occasions. To this day, having since listened to a hell of a lot of blues, jazz, and rock guitarists, I can honestly say I have never heard Joe's equal. What he did on the guitar was flat-out necromancy. An artist of the highest order, he created audiotectonic palaces in the air. Listening to him with eyes shut, you'd swear three guitarists were playing rather than one. I haven't the slightest idea how he coaxed such a soulful sonic symphony from that glorious Gibson L5.

As I look back from midlife on my nonlinear process of artistic evolution, the most compelling feature is the Memphis connection. The formative exposure to the powerful medium of blues provided an unwavering foundation for a lifetime's exploration of and dedication to musical forms created by African American artists and visionaries. When I left Memphis in 1976, blues was just about all I listened to, with some exceptions, and it remained so until I discovered my second love, jazz, around 1980. At that time, my artistic focus was writing crazed Jung-cum-Dylan Beat poetry and bastard haiku. My wife, Jeanne Ann, was getting a graduate degree in printmaking at the University of Georgia, and I worked for a book typographer. At one Atlanta printer, I met a very cool art director, Charles F. Robertson, who had a small press called the Tinhorn Press in his basement. I shamelessly showed Chuck some of my work and mentioned my attempts to get published and the resulting mounting piles of rejection slips. He must have liked something about the poems, because he suggested that I buy a printing press and publish them myself and offered to show me how to get started. I think, in retrospect, he must have simply recognized a nut when he saw one because, sure enough, I purchased a 1920s Chandler and Price clamshell platen letterpress that weighed an even ton. Good as his word, Chuck became a wonderful mentor, encouraging and advising me, suggesting various fonts and materials to buy. I began laboriously setting my poems by hand, character by character, in a composing stick. Before printing the first one of them, I had already named this publishing endeavor the Blue Dog Press.

Seeing the work produced—if a bit amateurishly—on fine paper was gratifying, but something was missing. Jeanne Ann told me she would teach me how to make linoleum cuts to illustrate the poems and transform them into "broadsides." So, in 1979, I began carving linoleum and experimenting. I was never trained as an artist, and my work has always exhibited a somewhat crude or raw style. My very first print was a portrait of Joe Willie Wilkins. I must have carved it in a completely unconscious state, because it remains one of the best prints I have ever done. Often I've said that the ensuing twenty years have been spent trying to match its effortless grace. Shortly after finishing the portrait of Joe, I produced the Blue Dog Press's first broadside, an illustrated, double entendre blues song I wrote called "My Parking Meter Baby" ("keeps running out too quick / Why don't you see what you can do / to make my money stick"). The complete song appears on page xv.

Over time, I abandoned words and focused only on the images. By the early 1980s, my work expanded to include new avenues of interpretation. I began making small votive shrines, "honkey *retablos*," which incorporated colorful backdrops and found objects. Eventually these retablos took on a more collagelike appearance; today I use international stamps and money and old postcards as well as found objects and "gris-gris" items to fashion these constructions.

The other avenue I began to explore at that time was learning to play the saxophone. Like that of my visual art, my saxophone education has been jaggedly idiosyncratic. It's fair to say that I'm self-taught. I learned by playing along with records and slowly began playing with other musicians. Today, after eighteen years, I enjoy playing jazz gigs as a hobby. We play small-band swing and hard bop in clubs, restaurants, and coffee houses for weddings, parties, and functions. It is a demanding hobby requiring regular practice, but it is one that rewards with the occasional ineffable performance, when the music is more than the sum of the musicians. Countless gigs in dim, greasy bars where your feet stick to the floor have helped educate me about the dubious lot of musicians everywhere. These experiences have also helped to authenticate what once was merely a secondhand understanding of the vagaries of band life, the unpredictable rhythms of performance.

The common element in these divergent artistic expressions is music, specifically blues and jazz. As a thematic vision, African American music has served as inspiration for the body of my work dating back to my first attempts. Many of the prints and retablos specifically have been celebratory tributes to musicians. Often the constructions tell "stories," imaginary mytho-poetic tales of sacrifice, challenge, and triumph.

Memphis made its way into my life again in 1992 when Naomi Kojima, an old friend from college, called with an offer to do a blues book for a Japanese publisher. Naomi, a well-known children's book artist and author in Tokyo, had shown some of my prints to her publisher, and the company wanted to do a series of prints accompanied by blues songs associated with the artists depicted (with, challengingly enough, Japanese translations). The resulting book, Carvin' the Blues, was published in 1994 by Libroport Publishers. This was the first occasion Fred Hay and I had to collaborate: he guided the song selection process and provided insight into picking little-known gems as well as several classics. The Japanese designer did an elegant job, and the book turned out beautifully. Fred advised me where to archive the few copies I was able to acquire. Long out-of-print, the book was a dream project, and I appreciated the publisher's belief in my work.

When I first began using musicians as inspiration for my art, it was hardly a "cool" thing to do. Blues music was not particularly popular then, nor was jazz enjoying the relative acclaim it does today. I simply followed my heart. It is said that writers must write what they know. I believe artists must interpret what they feel, and if the feeling is deep and abiding, then that sensibility will be conveyed in the work, much as a writer successfully evokes what is most dear to him or her. Why would a reasonably well educated, southern white boy make art about black music? Who knows, really. It's sort of like Ida Cox sang—"early this mornin' / the blues came walking in my room." To me it's just the Memphis connection. I went there at that time and it "did" me. That's all. Memphis is a city so deep in the funk, it evokes an image of one of the serpentine Mississippi's oxbow lakes, a figure scoured into the land and left by the passage of time to be itself—in Memphis's case, a fount of deep blue feeling that endures outside the constraints of late-twentieth-century commercial excess.

I have not been back to Memphis in more than fifteen years. I may never return. An old friend, artist, and writer was born there and returned recently to visit family. "The party is still going on," she said when I asked her what it was like nowadays. "It's like you never left." *Yeah, Memphis is a hound town, I've since thought to myself. It can't get up for getting down!*

My Parking Meter Baby

My parkin' meter baby
keeps running out too quick
Why don't you see what you can do
to make my money stick.

Parkin' meter baby
Parkin' meter fine
Don't tell me this is a tow-away zone
I park here all the time.

My parkin' meter baby
My parkin' meter maid
keeps handing out free tickets
just like Christmas every day.

Parkin' meter baby
Parkin' meter fine
Don't tell me this is a tow-away zone
I park there all the time.

Parkin' meter baby
Runnin' in the red
if I'm that long overdue
I might as well be dead.

Parkin' meter baby
Parkin' meter fine
Don't tell me this is a tow-away zone
I park here all the time.

George D. Davidson

Gus Cannon

Introduction

Goin' Back to Sweet Memphis

Well, if that's yo' man, you'd better buy a lock an' key, O babe! (2×)
And stop yo' man from runnin' after me-e-e.

Well, I goin' back to sweet Memphis, Tennessee, O babe! (2×)
Where de good-lookin' wimmins take on over me—make a fuss over me.

Now, a good-lookin' man can git a home anywaher' he go,
The reason why is, the wimmins tell me so.

She change a dollar an' give me a lovin' dime,
I'll see her when her trouble like mine.

—anonymous itinerant singer, Lafayette County, Mississippi, early 1900s

Memphis, on the fourth Chickasaw Bluff of the Mississippi River, was built at a place where the Chickasaw Indians would not live because they considered it unhealthy (the land along the river "leaked too much" [Roper 1970, 40]). Yet, the bluff was an important river port and hunting ground for the Chickasaw, and they had no desire to sign away their rights to this land. But they did. A new town was created about 1820 by entrepreneurs such as Andrew Jackson and James Winchester. Memphis was named after the Egyptian capital on the Nile River, and over a century and a half later, Memphis, Tennessee, even constructed its own pyramid (a sports arena).

Memphis is the capital city of the Mississippi Delta, which stretches out south and west of the city in the states of Mississippi and Arkansas. Actually, the Mississippi Delta is not the Mississippi River's delta but an alluvial floodplain of rich black soil and poor black people. This Delta of which Memphis is the primate city is not really of Tennessee at all but of these adjacent states. Memphians like to say that the Delta really starts in the lobby of the Peabody Hotel on Union Avenue and Second Street.

Memphis is a peculiar place where the Delta and hill and river folk come together. Although considerable interpersonal distance and frequent hostility exist between black and white people, Memphis is also a place where their ways have intermingled to a greater extent than elsewhere in the South. It is a place that gave us such peculiarly American institutions as the first supermarket (Piggly Wiggly) and motel chain (Holiday Inn) and that most peculiarly American of all cultural products, rock 'n' roll.

But before there could be rock 'n' roll, there was, there had to be, the blues. Memphis was a hotbed and a crossroads of the blues and of the South—river transportation met the convergence of three different railroad lines, and different styles of black music mixed to create a distinctive Memphis sound of blues and blues-drenched jug band music. During the first half of this century, Beale Street was the center of blues activity in Memphis. In the words of Beale Street chroniclers and personalities George W. Lee and Nat D. Williams, "Beale Street ain't nuthin' but de Blues an' de blues ain't nuthin' but Beale Street carryin' on" (Fox 1959, 132).

Beale Street, originally lined with fancy, white-owned mansions, began to change in character after so many whites died or fled the city because of a series of yellow fever epidemics. In 1899, African American businessman Robert R. Church Sr. purchased six acres of land on Beale and created Church Park and Auditorium. Beale Street quickly developed as a commercial strip for the African American community. Church hired W. C. Handy to direct the park's band, and Beale Street became the entertainment center of the black mid-South, featuring great jazz, blues, and jug band music in the concert halls and honky-tonks and on the streets. In this semifrontier river town—the town with the highest murder rate in the country—Beale Street also became the center for vice, for both black and white, for the entire region. Indeed, it was said "no other street in Memphis can vie with the colored thoroughfare for renown" (Fox 1959, 128).[1]

Memphis on the Mississippi: Blues Hearth

Blues music is an African American cultural product. Generated out of West African musical concepts—those primarily from what German ethnomusicologist Gerhard Kubik labeled the "West Central Sudanic Style Cluster"—the blues form evolved only in the southern United States. The most African of the early blues styles were those found in the Mississippi Delta of Mississippi and Arkansas and the Mississippi Hill Country adjacent to the Delta. It was this most African (and to the western ear most dissonant) of blues styles that came to dominate the future evolution of the blues genre.[2] The blues evolved in uniquely American ways but never lost their African character: "Blues is an African-American tradition that developed under certain social conditions on U.S. American soil, in the Deep South . . . yet it is a phenomenon belonging essentially to the African culture world" (Kubik 1999, 197). In Memphis, these early African-derived styles crossbred and amalgamated with other types of African American music, evolving into the prevailing strain of what is now known worldwide as the blues.

All of the important urban blues centers of the postbellum South were crossroads where people and musical styles came together, coexisted, blended. But in none of these other southern cities (not in Atlanta, Nashville, Birmingham, Dallas, or even in New Orleans, which had the added influence of Caribbean and Latin American rhythms) did such a mingling of black people and styles take place as it did in Memphis, Tennessee. Here merged the distinctive sounds that migrated to Memphis from what William Barlow called three "rural blues hotbeds" (1989, 202): northeast of Memphis in the Brownsville/Jackson area (e.g., Tommy Gary), the northeastern Mississippi Hill Country (Boose Taylor), and the Mississippi Delta (Bukka White). The mixing of these rural blues styles in Memphis joined rather than replaced the urban black music that already thrived in the city—its blues and ragtime piano (every joint on Beale Street once featured a piano player), jazz and brass bands (W. C. Handy, Jimmie Lunceford), "classic" vaudeville blues of female vocalists (Memphis Ma Rainey), the gospel singing and preaching of street evangelists and churchgoers (Memphis has an equally rich but even less well-documented tradition of gospel music), and its own indigenous guitar blues (Furry Lewis).

There were other influences as well. The music of New Orleans and St. Louis came with the riverboats and their cotton, roustabouts, dry goods, and prostitutes. The interior regions of the South were also tapped through the railroads that networked virtually the entire South through Memphis, and from the traveling shows, large and small, that played Beale Street's parks and theaters. Beale Street, as the river-town tenderloin section and the mid-South's primary African American commercial district, had a greater mix of peoples—rural and urban, rich and poor, black and white (including the Greek, Italian, and Jewish merchants and bar owners and the local whites who

patronized the brothels and white-only performances by black entertainers)
—than existed anywhere else.

This "savory pot of gumbo," as William Barlow described the making of
Memphis blues (1989, 202), gave it a fuller tone (more "bottom"), a richer
and more varied repertoire of sounds and styles, a lighter and more playful
(but always raucous) feel than the blues music associated with any other place.
Its blending of so many diverse styles of music; its technical sophistication as
well as its capacity for expressing the rawest emotion; and its flexibility, elas-
ticity, and inclusiveness make Memphis blues nearly impossible to describe in
concrete terms. It is a prime example of the creative amorphousness and
resilience that typify African-derived cultures throughout the Americas.[3]

The blues of Memphis, in the years preceding World War II, included all
the distinctive strains, cadences, and instrumental techniques of the original
ingredients that collectively made up the savory gumbo, but also a number of
new sounds resulting from the different combinations and medleys of the
various ingredients. Each bowl of gumbo from the common pot had its
unique proportions of this and that. An outstanding example of one of these
new sounds, distinctively Afro-Memphis, is the jug band.

Although jug bands existed in various places throughout the South in the
early years of the twentieth century, the Memphis jug bands were unique in
their bluesiness and Africanness. Early jug bands seemed (no actual recordings exist) to have played music similar in nature to the rural string-band music played by both white and black musicians (though the latter were often
more funky), but with the addition of a jug bass. In the Louisville/Cincinnati
area, jug bands added the innovation of brass and woodwind instruments and
jazz phrasing. Recordings of the Louisville jug bands were quite popular in the
1920s, and in an effort to capitalize on this trend, Memphis musician Will
Shade formed his own jug band, the Memphis Jug Band (Little Laura Dukes
was a member). Others soon followed: Cannon's Jug Stompers, Jack Kelly's
South Memphis Jug Band (Kelly also worked with Boose Taylor), and Jed
Davenport's Beale Street Jug Band. These jug bands were a mainstay of the
Memphis entertainment world (popular with both black and white audiences) for decades. Music journalist Bruce Cook observed that if there was
anything that was singularly a "Memphis Sound" (a phrase used by Stax, a
1960s soul label, to market their records), "it originated with the rhythmic
rumbles that issued forth from those Beale Street jugs" (1973, 121).[4]

Jug bands were only one manifestation of the variety of Memphis blues music in the 1920s and 1930s. And the Memphis Jug Band itself had a frequently changing lineup of musicians. Furry Lewis, who performed with the band, also played slide guitar and sang as a solo act or as a duet with other local guitarists, worked as a substitute in W. C. Handy's dance band, and traveled with medicine shows as a blues performer and comedian. The versatility of the Memphis blues has always sustained it.

Again, after World War II—and definitely on the coattails of Helena, Arkansas, radio station KFFA's extremely popular daily show, the King Biscuit Time (whose performers included Joe Willie Wilkins and Houston Stackhouse) —Africa, by way of the Delta, reasserted itself in the blues music of Memphis / West Memphis. It was this music, and in many cases these musicians, that moved north and popularized the sound that was later labeled the "Chicago blues," the "Detroit blues," and so on. And still later it was this music combined with gospel, mellifluous West Coast blues, and Memphis jazz (including the musicianship of such Memphis jazz luminaries as Phineas Newborn and George Coleman) that was the basis of what anthropologist Charles Keil referred to as the "Memphis Synthesis" (1966). The synthesized music—performed by such Beale Street personalities as B. B. King, Junior Parker, Bobby "Blue" Bland, and others—popularized blues with new audiences and became the source of many of the techniques and stylistic components that were later central to the development of rock 'n' roll and soul music. The Memphis Synthesis was disseminated daily over Memphis radio station WDIA—the nation's first radio station that featured all black-oriented programming— and through record companies based in Memphis (Sun), Chicago (Chess), California (the Bihari Brothers family of labels including Modern and RPM), and Houston (Duke). The Memphis Synthesis was to be Beale Street's last great contribution to the world.

Beale Street 1971: Blues Besieged

I arrived in Memphis in the fall of 1971 to attend Southwestern at Memphis College. I chose Southwestern (now Rhodes College), in part, because of its location in Memphis and Memphis's association with the blues. While still in high school, like so many other middle-class kids from around the world, I acquired records by Blind Lemon Jefferson, Robert Johnson, Bessie Smith, Muddy Waters, Big Joe Williams, B. B. King, and others and read blues books by the likes of Paul Oliver, Sam Charters, and Zora Neale Hurston. My high school in northern Georgia had been recently and violently integrated, and the older blues in addition to the popular soul, psychedelic rock, and country music provided meaningful context.

On a hot, sunny Saturday afternoon, soon after I had arrived in Memphis, a few of us freshmen decided it was time to see world-famous Beale Street. We arrived too late; Beale Street had been razed. Where there had once been shops, bars, cafés, funeral homes, dry cleaners, barber shops, churches, professional offices, music halls, and other businesses, there were empty, boarded-up buildings and vacant, litter-strewn lots. Where once people from all levels of African American society mingled together at the mid-South's primary black business and entertainment center, only a few lonely winos, drinking from bottles and cans in brown paper bags, remained. Sure, Club Handy was still there, but it was closed. Handy Park with its namesake's famous statue remained, but no musicians gathered there. Some pawn shops, a few bars, and A. Schwab's Department Store were all that was left of Beale Street.

We walked the streets, visited the pawn shops, explored Schwab's (especially the conjure section with its herbs, powders, potions, and dream books), went in a couple of bars and had a beer, shot a game of pool. At one bar we were threatened by a man; he put his clenched fist next to my head and demanded money. We refused him and he backed off.

What had happened? Where was the music? The crowds? We learned later that those white people in charge, in the governments of Memphis and Washington, D.C., had purposely destroyed Beale Street, using as their cover Urban Renewal—a federal program created to help poor people and revive decayed urban areas. (The similarity to what U.S. international aid programs have sometimes accomplished in third world countries—such as USAID's much too successful efforts to replace subsistence horticulture with monocrop-for-export agriculture in Haiti, the hemisphere's poorest, hungriest country, or the devastation caused by the implementation of "green revolution" ideology and practices in the adjacent Mississippi Delta—should not go unnoticed here.)

For about a hundred years, black Beale Street was vibrant and bustling. Only about a mile and a half in length, this east-west thoroughfare, immortalized in song by W. C. Handy and others, was "gorged with traffic. . . . Sidewalks were filled with displays of clothes, racks of shoes, and swarms of people. Pullers hovered in front of pawn shops and dry goods stores trying to attract customers. Street vendors sold a variety of foods. . . . Peddlers pushed their carts. . . . Farmers in overalls, in town to do their Saturday shopping, boarded their horses and wagons. . . . Handy Park echoed with the rhythmic pulse of preachers and bluesmen, as well as the awkward shuffle of winos. . . . After dark, the attention of the crowd shifted to the theaters, dance halls, and restaurants which lit up the street" (Raichelson 1994, 1–2).

Beale Street was the center, the heart, of black Memphis and the black mid-South. It was the hub for black business, religion, entertainment, politics, and civil rights activity. In the oppressive and dangerous Jim Crow South, Beale Street and the surrounding neighborhood was a place where black people could gather and be themselves and celebrate their community and culture. Saxophonist Edward "Prince Gabe" Kirby wrote that "Beale Street was the only street a black man could feel free on" (1983, 66).

In 1959, at the height of Elvis Presley's popularity, and long after his Beale Street clothes and influences had been widely publicized, Mayor Edmund Orgill announced that Beale Street would be transformed into a major tourist attraction. (But the transformation of the street had begun even earlier; Maude Greene wrote in 1941 of a "Beale before it was WPA'd into respectability" [1941, 4].) Before Beale Street could be transformed it had to be destroyed, and the Memphis Housing Authority (MHA) was given this charge. Following the riots in the aftermath of Martin Luther King Jr.'s assassination at the Lorraine Motel on nearby Mulberry Street, the MHA was able to speed up this process. Urban Renewal—"a better name would have been urban removal" (Kirby 1983, 71)—destroyed the heart of the black community; dispersed its residents, businesses and services, and musicians; and bulldozed its buildings. Urban Renewal demolished 474 buildings and "placed a blockwide barrier of empty lots and parking spaces between African Americans and Beale Street" (Lovett 1998, 54). Eventually the remaining black-owned businesses were forced out through condemnation and high resale prices. In 1979, long after the corpse was cold, the *Memphis Press-Scimitar* declared the obvious: "Urban Renewal destroyed Beale Street" (Lovett 1998, 53).

Beale Street 1999: Spurious Blues

In the spring of 1999, my family and I returned to Memphis to see what Beale Street had become. Before going to Beale, I drove my wife and son by a few of my old haunts: Bukka White's "office" and the site of Furry Lewis's duplex on Mosby Street, and harmonica blower/sign painter Coy "Hot Shot"

Love's small, one-room, second-floor apartment (shared with three women friends), which contained a double bed, an old refrigerator, a hot plate, and stacks of clothes and other goods. We went on to Carpenter Street in North Memphis and the neighborhood of Joe Willie Wilkins's extended family. We saw Joe's house, where I had spent so many hours hanging out, doing repairs, and talking to musicians such as Walter Horton, Floyd Jones, James Cotton, Calvin Valentine, and Woodrow Adams. On Warford Street, a block from Wilkins's house, recent widening of the street had caused the leveling of Joe Hill Louis's (the "Be-Bop Boy") former residence. The barber shop around the corner on Chelsea Avenue, where Houston Stackhouse had spent so many hours playing checkers, was also gone.

We had reservations at the King's Court Hotel on Union Avenue—turns out that it's the former TraveLodge Hotel next to the bus station. (For which king is King's Court named—Elvis, Martin Luther, Albert, B.B.? Or is it named after the true king of Memphis, its BBQ?) Now owned and being renovated by an Indian family (and what delicious cooking aromas emanated from their quarters behind the check-in desk), most of the rooms at the King's Court were in sad shape. Our room, with its peeling paint, stained carpet, lumpy and sagging mattresses, smoke alarm and cable TV connections wrenched from their wall sockets and hanging by a wire, was all that was available because our pilgrimage to Beale coincided with the Promise Keepers's pilgrimage to the Memphis Pyramid Arena. The Promise Keepers got to the better rooms first and were among the hundreds of visitors with cameras and camcorders who crowded us out of the way when we stopped by to watch the ducks promenade, on their red carpet, across the Peabody Hotel's lobby. The Promise Keepers, their minds no doubt on other matters, were not a significant presence that evening on Beale Street.

Around the corner from the Peabody, on Second Street, is the Memphis Music Hall of Fame. The Museum, laid out in roughly chronological fashion, starts with the slave trade and then moves on to the blues but devotes greater space and detail to soul and especially to rockabilly. Owned by a local attorney, this museum has collected an impressive array of materials and some very fine artifacts, but Memphis jazz is largely ignored and the blues exhibit is egregiously and misleadingly selective. For instance, the great Bukka White is not mentioned, and the only representation of Joe Willie Wilkins is in a group photo of the King Biscuit Entertainers. Yet, it was Wilkins who was the primary architect of the blues guitar sound of postwar Memphis and the Delta, a sound copied by the white rockabillies to whom the museum dedicates so much space and attention. And both White and Wilkins were important mentors for B. B. King, the blues musician most celebrated by the museum.

Beale Street itself was not familiar; it has been rebuilt as a tourist attraction. Handy Park was still there, and so was Schwab's (though the store had added a lot of tourist-related merchandise). But most of the buildings were new and, from B. B. King's Club to the Hard Rock Café (site formerly of P. Wee's Saloon, where legend has it that W. C. Handy scribbled out the words of what was to become the "Memphis Blues") to Willie Mitchell's Rhythm 'n' Blues Club, more white musicians than black were performing generic blues for generic American tourists (it could just as well have been Myrtle Beach, Disney World, or San Antonio's River Walk). The most interesting music, not surprisingly, was being performed for voluntary contributions in Handy Park.

Beale Street is now blocked off to traffic. Visitors can buy draft beer or mixed drinks from numerous sidewalk vendors and wander from shop to club to restaurant with their plastic cups. Police are now a noticeable presence and panhandlers are scarce—found only on the fringes away from the law and the more prosperous businesses. It is a street that honors Stevie Ray Vaughan and Eric Clapton with the same enthusiasm that it does Frank Stokes, Howlin' Wolf, and Memphis Minnie. Beale Street is static, not dynamic like the real music scene in Memphis and the Delta. Real Memphis music is an experience that today's Beale Street denies. Of the many shops on Beale that sell blues music, not one had recordings by currently active Memphis-based blues musicians like Big Lucky Carter or Little Jimmy King. Instead, the shops carried the music of those far removed from Memphis by either physical distance or death.

Robert Henry, former Beale Street business proprietor, said, "They declared Beale Street a shrine, wasn't nothing to be done about it, just keep it a shrine" (Yale 1978, 38). Beale Street is not a shrine to the blues but, like most popular American attractions, is a shrine to consumer culture. It flattens that which is layered, conceals that which is distinctive, dulls that which is brilliant, and glitters that which is subdued. It celebrates sameness and slights diversity. Generic American culture (or generic global culture, for that matter) is, in the words of Clyde Kluckhohn, "hostile to nuances" (1949, 269). The blues peddled on Beale Street today are without nuance. Yet, nuance is the essence of the blues. Contemporary Beale Street blues, no matter how well performed, is culturally spurious. It has been made safe for America but has lost much of its social meaning and no longer serves the vital role it once played in sustaining African American culture. Beale's new blues is, in Angela Davis's words, a "violation of the spirit of the blues" (1998, 61).

Which is the worse fate for a community—being destroyed and replaced by something entirely different (like what happened on Maxwell Street in Chicago or Hastings Street in Detroit) or being co-opted into a shrine to American banality? Which is the worse fate—complete erasure, or a Beale Street "toned-down, cleaned-up, and guaranteed safe for the white, middle-class tourist," a Beale Street transformed into "the white man's fantasy of black culture"? (Bowman 1977, 76). In the spring of 1999 I also visited Hastings Street, another place that Urban Renewal had destroyed, another dispersal of a neighborhood and scattering of a community of musicians. Most of Hastings had been bulldozed to make way for an expressway, but a few blocks still exist. (Several African American cab drivers refused to take me there. Eventually a white Appalachian expatriate from Tennessee agreed to give me passage to that street once made famous by the music of black migrants from another distinctive and purposely and systematically impoverished but culturally rich southern region, the Mississippi Delta.) Those remaining blocks were truly desolate, and the only living beings I saw appeared to be engaged in illegal transactions.

Destroy the Street, Steal the Culture: The Saga of Gus Cannon and "Walk Right In"

Born in 1883, Gus Cannon was one of the oldest of the first generation of black musicians to record commercially. The material he performed was a diverse mixture of old fiddle songs, minstrel show pieces, rags, and blues. Cannon's recorded repertoire was typical of the music played by southern, especially rural, black musicians in the early years of the twentieth century, before the blues became the dominant, secular performance genre in African American culture.

Cannon's music had deep roots in Africa. Both blues researcher Sam Charters (1993, 15–16) and ethnomusicologist Harold Courlander (1970, 298) have commented on the similarity of Cannon's banjo playing to that of the West African *halam*. (For Courlander, this was especially true of Cannon's version of "Old John Booker," the first song Cannon learned.) "Gus Cannon played banjo passages that resembled in pitch, pattern, rhythm, and tempo the sounds produced on West African lutes" (1970, 214). And David Evans even interpreted Cannon's jug blowing as an African cultural survival: "The jug and kazoo. . . . were derived from African 'voice disguisers,' which were used frequently in connection with masked rituals to represent spirit voices" (1993, 39).

But Cannon was also an innovator. As the leader of the best of Memphis's great jug bands, Cannon's impact on American music was profound. Old-time country musicians such as Sam and Kirk McGee studied Cannon's early records (Burton 1981, 131), and folk revivalists such as the Rooftop Singers learned Cannon's songs from commercially released field recordings made in the mid-1950s. It was the Rooftop Singers's recording of Cannon's composition "Walk Right In" in 1963 that rose to the top spot on *Billboard*'s sales chart, bringing Cannon new recognition and some much-needed cash. Other folk revivalist and rock 'n' roll groups followed—from the Lovin' Spoonful to the Grateful Dead—recording their own versions of Cannon's and the Jug Stompers's songs.

In 1927, Cannon went to Chicago, in the company of fellow medicine show veterans Jim Jackson and Furry Lewis, to audition for Vocalion Records's Mayo Williams. Williams sent Cannon to Paramount Records, where he recorded six songs, either solo or accompanied by guitar wizard Blind Blake. The songs were released under his old medicine show moniker "Banjo Joe." He also accompanied Blind Blake on his classic recording of "He's in the Jail House Now."

The following year, Cannon, Noah Lewis, and Ashley Thompson recorded for Victor as the Cannon Jug Stompers. On future Jug Stompers recordings, Elijah Avery or Hosea Woods replaced Thompson, but the brilliant harmonica player Lewis and the jug and banjo rhythms of Cannon were constant features of the Cannon Jug Stompers's recordings. In 1929, Cannon also recorded as a duo with Hosea Woods for Brunswick as the Beale Street Boys. Between January 1928 and November 1930, Victor released twenty-six songs recorded by the Cannon Jug Stompers. The Brunswick session with Woods resulted in one released record.

From 1930 until Sam Charters's historic visit to Memphis in 1956, Cannon continued to play either solo or in small jug band ensembles, on the streets or for white parties. Charters taped some of Cannon's repertoire, which subsequently saw release on a Folkways anthology. These were Cannon's first known recordings since 1930. Cannon recorded a limited edition LP for the fledgling Stax label in 1963 and recorded his last commercial sides for Adelphi in 1969 (one song each on their anthologies *On the Road Again* and *Memphis Blues Again, Vol. 1*).

Cannon states on his Stax LP that he and Hosea Woods commenced to playing "Walk Right In" in 1913 out on the Macon Road (on the outskirts of Memphis). He also made a statement about the song's origin. Samuel Charters reports that Cannon told him the following version of the story in the late 1950s: "I went to an old lady's house one day, and she told me, 'walk right in.' She said, 'Well, will you sit down?' Said, 'Thank you, ma'am.' . . . And so that night . . . I commenced to dreamin'. . . . So I got hold of my old banjo. I said, 'You know one thing Bessie? You told me to walk in here. Now you know I'm gonna get somethin' or other on that'" (1977, 38). (This text was not, as Charters states, reprinted from his 1959 book *The Country Blues,* but was apparently transcribed from Cannon's Stax LP. Bengt Olsson also quotes this passage without attribution in his 1970 book.)

In 1963, when "Walk Right In" was a hit for the Rooftop Singers on Vanguard Records, Charters, Maynard Solomon of Vanguard, and a copyright lawyer flew to Memphis. Solomon got Cannon's banjo from the pawn shop and bought him coal to heat his house. They took Cannon to the courthouse to make statements and were able to get Cannon "composer's royalties for the song" and "a small income from it over the years" (Charters 1977, 41). (The copyright holder was Southern Music Company, the company for which Ralph Peer of Victor Records published the songs he recorded for the label.) The rumor in Memphis in the early 1970s was that the group visiting from New York City bought Cannon's interest in "Walk Right In" for $500. I have never discovered any evidence confirming this rumor. In fact, Olsson quoted Cannon as saying that "one day, when I had gotten some royalties for 'Walk Right In,' I went out to get a beer down around Beale. When I was there someone must have heard about me having all that money, so they followed after me when I walked home, and tried to rob me" (1970, 54). In 1973, Olsson wrote that "Sam Charters said that Gus got BMI royalties for airplay but never anything for each copy sold, since he had 'signed away' his royalties in 1929, consequently leaving the royalty rights to RCA Victor" (4).

Time magazine reported in its April 5, 1963, issue that for "publishers' rights to the song Vanguard Records gave him $500, plus the promise of a one-third cut in royalties if all goes well." In an article in the February 16, 1963, issue of the *Memphis Commercial Appeal,* K. W. Cook stated that the rights were purchased by Willard Svanoe and Erik Darling, "the two men whose name appears on the record's label as the song's authors" and that their publisher, Ryerson Music, was also party to the agreement with Cannon. In this article, Cannon got $500 and one-fourth of the royalties. Cook quotes Cannon as saying, "That man from New York told me I'd get a check every month. This is for 20 years and I can renew it if I want to."

The person working behind the scenes in an effort to get Cannon his due appears to have been John Quincy Wolf (the same Professor Wolf who had Cannon's last jug fabricated in the machine shop at Rhodes College, where he taught). According to Gene Hyde, Wolf's widow, Bess, remembered how he had convinced a Memphis lawyer to work pro bono on Cannon's behalf (1998). And in the Wolf Papers at Lyon College there is a letter, dated March 7, 1963, in which Alan Lomax responds to an earlier letter from Wolf addressing ways in which Wolf could help Cannon obtain his royalties. (The Wolf Papers also include a letter from NBC News anchorman David Brinkley thanking Wolf for his suggestion for doing a story on Cannon.)

According to Robert Gordon, in the early 1960s white Memphis musician Jim Dickinson used Sam Charters's 1959 book *The Country Blues* to track down Gus Cannon. He found Cannon working as a yardman and living in a room above his employer's garage. "He took us up into his room, and on the wall he had a certificate for sales from 'Walk Right In,' for which of course he didn't get any money. And he had a copy of the record that Charters had made for Folkways, but he had no record player. That was a real good introduction to the blues" (Gordon 1995, 78).

Fred Davis wrote in 1968 that when the Rooftop Singers hit big with "Walk Right In" in 1963 Cannon was "really down and out." Gus was "quite elderly now, and had pawned his banjo to buy firewood to heat his rundown shack. He was too weak to cut wood himself. After the initial notoriety of the song, Jimmy Stewart, owner of Stax, went over to Cannon's shack, put 500 dollars in his hands and told him to come over to the studio for a session." The musicians that Stewart had lined up to accompany Cannon did not work with Cannon's old-fashioned style, so two old-time jug band musicians were brought in and helped Cannon make "a sound that is really archaic" (1971a, 145).

Stax Records historian Rob Bowman wrote that neither Jimmy Stewart nor his sister Estelle remembers much about the Cannon LP. Estelle recalled that Cannon lived in the neighborhood and would often visit her Satellite Record Shop. Jim remembered that Atlantic did not pick up the distribution rights to the LP and that Stax pressed only about five hundred copies. He recalled that "it was really difficult to work with him. He wasn't really all there because of his age." A *Time* magazine article was more upbeat. It noted that "an English professor named John Quincy Wolf stood by as a consultant on ethnic authenticity" ("I'm a Yard Man" 1963). Stax issued three LPs in 1963: Stax 704 *Walking the Dog* by Rufus Thomas, and two LPs numbered Stax 702 —Cannon's *Walk Right In* and the anthology *Treasured Hits from the South* (Bowman 1997, 45).

Corporations and white entrepreneurs stole the music and the poetry (and the revenue they created), governments destroyed Beale Street (and Hastings Street, Maxwell Street, and so on), and then "liberal" journalists and cultural commentators re-created cultural history in their own image. Consider, for example, how Gus Cannon is used in music journalist Robert Gordon's well-received 1995 book. In *It Came from Memphis* (a book described in a dust jacket blurb as one in which "Gus Cannon is more important than Elvis" but that contains very little information on Cannon or any blues musician while giving extensive coverage to white, and often obscure, local performers), Gordon reports that Cannon told young white musician Jim Dickinson in the early 1960s that he had learned his material "from the radio." "'It really surprised me,' recalls Dickinson. 'That's where I learned stuff. These guys had learned it exactly the way we had'" (78–79). The first commercial radio broadcast was in November 1920. Most all the songs in Cannon's repertoire predate that event; "Feather Bed," recorded by Cannon's Jug Stompers, even predates the Civil War. The sad fact is that Dickinson rather than Cannon is the star of Gordon's book, and the cameo roles of Cannon, Furry Lewis, and other blues musicians are included in a ludicrous attempt to legitimize Dickinson and his associates as the *real* Memphis musicians.

One need not wonder why Cannon told us in 1972, "I just showing y'all I got be a huckleberry at a bird meeting."[5]

Genuine Blues: The Blues in Black and White

It is ironic then that the blues, a music which so many feel familiar with, is probable the most misunderstood product of African American culture.—Dwight D. Andrews

Nineteen ninety-eight was an exceptional year for blues scholarship. The two most insightful analyses of the blues yet published appeared in this year: Angela Davis's *Blues Legacies and Black Feminism: Gertrude "Ma"*

Rainey, Bessie Smith, and Billie Holiday and Clyde Woods's *Development Arrested: Race, Power, and the Blues in the Mississippi Delta*. What Davis and Woods have in common, other than being African Americans writing on a topic dominated by whites ("the guild-like fraternity of White Black music scholars" [Woods 1998, 38]), is their understanding of the crucial social role played by the blues.

Terms like "blues consciousness" and "blues epistemology" are used by these scholars to describe the indigenous knowledge system that enabled the creation of community and the survival of a people. Davis explains how blues evolved and empowered, from the turbulence of emancipation through Reconstruction, the institution of Jim Crow, and the onset of the Great Depression. Woods documents the same process, from the reestablishment of the Delta Plantocracy through the Clinton administration. The discussion of the blues presented in these two books is much too involved and far reaching to be adequately summarized here, but they should be considered mandatory reading for anyone with an interest in the subject.

The blues, according to Davis and Woods, embody a fully developed philosophy and worldview, and these deceptively simple songs are in fact layered with subtle and complex meanings. For instance, Davis discusses the political, social, and spiritual resonances of the sexuality portrayed and celebrated in the blues. Accepted at face value, these blues would seem to be about only sex and desire, yet, in reality, they often express a full range of the complexities of African American social organization and African Diaspora worldview. These same songs performed by individuals from outside the African American cultural tradition do not convey these deeper meanings and sometimes seem simply vulgar, sometimes ludicrous.[6] (Woods appropriately refers to *The Blues Brothers* as "minstrel film.")

Blues musician and author Julio Finn observed that it is ignorance of the "spirit of the blues" that has been the source of so much distortion and inaccuracy in the blues literature. He claims that blues researchers have "invariably asked the wrong questions. These have been historical and sociological; they should have been psychological and spiritual" (1986, 1). Many authors (e.g., Cone 1972 and Hay 1981) have commented on the superficial similarities between worship in the African American church and participation in the blues performance, but Finn does not limit himself to a comparison of these two African-influenced cultural institutions. Instead, he examines the blues in the larger historical context of the African Diaspora in the Americas.

Finn bases his discussion of blues evolution on respected historical and anthropological scholarship in which Catholic Latin America is depicted as less dedicated to the forced eradication of all things African than was Protestant North America. Furthermore, Catholic cosmology allowed for a "syncretism" of Christian and African religious belief and practice (for example, the identification of African deities with Catholic saints) not possible within the more severe and less flexible Protestantism of the United States.[7] Instead, African psychic/spiritual life had to be "reinterpreted" in the guise of Anglo-American culture.[8] Just as the African spirit-possession trance was in the United States reinterpreted as a personal visitation by Christianity's Holy Ghost, other aspects of the African worldview were expressed in the blues, an audacious music often imbued with a supernatural, if not always heavenly, allure. It was only in British America, where Africans' spirituality (and resistance) was so suppressed (and their worldview so regimented by Cartesian dualism), that their salvation could be assured only through their rebirth in the polarized domains of the church and the juke joint. If scholars who specialize in the blues have failed to understand this spiritual genealogy, is it any surprise that those white musicians, often quite removed from African Americans and their cultural history, sometimes sound ludicrous and vulgar when performing the blues?

Davis wrote that "the symbolic economy of the blues refutes and simply refuses to be subject to the symbolic economy governing mainstream American popular forms" (1998, 106). White America's institutionalization of the blues in museums, tourist attractions, foundations, award shows, and so on threatens the loss of the great intellectual and spiritual richness contained in the genuine blues. And when non–African Americans proclaim as their mission "keeping the blues alive" one wonders what part of the blues, as they understand it, they wish to preserve and for whom they wish it preserved. The genuine blues, poet Jackie Kay reminds us, "don't allow you to forget anything" (1997, 139).

Aspects of the blues's capacity to empower, resist, and reveal live on in subsequent African American musical, artistic, oral, and literary forms. And the blues have had an unimaginable impact on the music, literature, and worldview of non–African Americans worldwide. The blues are one of the foundation pillars upon which contemporary civilization is built, and it behooves us to learn more about it. (Finn describes white American culture as "mulatto" because of its unconscious assimilation of aspects of African culture, especially the blues.) If we wish to better understand the antecedents of rap and rock, or the consciousness that demanded humanity and created community where both were violently and systematically denied, if we want to comprehend the beauty, fears, wisdom, and spirituality intrinsic to the genuine blues, we must first listen to the voices and stories of those who made and performed the blues.

Blues Conversations: Notes on the Interview Text

If I'm lying, I hope God kicks me in the ass.
—Joe Willie Wilkins

The interviews presented in this book were conducted by two college freshmen, Fred J. Hay and Bill Lyons. On some interviews we were assisted by others. Bill and I were both blues enthusiasts, but neither of us was particularly knowledgeable about blues music, culture, or history.

I had been a student for two semesters in John Quincy Wolf's folklore classes and for one semester in Richard C. "Doc" Wood's American Folklore class. Bill had joined me in one of Wolf's classes. Through Wolf, I became acquainted with Steve LaVere, who was at that time living in Memphis and working in blues promotion. Steve supplied us with a list of blues musicians and their addresses, and Doc Wood encouraged us to design a credit course in which we visited and interviewed local blues people.

We arranged each interview by telephone; we volunteered to bring beer but were often asked for whiskey instead. We did not offer payment but were asked for such by about half of the interviewees. When asked, we negotiated a small sum (usually about twenty dollars) in advance of our arrival. Tommy Gary demanded additional payments, and the difficulties of interviewing him are evident. On Steve LaVere's advice, we laid a ten-dollar bill on Joe Willie Wilkins's amplifier in an attempt to get him to sing. It worked, and he later sent us to the store with the same ten dollars to buy more beer for everybody. Prior to these interviews, and with the exception of Wilkins, Stackhouse, and Kennibrew, we had not met, other than briefly at public performances, any of the people featured in this book.

The eight interviews prepared as chapters for this book were among those we conducted for Doc Wood's class in May 1972. The blues people interviewed include representatives of early blues and preblues music (Boose Taylor), but also one who had a few years earlier recorded soul-inflected blues (proto soul-blues) for Willie Mitchell's Hi label (Amos Patton). The featured musicians range from the internationally famous (Furry Lewis, Bukka White), to the locally popular with mostly white audiences (Laura Dukes), to the completely unknown (Boose Taylor). They performed in different blues genres such as the classic blues (Ma Rainey), country blues (Bukka White), jug band blues (Laura Dukes), and tough, postwar electric blues (Joe Willie Wilkins, Houston Stackhouse). They played a variety of instruments, including fife, fiddle, acoustic and electric guitars, bass guitar, ukulele, piano, and harmonica. Some performed mostly for white blues/folk revivalist audiences (Furry Lewis, Bukka White), some played mostly for black audiences in Memphis and the small cafés that dotted the Delta (Joe Willie Wilkins, Houston Stackhouse), and some did not perform at all (Boose Taylor). There were veteran interviewees (Furry Lewis, Bukka White), reluctant interviewees (Joe Willie Wilkins, Tommy Gary), and those who had never been interviewed previously (Boose Taylor). Among them were the naive (Boose Taylor), the bitter (Tommy Gary), and the especially polite (Laura Dukes). In all there was, not by design but by accident, an excellent mix representing the state of the blues in Memphis in 1972.

As relatively inexperienced interviewers and blues novices, Bill and I asked a lot of dumb questions, but we also gave the speakers free rein to talk about what they wished, and it is in those moments that we got some of the best material on tape. In short, these conversations succeed in revealing something about the lives and art of genuine blues people primarily because those people allowed the interviews to succeed.

I personally transcribed, edited, and annotated the eight interviews to create the conversations that make up this book. In transcribing, I tried, of course, to be as accurate as possible. If I was not sure of something said, I used brackets and a question mark, e.g., [Casey?]. Inaudible or unintelligible words are noted with three-em dashes (————). Omissions and incomplete or interrupted statements are indicated by ellipses.

In editing the interviews, I wished to privilege the voice of the blues and downplay the presence of the interviewers without destroying the context in which these people spoke. To this end, I collapsed all interviewer voices into one voice. I also removed the interviewers' unnecessary "uh-huhs," "yeahs," and so on to minimize the interruptions in the flow of the interviewee's speech. Only those song lyrics without copyright were transcribed for these conversations. With the exception of some of the less significant utterances made by the interviewers, some false starts and stutters made by all speakers, and copyright-protected lyrics, everything on tape is included in these conversations.

The importance of presenting the total discourse and discourse environment is well-established practice among anthropologists, linguists, folklorists, and others who study expressive culture. I share anthropologists Richard and Sally Price's conviction that the two evenings of Saramaka tale-telling they transcribed would "make little sense outside the setting in which they were told." They therefore published their transcriptions "relatively 'intact'":

> Rather than distilling tales into idealized story lines or grouping texts by analytical categories of one sort or another, we have attempted to present seriatim everything that fell within our tape recorder's range—from a mother reprimanding her child for knocking over a lantern and people arguing about the right way to chorus a particular song to the tale-teller excusing himself for some slip of the tongue or a listener announcing that she is sleepy and is going to stay for only one more story.
> We include (as post facto "stage directions" in our texts) nonverbal aspects of the recording, such as various kinds of laughter, clucks of moral disapproval, murmurs of condolence, exclamations of indignation, and so forth, as well as indications of the gestures and dances that contributed to the appreciation of the performance.
> It is our conviction that an understanding of what devices, routines, and incidents make Saramakas laugh, exclaim, feel sad, and so forth, is the main avenue leading to the understanding of meaning. (1991, 24–25)

I feel that the Prices' argument is also valid for the performances/interviews included in this volume. Unlike the "distilled" interviews presented in blues periodicals—interviews transformed into interviewer-authored narratives whose sole purpose is to identify and disseminate "facts"—these conversations provide the context and reveal the moment's playfulness, impatience, anger, joy, hilarity, sadness, or wonder. They give voice to a core sample of the men and women who created, nurtured, and re-created a twentieth-century musical genre and to some of the finest raconteurs, show people, and just plain folk one could ever hope to gather together in the pages of one book.

In the presentation of these interviews, I have been influenced by Richard Price's innovative work in presenting ethnographic history, especially in his *Alabi's World* (1990). In this work, Price presents four distinct voices: Saramakan (the Saramaka are the descendants of escaped slaves who created their own society in the Suriname interior) oral histories, Dutch colonial government documents, German Moravian missionary memoirs, and his own analysis and synthesis—each in different typeface. Accordingly, I present these conversations in different type styles; one for interviewer voice, one for the voice of the blues person (and the same for their attendant family and friends but also with their names preceding each of their statements), and a third for annotations. In some cases, the annotations are extensive; a full bibliography of cited sources is appended to the text.

Price writes of his Saramaka text: "The reader who wishes to embrace this experiment fully might try to 'hear' . . . the accent of a working-class eighteenth-century German Moravian . . . the Dutch accent of a bewigged colonial governor or his soldier-administrators, and . . . the speech cadences of the elderly, dignified Saramaka men" (1990, xx). I invite the reader of this volume to approach this experiment in like fashion, to embrace it fully, and to "hear" the words of these blues people.

When initially handling this book, a person will first notice the striking illustrations by George Davidson. Our collaboration in the presentation of these blues people has been inspired by the work of artist/folklorist Art Rosenbaum. First in his *Folk Visions and Voices: Traditional Music and Song in North Georgia* and more recently in *Shout Because You're Free: The African American Ring Shout Tradition in Coastal Georgia*, Rosenbaum has combined his own artistic renderings of folk performers with descriptive text. His illustrations add a vividness to the text that words alone could not convey. Likewise, George Davidson's art captures the spirit of the people it portrays in a way that a camera never could. Houston Stackhouse said, by way of tribute, that Joe Willie Wilkins's guitar case had a "scound" in it. George Davidson's art puts the scound in this book.

Notes

1. Pianist Sunnyland Slim said, "Memphis was one of the fastest towns in the world. . . . around 1925, and it was about the biggest town there was for hustling. Gambling, hustling, and all the best-dressed fellas in the world were there" (Trynka 1996, 44). When interviewer Kip Lornell asked Sleepy John Estes which town was tougher, Memphis or Chicago, Estes responded, "Memphis, no doubt about it. Memphis has always been the leader of dirty work in the world" (1975, 13).

2. "There is even one rule of thumb for our research. Whenever Western music theoreticians find a harmonic pattern in jazz or blues to be strange or unusual . . . it might

indicate retention of one or another African concept. One could devise a "negative" test method for detecting Africanisms by registering the reactions of cultural outsiders. Whenever they use labels such as 'strange,' 'unusual,' 'unorthodox,' 'deviant,' 'weird,' 'unstable,' 'uncertain,' 'idiosyncratic,' 'extreme,' or even 'fascinating,' a signal flashes up somewhere on the map of Africa" (Kubik 1999, 117).

3. "The dissonance of the blues note lent it its subversive character. . . . Its polyrhythm connected it with its African roots against the impingement of Eurocentric Standards. . . . Its fluidity is a lyrical response to the rigidity of norms, of restraints and constraints, and an expression of freedom" (Fabre 1990, 114–15).

4. Jazz critic Max Harrison suggested even more originated with these jug bands: "It seems plausible that such ensembles are the earliest known direct ancestors of the jazz band" (1986, 229).

5. When we interviewed Cannon, in the spring of 1972, he was already having difficulty hearing, focusing, and remembering. McKee and Chisenhall declined to interview Cannon for their book on Memphis blues (their interviews were conducted 1972–76) because of his "debilitating illness" (1981, xi). In 1974–75, I lived a few blocks from Cannon and would stop by and visit occasionally. After many years of robust health, Cannon was finally succumbing to the many years of hard living in an especially cruel world—that of a black person in the years stretching from the untimely end of Reconstruction to the eve of the Reagan presidency. The *Living Blues* obituary, citing the *Commercial Appeal* death notice, states that Gus Cannon died at Memphis Methodist Hospital on October 15, 1979 (O'Neal 1979, 57). In 1995, Robert Gordon reported his death date as November 16, 1979 (256).

6. According to Mark Humphrey, Delta blues pioneer Son House said in a 1968 television appearance, "Blues is not a plaything, like people think they are. Like youngsters today, right now, they take anything, and make the blues out of it, just any little ol' jump somethin' or other say, 'This is such'n-such a blues.' No it's not. . . . That's no blues. That's monkey junk" (1996, 176).

7. "In the New World, where Africans came into contact with Protestantism, retention of individual gods was impossible, since no identification with subsidiary beings could be effected, as under Catholicism. Reinterpretations thus took the form of emphasis on the power of the Holy Ghost, or stressed the importance of the River Jordan, the equivalent of the rivers that, in Africa, the spirits must cross to reach the supernatural world" (Herskovits 1967, 190).

8. Anthropologist Melville J. Herskovits, pioneer student of African Diaspora cultures, based a whole theory/model of culture contact and change on his ethnographic and historical studies of African-derived societies of the Western Hemisphere. Herskovits proposed the concept of "cultural focus," which designated "the tendency of every culture to exhibit greater complexity, greater variation in the institutions of

some of its aspects than in others" (1967, 182). In situations of culture contact, especially enforced acculturation, it is the cultural focus that is most likely to persist, in one form or another, in the new culture(s). The mechanisms that operate for the survival of the dominated group's cultural focus include syncretism and reinterpretation. The cultural focus in West African cultures—those from which most Africans imported as slaves to the Western Hemisphere originated—included both religion and music (1966).

Acknowledgments

First and foremost my gratitude must be expressed to the blues people who allowed us to interview them. Most of them I got to know much better in the years that followed, and some of them became good friends. I am especially indebted to my adoptive family, Joe Willie and Carrie Wilkins and their bilaterally extended families of siblings, cousins, uncles and aunts, and quite real "fictive" kin. I also want to thank Bill Lyons for being my partner in the original interview project and the late Professor John Quincy Wolf and Professor Richard C. Wood—the most brilliant and inspirational of teachers —for their classes and encouragement. I thank Steve LaVere and Bob Eagle for their participation and for sharing information and Gene Hyde of the Lyon College Special Collections, who helped me with many materials from the John Quincy Wolf Papers that he curates. Libraries and their personnel are always essential components in doing this type of research, and I want to es-pecially thank Maureen Mahoney and Diana Moody, who coordinate inter-library loan for Harvard University's Tozzer Library and Appalachian State University's Belk Library, respectively. I also thank Thomas Jones of the His-tory Department of the Memphis/Shelby County Public Library. I am in debt to my old friend and collaborator on this project, George D. Davidson, for his advice, wisdom, encouragement, editorial suggestions, and these extraordi-nary illustrations. I have learned a great deal from George through the years and continue to benefit in many ways from my and my family's friendship with George, Jeanne Ann, and Sam Davidson. And last to be mentioned but never last in importance are my wife, Valentina, and my son, Nikolai. With-out their love, encouragement, and support and Val's superior editorial eye, this book would never have been completed. They, too, have come to love the blues and the people who created them.

Goin' Back to Sweet Memphis

Bird Blues

1 Blues Really Ringing Around There like Birds

Bukka White at the Office

Booker T. Washington White was born near Houston, Mississippi, in the first decade of the twentieth century. He was one of the second generation of Mississippi blues musicians, a group that also included Robert Johnson and Tommy McClennan. Like Big Joe Williams and Howlin' Wolf (Chester Burnett), White was from the Hill Country, a region where blacks were more dispersed and isolated from each other than in the Mississippi Delta of the southern Black Belt. This isolation helps to explain why the Hills bluesmen tended to develop such distinctive performance styles. White's non-Delta childhood and idiosyncratic sound have led some writers to describe his music as derived primarily from old-time Anglo/"hillbilly" folk traditions. In the 1960s, some critics even referred to White as an "Uncle Tom" (P. Oliver 1984a, 288).

It is a mistake to think of White and his music in these terms. Although influenced by traditional Anglo-American music, the "fierce intensity" (P. Oliver 1970, 81) of White's singing and playing and his gift for improvisation are pan-African/African Diaspora characteristics. White was also a wonderful raconteur and poet in the African tradition. He was a man of great pride and dignity, and those who failed to recognize these qualities in White's personality and music did so out of ignorance of African culture. They were easily deceived, and White played on their ignorance.

After his "rediscovery" by white America in 1963, White often gave contradictory information about himself to interviewers. Based on his report of an interview with White (conducted by Bruce Jackson, Phil Spiro, Laurie Forti, and Al Wilson in Cambridge, Massachusetts, in 1964), Dave Evans wrote: "It

3

is very difficult to write a factual article on a person like Booker since he has a vivid imagination which is displayed both in his blues lyrics and in statements about himself. . . . His autobiography is told as a series of legends in which he is the protagonist, the centre of his wit and imagination" (1971a, 246 – 47). Indeed, White was a master of the African American oral tradition—signifying, telling the tale, and improvising—which is evident in the following interview.

In 1930, White made his first recordings for Victor in a mobile studio setup in Memphis. Columbia Records (ARC) recorded White in 1937 (when he waxed his widely copied hit "Shake 'Em On Down") and in 1940 (Okeh / Vocalion) in Chicago (where classics "Fixin' to Die," "Parchman Farm," and his theme song, "Aberdeen, Mississippi," were recorded). Jack Hurley and Dave Evans wrote that the 1940 session was "the artistic high point of Bukka White's career" (1981, 186), in which he recorded music that the British blues researcher Simon Napier described as "astonishingly beautiful" (Napier n.d.). (For an excellent overview and analysis of the songs recorded at this session, see Hurley and Evans 1981.) The 1937 and 1940 recording sessions were held, respectively, just prior to and just after White's two years of incarceration at Mississippi's infamous Parchman Farm. While an inmate at Parchman, White recorded two songs for the Library of Congress.

White did not record again until 1963, when he cut albums for Takoma (Takoma B-1001 *Mississippi Blues*) and Arhoolie Records (Arhoolie F1019 and F1020 *Sky Songs*, vols. 1 and 2). Chris Strachwitz of Arhoolie allowed White free rein to improvise, and the resulting albums are a brilliant statement by an accomplished blues artist. White continued to make records during the remaining years of his life. He used these occasions to introduce new compositions, such as "Fried Chicken," recorded for Adelphi in 1969.

As was the case with many blues musicians, White did not support himself solely from his music. He also farmed, boxed, played baseball, made whiskey, and worked in a factory—but he never entirely gave up his music. In the last decade or so of his life, White achieved international fame, made several excellent recordings, toured widely, and finally made sufficient money from his music to not have to work a second job.

When we arrived at White's residence on Mosby Street—a location immortalized in bluesman Johnny Shines's recording of "Southern Fool" (on the LP *It's a Mean Old World: A Collection of Songs by Artists Featured on the Southern Folk Festival and Old Time Mountain Music Tours between 1966–1972*)—

he was sitting on a chair in his "office," waiting for our appointment. Three years later, Sam Charters described this office: "He's set up three or four wooden seats and an old bench against a brick wall not far from his apartment in Memphis, and he spends his mornings there. He calls it his 'office,' where he 'does his business'" (1977, 36). We joined White in his office for greetings and conversation. After a bit, White led us up to the small, neatly maintained apartment that he shared with his wife. It was here that the interview was conducted.

In later years, White frequently told his audiences that he lies "some of the times but not all of the times." Keep White's warning in mind as you read the following performance.

[White tunes guitar.] I always keep the strings run-down. If you keep the strings tight. [Plays riff.] . . . Ah, when you get ready now. You want to ask some questions or what? Or how you want to do it?

Yeah, we'll ask you a couple of questions and then have you play a little. . . . We're at Bukka White's house and the date is May 9, 1972. First let's find out a little bit about yourself. Where were you born?

Named for the famous African American educator, White reportedly preferred to have his name spelled "Booker." The spelling "Bukka" was created by Okeh/Vocalion Records. It is by this spelling that Booker T. Washington White is known throughout the world.

I was born in Houston, Mississippi. . . . I was 1909. What I mean, I was born in 1909 and left there and went to the Mississippi Delta. . . . I went to Mississippi Delta in Clarksdale. . . . That's where the blues were really ringing around there like birds then.

White gave both 1909 and 1906 as the year of his birth to interviewers. Harris reports White's birth date as November 12, 1906 (1979, 552). Hurley and Evans state it as November 12, 1909 (1981, 201). Harris writes that White stayed with his uncle near Brazell, Mississippi (1979, 552); Hurley and Evans write that it was in Grenada, Mississippi (1981, 158); and McKee and Chisenhall claim it was Glendora, Mississippi (1981, 122).

Who was playing in Clarksdale at that time?

Playing with the slide? Uh, playing in my style? Well, you didn't find many guys, not too many guys back there in them days. They was playing some but not too many with a bottleneck, and a lot of guys come along with Charlie

Patton. They was playing—oh, they wasn't playing with a bottleneck, but they playing with a knife between their fingers, their little finger and their second finger. And so, I started off with a bottleneck, too, but now I had to get away from the bottleneck because you liable to drop it anywhere, and wherever you drop a bottleneck at—and that thing kind of solid—it going to bust on you. And so, we started from that, then old man was eighty-six years old told me, said, "Son, say, I tell you what you do. I'll be dead and gone, but I can tell what to do." He said, "Start with your steel pipe; start on that." He said, "That just come to me." So he made me an old pipe. Slide like this. Rusted. And that's where I started off then. Mostly after I turned the bottleneck loose, then I started with a steel slide.

Do you remember this man's name who told you this?

Yeah, named Charlie Brice. He's dead. He was a harmonica blower. He blowed a harmonica. Blowed a little guitar, but he wouldn't trust himself too much with a guitar like he did with a harmonica. . . . He was a great friend to my father. You know, my father, he played more, he played four instruments. . . . He played a guitar, piano, violin, and a mandolin. And them was his main favorite instruments that he used.

According to Hurley and Evans, harmonica player Luke Smith, a friend of White's father, John, introduced the younger White to the slide. They quote White describing his father and Smith playing at a local frolic: "We're going to have a frolic tonight! Who playin'? Luke Smith and John White! . . . And the guy named Billy Cocker was calling the set. . . . I'd have my arm on Daddy's shoulder and you could hear that guitar and fiddle from here to Main Street, look like" (1981, 157).

. . . Well, he showed me, one time, he said now, "If you don't play 'Goodnight Irene.'" He said, "I done bought the guitar and done tuned it for you, and if you can't play 'Goodnight Irene.'"

Leadbelly (Huddie Leadbetter) is usually given credit for composing "Goodnight Irene." He first recorded it for the Library of Congress in 1934. Leadbelly's biographers document the existence of "Irene" predating Leadbelly's use of it (Wolfe and Lornell 1992).

That's what he said and he walked on away. And I held that in that tune as long. 'Cause you see the first thing about music I play is learning how to sing and play is you first got to learn how to tune it. See, you don't want to play in the same tune, which a lot of people do do it, but I never could do like that. I have to change mine in different tunes. . . . And so me and my sister got to fighting over it one day, and in a way she was helping me. She got it out of tune, and I had to pull my brain to death to try to get it back where it been, and that was in open key, like I got it now. So after then I learned how to tune it and so they ain't been no more problems since. I left there and went down to the Mississippi Delta, down where my uncle was. He bought a piano for me and his boy Buster. That's where I started; I could play a piano. I don't go for no piano player, but I can play good enough until the piano player get there. And so, that's just the way that started off.

White was a less accomplished pianist than some of his Memphis colleagues, but his style was very similar to the barrelhouse piano playing of his friend John "Piano Red" Williams and other Memphis musicians. His vocal style changed when he was accompanying himself on the piano rather than the guitar. It became more of a shout reminiscent of Piano Red and other pianists who had to sing loud to be heard over their pounding of the ivories.

You play in open G?

Yeah, I play in open G. Uh-huh, I play in open G, I play in Spanish, I play in cross G and D-flat. I like, I got to switch around. I can't just play all my stuff in one tune.

Mr. White, some people, in books and all, make a connection between your style and the style of Charlie Patton. Could you. . . ?

Well, you want to hear a little Charlie Patton? Now, I can't play him, and I seen Charlie Patton wasn't using no pick. But I can play it, but I can't slap it with these picks on. If I take these picks off I can't, I can't play it long 'cause my fingers are too tender. I've been playing with these so long, you see. And, but I still can play, you know.

Charlie Patton (1891–1934), the pioneer Delta guitarist who, more than any other individual, established the early Delta blues style, has been the subject of several biographies, most recently Calt and Wardlow's *King of the Delta Blues: The Life and Music of Charlie Patton* (1988).

Did you pick anything up from Patton?

No. I just—well, yeah, I did, about a piece or two, now, but I don't think I'm good on about one piece, and what got me going, for myself, I tells everybody, white and black, if you playing music you got to learn something yourself. Don't sit around these record players and learn all the other fellow's stuff. When you go to do the recording, the man going to get a book and show you who made those records. So I went to Chicago, in '37, I had every record I ever heard come. And he said, "Well"—that's Lester Melrose—he said, "Well now, you can't do no good on that. I'm going to give you a meal ticket and I'm going to let you stay here two weeks to get yourself together." So I got something of my own.

White recorded twice for Melrose: two songs in 1937 (for the then independent ARC) before being incarcerated at Parchman Farm and twelve songs in March 1940 (for the Okeh/Vocalion labels) after his release. Melrose, a native of Olney, Illinois, was a music store proprietor who entered the music publishing business and later became an agent, recruiting and recording blues musicians for several labels. Melrose helped shape the sound of early urban blues: "But in Chicago Bluebird was beginning to grab most of the blues market with what Sam Charters characterized as the 'Bluebird Beat.' It might have been called with even more justification the 'Melrose Mess,' for it was a white businessman, Lester Melrose, who was really responsible for shaping the Chicago sound of the late '30s and '40s" (Rowe 1973, 17). Melrose also sought out and recorded singular blues stylists from the South, including Tommy McClennan and Bukka White.

According to Hurley and Evans, Melrose was one of the rare honest blues businessmen: "For years Melrose continued twice a year to send royalty checks, or statements if no records had sold. Even Melrose's daughter when she inherited the business continued to send Bukka a statement (and sometimes a check) twice a year" (1981, 186).

Hurley and Evans wrote that White showed Melrose handwritten transcriptions of songs that others had previously recorded. Melrose "got out a book and showed me who had put them out. He said, 'You see. You couldn't make a quarter. They'd sue you from the first to the end.'" Melrose gave White a meal ticket and a hotel room and told him, "'I'll give you two days to come up with something of your own'" (1981, 177).

. . . Okeh, that's right. Okeh, Bluebird and Decca back there in them days there, you know. And so that put me hip and so I ain't had no problem from that day to this and I learnt what to do. . . . Well, I'm going to play a little like this—like I say, I can't slap it, but I can pull it; I got to use my pick. [He plays "Give Me an Old, Old Lady." Ends with deep bass spoken aside: "She's going out there with Charlie Patton."] I always did want that piece and I, uh, one time, right after he got killed, his brother live in Clarksdale and he had that record. So he gave me that record and somebody stole it. Man, I cried for about a month over that. I don't know who in the devil stole that. I had it at a party, you know, carried a lot of records. And they picked that particular record out of it and they stole it.

This song is most likely White's own composition. Charlie Patton never recorded it. White first recorded "Give Me an Old, Old Lady" in Memphis in 1968 for Blue Horizon (BH 7-63229).

Well, I stayed in the Delta until I was growed up, around twelve or thirteen years old, and I slipped off from my uncle. And I got tired, you know, looking at them mules every morning. And I caught the freight train on the Dog. And I came, went to St. Louis. I stay with an old man up there named Old Man Ben.

White told Margaret McKee and Fred Chisenhall that this man was named Ben Wright (1981, 123). "So I got to Saint Louis the next morning about eight o'clock, soda cap on, knee pants and barefooted. . . . So there was an old man, Ben Whitley, sittin' on his back porch, and he told me, 'Come here, boy, what are your crying about?'" (Hurley and Evans 1981, 161).

Dog, short for Yellow Dog, was the local name for the Yazoo and Mississippi Valley Railroad. White was famous for his train imitations and always had a train song in his current repertoire. He recorded "Panama Limited" at his first recording session in 1930, "Special Streamline" in 1940, and "New Orleans Streamline" and "Bald Eagle Special" in 1963.

And he really the one who put me on the track. Old Man Ben then was about sixty-four or -five, and he didn't have any kids. He had a big nightclub there. He had a baby grand piano, so he told me he'd send me to school and all I had to do was stay around there and, uh, what I knowed, and still, I would know more. And he said he would call my peoples up and let them know where I was. So he did; he called them up and let me talk to them. Asked me did I want to come home. I told them no, I wouldn't be home in about five or six years, I think, if things keep going like they was. 'Cause I wasn't used to all of that, you know, all that excitement. Had a pretty Buick there—two spares on the side and one behind. And he was learning me to drive that and, you know, I wasn't studying about no home. If I went back home, I'd had to catch one of those mules, you see, and so that started my mind getting off that farming stuff, you know. Which every, everybody can't get away from that—somebody got to farm—but I didn't think I was the kid, you know, who was supposed to farm. So I left there. I stayed with him about two or three years. He give me money and I . . . Oh yeah. I come to be pretty famous there. I was young and the girls would kiss me, you know. And I just felt big, I telling you the truth.

I had on knee pants when I went there. He said, "You got to pull them off now; you a big boy to your size." He said, "Come on and go down to the tailor. I'm going to have you a suit made." I never will forget it. He had me a dark blue-grey made. Man, that suit was a bad suit. So, I'm telling you, I went on down there and about a week or two they had it out. And so, here's the first piece, I never forget the longest day I live.

He opened up that there nightclub up that night in my name: This is Bukka, this is Bukka night. That's what he had on the outside. The poster's on the outside. And at that time they was trigger toeing, you see. Way back there—y'all don't know nothing about that trigger toeing. But it's a pretty dance—just bad on your shoes. And so this is the way I was playing. [Plays "Jitterbug Swing." Ends with spoken aside: "St. Louis trigger toeing."]

White first recorded "Bukka's Jitterbug Swing" for Lester Melrose in 1940.

Is that your own song?

Yeah, I don't fool with nothing but mine if I'm playing around like this or recording. No, I told you about that Chicago give me, put me on the hip. So, don't fool with other folks' stuff. . . . Yeah, I commence to playing then. After that night everybody enjoyed it so. So I was just one of the main mens there, you know. I was young but I was large for my size. I was might large as you are and so, the girls just went for me, you know. I was a little bashful, you know. About the girl proposition. But about the music I wasn't, you know. I didn't know nothing about no courting or nothing. . . . Oh, I learned fast. That's the truth. I come in on that pretty fast, you know.

And so, after then that gives me a pretty good start. And so, I told Old Man Ben I was going to Cleveland. Some boys wanted me to go to Cleveland to do some recording with them. Had a band there. And so, they had a band there they called the jug band and they had some jugs, you know, like they do, used to do here in Memphis here. And so, he could blow that jug 'cause he had drums and things. So we went on up there and did good. We did good. Left there and I came to Chicago. And we stayed around there and we left there and went to Milwaukee. We fool around there. Then we left there and came back to Chicago. And then I began to want to see my parents, then, so I came back to St. Louis, so, and me and Old Man Ben jumped into that Buick and jumped on down South, where my parents were. Man, it was so glad when we got there. It's Sunday morning. So, we got out there and we washed up and cleaned up, changed clothes, and went on to the church. Now, I broke the meeting up; they was so glad to see me. The preacher thought Jesus had came down, you know. Really, they thought Jesus had came down. Everybody was running and jumping. That's the honest truth. Hugging and kissing me and so one of the deacons told me, said, "I tell you what to do. I tell you stay outdoors 'cause you done broke this meeting up, everybody so glad to see you and all and seen that pretty car, too," you know. Wasn't nothing around that church but old raggedly T-models, you know, and so that long Buick—we had the top dropped back, you know, and we was just cooling. That's all.

White's rhetorical use of the expression "you know" dated at least as far back as his 1930 recording of "Panama Limited" for Victor.

When you were in Chicago, how long did you stay in Chicago when you went up there?

Well, when I was in Chicago—I was recording for Lester Melrose and them—I was there, well, I wasn't there too long. 'Cause I had done went everywhere back South and Melrose got in his car and he headed back, and then he got hold of some of my tapes. He came down South and he find me. He brought me back. And so, I stayed up there then about four or five months. . . . Oh yes, you take a ole Big Bill, Tampa Red, Washboard Sam, you know, all them guys. Yeah, we were right in there. Memphis Minnie, she was red hot. I was playing the same place she was playing a lot of times, you know. . . . And so, they just; everything I did look like everyone enjoyed it, and so I didn't have no problem. No problem. They was taking care of me. That was one of the greatest things, too, you know.

I have a tape here now, guys, I'm going to sell it, you know, if somebody give me the right kind of price on the ———. Some tape I say I going to sell it. Wasn't doing no good. You know, it just laying up here. One of my tapes out, somebody recorded it, you know, I carried it sometime where they record it. I let them check it out. Let them have it, you know. 'Cause that's just the way you have to do things. In the music line you got to be, kind of, steady moving on. 'Cause when you go, here to be off of it for a long time, rats go to getting in your barrel, you know. And rats don't care nothing about no music; all they steady looking for some what the music's done brought in. [Laughs.] I can't get started all the time, you know. Yeah.

William Lee "Big Bill" Broonzy (1893–1958) was an exceptional guitarist and prolific composer of blues songs. The Mississippi born Broonzy was a major influence on the development of the Chicago blues sound and later a world famous purveyor of "folk blues."

Hudson "Tampa Red" Whittaker (ca. 1900–81) was born in Georgia and lived in Tampa, Florida, before migrating north to Chicago. Whittaker's sophisticated slide guitar playing helped a later generation of Delta guitarists to develop the postwar slide guitar styles made famous by Elmore James, Robert Nighthawk, Muddy Waters, and others.

Robert "Washboard Sam" Brown (1910–66), a native of Arkansas and half-brother to Broonzy, recorded prolifically under his own name and as rhythm accompaniment on many other artists' (including Bukka White's 1940 session) recordings.

For more on Memphis Minnie, see Memphis Ma Rainey and Little Laura Dukes chapters.

When you came back down through St. Louis, did you spend long there?

Oh yeah, but St. Louis was the first largest place that I ever, you know, going to at that time. 'Cause as I say, we hoboed up there, bunch of us boys, before we went to the Delta. I came back to the Hills. Bunch of them from the Hills went to St. Louis and then we came back. And then I left there and went to the Delta where my uncle was. Where Charlie Patton and them, and all them guys. Ole Nathan Scott and a girl named Laurie [Lurie?]; she was a—she didn't play music, but Lord she could sing, though. So she sung behind Nathan Scott. And so, when I went back to the Delta, I beginning to have a lot of enemies. 'Cause where them guys were playing at, I went there and played one night and so they give me a job while I was around there and so Nathan and them fell out with me. I begin to feel shy; somebody liable to be on the outside and it get dark and do something to me, you know. 'Cause, I was young and had a voice like a bull and I could go, you know.

Me and a guy, he was playing with me, George Bullet Williams. I run up on him. You about done heard talk of him 'cause they still got some of his old records. Some people got them now. George Bullet Williams, the best harp blower I ever heard from that day to this day. He's from Alabama. I don't know whether living or dead. . . . Yeah, that's right. And I just don't see how he could be living because George would drink denatured, strained shoe polish. I'm telling you the honest to God truth, anything with alcohol on it, he would drink it. . . . Yeah, I know if he living, he got an iron stomach. . . . I believe he's dead now. Got to be dead. Uh-huh.

George "Bullet" Williams, reportedly from Alabama, recorded four songs for Paramount in Chicago in 1928. Other than what White could remember, almost nothing is known about this brilliant harmonica player. White said, "The first time I met George that was in West Point, Mississippi. . . . At Bapterville, a colored settlement there. I met George in '28, in January; I was real young then; George was a grown man then." White and Williams played together frequently for a spell. "George would go down on me 'fore day. . . . God knows he'd be in the kitchen under the table drunk. . . . He'd drink 'till you could hear it comin' up like a pump, honest to God" (Stephens 1991, 84). In the early 1930s, White was married to Williams's wife's niece.

When you were in St. Louis did you meet people playing blues in St. Louis?

Yeah, I met, uh, you know, uh, me and St. Louis Slim. His home was down in Clarksdale down below.

White told McKee and Chisenhall that he had met St. Louis pianist Jimmy Oden (1903–77) at this time (1981). Oden was born in Nashville, Tennessee. St. Louis Slim is an unknown.

Yeah, I met him, me and him, ole Peetie Wheatstraw. All them old guys, yeah. . . . Yeah, uh-huh, I was in St. Louis first. See, I met them before I went to Chicago. I didn't know much about Chicago. And so, that what's being around with them guys, that what put me hip were those St. Louis Slim, Peetie Wheatstraw. Another old guy named Bubba Jones. He about the best thing going in St. Louis. That guy could play a guitar out of sight. And he was about sixty then, you know. And we just had a nice time. Other words, I was—I had determine to do this, what I'm doing now. And so, if you want to do something, you can might near do it. And so, me and him, all them old musicians, we'd get together, two or three o'clock, four o'clock. That night, then, they'd book us out to a party, you see. Then they was booking you out. See they had an office and they was booking you out. Different people wants you.

William "Peetie Wheatstraw" Bunch was born in Ripley, Tennessee, in 1902 and died in an auto accident in St. Louis in 1941. This pianist/guitarist was one of the most popular blues artists of the 1930s. An influential artist who composed many original blues, Bunch billed himself as the "Devil's Son-in-Law" and the "High Sheriff of Hell." Wheatstraw's life and music were described in Garon's 1971 biography *The Devil's Son-In-Law*. Bubba Jones is an unknown.

Who ran this business in St. Louis?

A guy named Richard. He was a colored guy.

Do you know, do you remember the name of the. . . ?

No, I really, I can't, you know. Let's see now, but it was on Gambling but they've done torn all that stuff down now. They've done torn down just like they tearing down here. You go to St. Louis and you really don't know it, you're lost they done tore.

So, when you came back down here did you start playing again?

Yeah, yeah. I went wide open then. . . . The guys from everywhere. My first recording without being just a little place up here to the Auditorium on Main and Popular. I never forget that the longest day I live. I say I was in the Delta and a fellow brought me up here from Itta Bena, Mississippi. Ralph Lembo, he brought me up here. Brought . . . let's see now, there were three of us. Three colored and two white. The white boys, I don't know what happened to them, they got, I don't know whether . . . They should of knowed it before they left Itta Bena, but they got out, they put us down at Webb—that's in the Delta. They got out. That left me, [Poia?], and Fount Massey. Hell, he got up there and he got to drinking that apple brandy and he got drunk. Well, he couldn't make no record. We had to . . . Kind of delayed us a couple of hours. Now he was doing alright, but when they give that sign to stop, they couldn't stop him. See, that brandy was kicking in him like a mule in a stable. He wouldn't stop. He went over. This only plays three minutes, and he was playing about six minutes. So he was just running, running the red light. Just running. But when he got straight we made it. And so I was singing church songs, you know, and he paid me good. Yeah, he really paid me good. . . . Well, I'll play you one. Then you'll know. Now, my first church song that I ever put out in my life, "I Am in."

According to Robert Dixon, John Godrich, and Howard Rye, neither a Fount Massey nor a [Poia?] recorded for Victor that day (1997). White later told McKee and Chisenhall that it was the preacher who was drunk at this recording session (1981). That would have been Rev. Holt. Hurley and Evans quote White speaking of a "Polean" and an "Old Man Fountainathie" who accompanied him to Memphis to record. According to these authors, Polean is short for Napolean Hairiston, who accompanied White on guitar on these recordings, and Old Man Fountainathie was "probably Reverend M. H. Holt" (1981, 165).

Sicilian-born Ralph Lembo was an Itta Bena, Mississippi, furniture store owner who acted as a talent scout for record companies looking for blues artists. His reputation among blues musicians was not a good one; they complained of being cheated by Lembo. "Finally, Lembo himself withdrew from the field of scouting altogether with the complaint that he was being bilked by record companies out of royalties or finder's fees" (Calt and Wardlow 1988, 177).

White recorded fourteen songs for Victor on May 26, 1930. Two records (four songs) were issued. One was blues. The other, a gospel number, was released under the name "Washington White, the Singing Preacher." This included a version of "I Am in the Heavenly Way." A "Miss Minnie" sang harmony behind White on the gospel songs.

[Plays "I Am in the Heavenly Way."] I am in the heavenly way. Yeah, I am in the heavenly way. I use to sing in the church, you know. I use to be a great church member 'cause my grandfather was a bishop. And my daddy was a musician, and so that church stuff was too slow for me. So, I cut out and went on my daddy's side. You see, I thought I come, you see, other words, I'd make more, I figured, doing this than I would singing in the church, you know. So I picked up on my daddy's side. And I been sliding ever since.

White's clever use of "sliding" here to denote both his slide playing of the guitar and his back-sliding from the church is reminiscent of his use of "ringing" to denote birds singing and his own slide guitar playing.

Punk Davisson, White's maternal grandfather, was a "fundamentalist preacher who owned more than four hundred acres of farmland and managed to keep four churches under his control" (Hurley and Evans 1981, 147).

Did anyone else in your family play any music?

Yeah, my father did . . . and my sister. . . . Yeah, my sister. My sister Etta, she played guitar. She could sing, I'm telling you the truth. She fell dead in '67. I was getting ready to go overseas. So she went up to check her son's house. He was in some part of . . . Indiana. And she went up there to check the house to see if nobody had bothered it. And so, and turned around and coming on back she must a had a heart attack; she done fell dead. Yeah, she . . . got a son can play, too. She got three sons can play. Ole Monk in Detroit, he over B. B. King. He can go. Yeah, he can go.

B. B. King's your cousin, isn't he?

Yeah, B. B. King. Yeah, we two sisters' children. . . . Well, when B.B. was about six or seven years old, I give him a brand new Stella. And he was setting on the floor. He was just quiet, you know. And that was the only cousin my auntie had and he looked so pitiful. I had a Stella—I used not to play nothing but a Stella guitar. Anyway, when I got ready to go that morning. I was going to Moorhead. And me and George, we was together then. And B.B. looked so pitiful. George said, "Why don't you give him that guitar and buy you another one in Moorhead?" Said, "They got plenty of them there." So I just turned around and pulled it from over my head, the string I had over me, and give it to him. And so, that give him a good feeling to start. He been going ever since. Yeah.

Hurley and Evans quote White telling a very similar version of this story (1981, 190).

Did you ever used to do any traveling with him?

Oh yeah. You know I used to do. I came here the first time . . . I made them records in '30; in 1930 I made it here. At the Auditorium.

With B.B.?

No. Me and B.B. never cut no records together. I don't know, it's a funny thing, but I just have to say it. Me and B use to be together and play right smart, but the guys would tell me, say, "Why don't you get rid of that punk there? He can't play no guitar." And just commence to feeling downhearted. Other words, he always figured people had me way over him, you know. And he just never did want to fool with me too much. Everywhere we'd go, . . . I wouldn't know what a fellow going to say, you know. I wasn't no mind reader. And everywhere we'd go along, they would say that word. I don't know why. And I would tell them, "Don't do that," I say, "'cause B's young. He got a chance to get on up the road." Like he is now. And so, he just never did. One thing—he was always shy of this—he can't play with a slide too good. And he knew if we hang up, I'm going to use this slide on him. And he going have to jump and shout. 'Cause I'm going to bear down on him with this slide, you know. And so, I said that why he just be like that, you know. Well, down here to the Paradise, he tried to get me to go on stage after they come up, but I didn't have my picks and I didn't have my slide, and so, I didn't get on there. If I . . . knew he wanted me to play I would have brought this along with me, you know. And brought my guitar because I couldn't play his guitar.

According to B. B. King's biographer, Charles Sawyer (1980), King lived with White for ten months when he first came to Memphis and learned a great deal from him about guitar playing. King even bought his first electric guitar and amplifier with money he had borrowed from his cousin Bukka. Sawyer states that King and White never played together publicly. The Club Paradise was, at that time, Memphis's largest showcase for black entertainment.

Mr. White, like, were there any guitar players or singers or anything that had an influence on you like Charlie Patton did? Any other one along the way?

Oh, talking about influence, interest in me. The way I was playing then? Oh well, just like I say. I never did see Charlie Patton, but a lot of them other old guys—like Son House and all—he was down in there then, you know. . . . Yeah, we played a lot. . . . I play with him now whenever we get a program on or something.

White recorded the remarkable "Remembrance of Charlie Patton (Talking)" for John Fahey's Takoma Records in 1963. In this piece, White relates how Charlie Patton gave him his first taste of whiskey in a spoon.

Son House (1902–88) was a pioneering and superb Delta blues guitarist and vocalist, and sometimes preacher. He was an early associate of Charlie Patton and a later mentor to Robert Johnson and Muddy Waters.

Did he help influence the style of your slide playing?

Yeah, he was, . . . if you want to hear the truth. Son House probably wouldn't say it. That's where Son House got that slide from me. He wasn't using no slide when I run up on him. He wasn't using even the bottleneck, too. And after, the next time I see'd him, he had a bottleneck. And so he's been bottlenecking ever since. See, in this style of playing every man play like he wants to play, but in this style of playing you take care of your fingers so good. Now, I don't play everything with this slide here, but the mostly I play with the slide. 'Cause now my fingers just so, is just so tender. They may not look like they be tender. But it's tender there. This keeps the weight off you. You can play so much longer with this slide than you can with your naked hand. Have all that 'telligence stuff on it. I see guys' fingers that the strings done dug into their flesh, man, just be. Well, they got to play because they don't have no protection. And so this is the way I go ringing. I can stand up playing so long, you see.

Simon Napier (1971) wrote that White didn't remember meeting Son House prior to White's rediscovery in 1963.

Did you ever do any traveling to the southern part of the country? Like out west or over into Alabama?

Oh yes, my God, man. Georgia and way, and L.A., and all them places. I've been playing out in the West ever since 1963. The first job I got there for Ed Pearl. . . . Yeah, the Ash Grove. [Laughs.] Eight-one-six-two, I'm telling you the truth. [White is recalling the Ash Grove's address: 8162 Melrose Avenue in Los Angeles.] . . . I played there three weeks straight, and this here Indian girl come behind me. What was that girl? Oh, Sandra? Sanja? Sanja? She sings and plays to an Indian girl. I seen her on television last week. Sanja and something. And that was the first time she was there, and that was my first three started, and she was there every night. And do you know she picked up some of my stuff and recorded it? [Laughs.] . . . Sanje Indian girl. She did that, yeah. She told me she was going to do it. I told her, "Go ahead; I don't care." Yes, she done married now, but she—I seen her at Newport, Rhode Island. We played there together. And I seen her out there. And we had a nice time, but she done married now.

The "Indian girl" was recording artist Buffy Sainte-Marie. Sainte-Marie and pop crooner Andy Williams even performed White's "Fixin' to Die Blues" as a duet on Williams's TV show in 1967 (Groom 1971, 40).

While you was traveling through Alabama, Georgia, Carolinas, did you meet other blues singers and players?

Oh yeah, I met a guy out there in Atlanta, Georgia, and me and him were at Sewanee College about three years ago. And this guy was named Robert, named Robert Mim. He was an old settler like . . . And we didn't think we'd ever see one another again. But that cat still play just like he ever. And man, we played at Sewanee College. That's out from Chattanooga there. And Willie Dixon, he had his band there, too, you know. And man, I'm telling you the truth. See in playing music and you run up on some guys, you know, you can just play so much better, you know. It looks like, I don't know what it do, but it just gives you a uplift, in the gill. Sunnyland and, uh—who else he have with him down there? Let's see, now. Sunnyland and another boy who blows the harmonica—he from Alabama there. I forgot; I can't 'call this boy's name. DeWitt—that was his name—a boy named DeWitt. He a young cat there, but he can blow that harp. Oh, Willie Dixon, he's going to try to get the best because he do a lot of recording, you see. That's the way he makes his living. He makes, Willie Dixon makes a hell of a lot of money, too. See, he got one home and he's buying another, uh, a brick house got about six or eight rooms in it, got a basement down there. And got a station wagon to haul his stuff, you know. Oh, he's doing along all right; he ain't living too bad.

After his "rediscovery" by John Fahey and Ed Denson, White played to appreciative audiences at clubs, concerts, and colleges around the world.

Big Willie James Dixon (1915–92), bass player and song writer, was a native of Vicksburg, Mississippi. Dixon moved to Chicago, where he was active as musician, talent scout, song writer, and producer. His impact on postwar Chicago blues was immense. Dixon's autobiography, *I Am the Blues,* was published in 1989.

Albert "Sunnyland Slim" Luandrew (1907–95) was a native of Vance, Mississippi. Sunnyland was a mainstay of blues piano in postwar Chicago, recording under his own name and as accompanist to many other musicians, including Muddy Waters.

No, I never did meet Blind Blake, but I, you know, I always had some of his records and I listen to them. I didn't try to take no pattern out of them. So I managed to meet Lonnie Johnson in Toronto. Yeah, I run up on him in '65 and I run up on him in—let me see, I was in Toronto, I believe—year before last. He got struck, you know, a car. He was standing on the corner and the car struck him. He got back up and started to playing again then. He passed, you know, he passed. Yeah. But, you know, he was cool cat playing the guitar. Lonnie Johnson was cool cat, I'm telling you, and all them peoples there crazy about him. Yeah, I'm leaving here on the 29th, going to Toronto. . . . Yeah, I be there five nights. Yeah, I played there about three years ago, four times in one year. So, I commenced getting other places, so I had to turn them down. I just got tired of going there. You can go to a place so much, it get old to people. But they was paying me, they was paying me alright, now, they was paying me a nice salary. But I commenced going back out on the West Coast, going to New York, up in New York, and all them places. So I just give them—so they finally caught me kind of a little vacant, you know. So I go out, I leave here on the 29th. I done signed the contract, and so, I got a contract and they got a contract.

For more on Blind Blake, see the Joe Willie Wilkins chapter.

Alonzo "Lonnie" Johnson (1889–1970), jazz and blues guitarist, pianist, and fiddler, was a native of New Orleans. Johnson was an extremely gifted guitarist whose influence on jazz and blues guitar playing is profound. He died of a stroke at his home in Toronto in 1970.

While you were back playing in the Delta, did people from other parts of the country, blues singers, travel through? Like did Blind Lemon Jefferson come through?

Oh yeah, they know had been through, but, like I say, I never did, I never did meet them. They always be just going. But a lot of them, over there, would tell me about it, you know, and a lot of them younger kids like me was catching hold of their style. And I always thought if I could get something of my own, it would last more than the other fellows' stuff, and so I would sit around and go to them roadhouses, you know. And I couldn't understand them guys. They wasn't making nothing. They just play. But they paid me, though. 'Cause I told them they had to pay me, you know. I beginning to going to depend on my work, you know.

And so, old fellow in the Delta named Old Man, Old Man Ben Smith. He was about eighty-six years old. And had one of the prettiest old houses you want to most ever look at. And so, I played there most every Friday and Saturday night. Back there in them times—I wasn't nothing but a kid—he give me fifty dollars. Yeah, he give me fifty dollars. And them guys just been through, like Blind Blake and all them different guys. Well, he said, "They didn't want nothing, they didn't ask for nothing, I didn't give them nothing." Well, I said, "I want something; you got to give me some." 'Cause I begin to go on my own, you see, then. I couldn't set up there, and about two or three hundred peoples in there, man. Good God Almighty. All frying fishes, you know, and quails and all that kinds of stuff. They had some kind of drink—I don't know; it wasn't no beer. I don't know what it called was, but I wasn't drinking nothing then. I didn't want nothing.

I don't drink too much now. But the way I do when I'm at home, I drinks at home. I makes it in medicine at night. Keep that cold down. I can go out, I can start drinking right now and go out in that air there, and you can't hear me talk. It just clip my wind like that, you see. I've been singing so long. At night, I take that whiskey and get me about four lemon and pour about half of it in there and shake that around, put about a teaspoon of sugar in there, and set up here and look at the TV, and them songs start to rolling into my mind. And that's the reason I don't like to start to thinking about playing too much. 'Cause them songs just come in rotation, just like peoples in the line to catch the airplane or something. So helps me God, that's just the way they do. See, I studied that so hard, I used to sing in my sleep. I had to stop studying it. I, uh—take a lot of numbers I put out. I done already sung them in my sleep, and when I wake up I go right on the my guitar and go to playing ———. I'm going to play. Now, I'm going to give y'all one of my Chicago—you know my girl I was liking—and when I play that, then I'm going to cool off. 'Cause, now, that be right now. When I play this number? I have to tune up now. [Tunes his guitar.] Anytime when you get ready, let me know, now. They still like to send me to the penitentiary, and if I hadn't the sense I had, I being young, I be in the pen now, 'cause they can give you life where you won't never get out. And I writ this record up in her name, to keep from killing her, you know. I caught her kissing a guy at this roadhouse, and when she kissed him . . . I was pretty bad back then, totin' a pistol. When she turned around I had that .38 right in her face, and she hollered and said she never would do that no more. And so a cousin of mine hit my hand, knocked it down, and the [bullet] shot the toe of her shoe off her. The shot tore the toe off her. That was just how close it was getting to her then. This here song it—Gibson's Hill—it was written by Miss Rosa Lee. [Plays "Gibson Hill." Spoken aside at end of song: "She went out on Gibson Hill."]

For more on Blind Lemon Jefferson, see the Furry Lewis chapter.

White recorded "Gibson Town" for Blue Horizon's *Memphis Swamp Jam* (BH 63229) in 1968 and "Gibson Hill" for Adelphi's *Memphis Blues Again* (Adelphi 1010) in 1969.

Now, you see, that's what I tell y'all about this stuff. It just like I say. It's like what I'm doing now. I've made a heap right smart of change. Now, this is hard work. This is not no plaything. This is hard work, playing this thing here. And so, I think I've kind of done give y'all a day's work and gave you worth of your money, and I played it from my heart. But I've got to leave you with "Aberdeen." I'm going to play you "Aberdeen," if y'all would like to have it. . . . I figured, you know. [Tunes his guitar.] You know, I always do more than what I supposed to do. Like I said, I've always been a fellow easy to get along with and I likes to do the right thing. And everybody what's been dealing with me know that I am like that. I have went to places charging fifty dollars and they give a hundred. So many times. I thought done shoot. Because I didn't want to be charging them too much. You know what I mean? I just didn't know it was worth no more than that. Now this is open G, getting back in open G now. I done recorded this record, I bet you, six times. I done recorded it. [Plays "Aberdeen, Mississippi." Spoken aside ending song: "She going out now, in Aberdeen, Mississippi. Bye."]

White first recorded "Aberdeen, Mississippi, Blues" for Melrose in 1940. (Aberdeen is a town in Mississippi's northwestern hill country.) It is possible that Bob Dylan's inspiration for "Memphis Blues Again" was the following line: "Sitting in Aberdeen with New Orleans on my mind."

I just want to ask you one more short question. You said you use to play the Stella.

Yeah, yeah.

Well, did you switch to the steel guitar before the Okeh recordings, or were you playing a Stella on the Okeh recordings?

I was playing the Stella. I switched back to a steel guitar along, in, let's see, '39, in '39. . . . What?

According to Hurley and Evans, White borrowed Big Bill Broonzy's "big Gibson" for the 1940 recording session "because his own little Stella did not record well and Big Bill's 'cut through better'" (1981, 178).

The recordings you made when you was in Parchman Farm?

That was a wooden guitar. Naw, naw, that was a wooden guitar. That was a guitar I was playing. I didn't have no Stella then. I had a Gibson. Yeah, the Farm, the peoples down there bought me a guitar. And when I got there, they set up a big band.

White served time in the Mississippi state prison, Parchman Farm, in the late 1930s. "Throughout the American South, Parchman Farm is synonymous with punishment and brutality, as well it should be. Parchman is the state penitentiary of Mississippi, a sprawling 20,000-acre plantation in the rich cotton land of the Yazoo Delta. . . . Parchman is the quintessential penal farm, the closest thing to slavery that survived the Civil War" (Oshinsky 1996, 1–2).

In *The Story of the Blues,* Paul Oliver wrote that White served time because he killed a man (1969, 121). Hurley and Evans quote White as getting into a fight and shooting a man, but not fatally: "Well, I had a .38 Colt in there and I let it loose. And I just shot him where I wanted to shoot him. Broke his thigh" (1981, 171). White told Chris Strachwitz, "I had to burn a guy a little and they gave me a little time down there on Parchman's Farm—they treat you like you treat yourself—they called me 'Barrelhouse'—and I seen better days there than I did at home—on Sundays girls would come by and take for a ride—bring me food and cakes—I became famous down there—was of too much service to them to let me go—when I got out I felt like shootin' somebody else!" (1965). Here's another version of the story: "Booker was caught up in a shooting scrape near Charleston, Mississippi. . . . He insisted he was threatened by a gang of men resentful of the fact that he was playing his guitar and courting the women while they were working in the fields. At any rate, one man lay dead after the fracas and the judge sentenced Booker to Parchman" (McKee and Chisenhall 1981, 125). Charleston is in Tallahatchie County in the Delta. Gayle Wardlow discovered the Monroe County (northeastern Mississippi) court records that show White was convicted of murder and given a life sentence. How White got out after only two years is unknown (1998, 103).

Before his incarceration, White was allowed to make a short trip to Chicago to fulfill a contractual agreement to record with Lester Melrose. One of the two songs he recorded, "Shake

'Em On Down," became an immediate hit and was widely copied, becoming a genuine blues standard.

While he was an inmate at Parchman, White recorded two songs ("Sic 'Em Dogs On" and "Po Boy") for John Lomax of the Library of Congress. Apparently, White felt that he should be paid for his performance and refused to play more than the two songs.

I would of got out the next week, but they said, "No, you too much service here." I swear to God, they wouldn't let me out. I hold my hand to God, that made me so doggone mad, I hate I ever seen a guitar string. They say, "No, you can't get this man till his two years out." Nobody. Melrose come in, man, he came in. Couldn't nobody get me out. They said money won't get him and . . . President Jackson White—he was on then, President White—he said, "'Cause we done already called him for the ——— let nobody have it. Just going to be here two years, and you got to do it." He said, "You going to live better here than out in the world," but that didn't sound good to me, you know. Regardless of what they was doing, it wasn't like at home, you know. 'Cause I had left a wife and things there. I was railroaded anyway. They really didn't tell you how I was railroaded, did they? Okay. I's good. They could throw a block on you, you know. And so, I just played it self-confident, you know. I could go anywhere I want to, you know. Walk around there . . . Yeah, they made me, you know, a straight. I was a trustee, you know. I was a trustee, and I would go to the white and colored camps and play, you know. Go to the women's . . . some of the prettiest women down there you ever . . . I try to get one out and I wasn't out myself. But I know if I got her out, I have somebody out. . . . And a man caught me on the outside of the camp and he said, "Man, what you want to get that woman out? You going on about her 'cause she's pretty and made up." And he said, "That woman done cut two niggers' heads off they shoulders." And that's just the way he told me. "And throwed the second, the colored, she throwed it under the house." And that kill that feeling then. I didn't want that.

McKee and Chisenhall also recorded a version of this story (1981, 121). It is similar in part to the magnificent, surreal blues vision, "My Baby," which White recorded for Arhoolie's two-volume *Sky Songs* (Arhoolie F1019/F1020) in 1963. The Library of Congress also recorded women inmates at Parchman, and some of these recordings were issued in 1987 on Rosetta Records 1316 *Jailhouse Blues: Women's A Cappella Songs from the Parchman Penitentiary, Library of Congress Field Recordings, 1936 and 1939.*

I said, "Well, she'll be here from now on, then. Forget about it." He said, "I know you got a man, say Ervin Henry ———. If they any way in the world to get out and you want out, say Ervin would get them for you. That's a man I liking for you. Say Ervin will do anything, Bukka. I don't believe too many man around here that people do for like they, uh, but they done put the clamp on you. Got to be here for two years. You can't go." I just made a sense of that. I wasn't doing nothing but playing, practicing—the Sergeant and the driver, them boys I was teaching lessons, you know. And so, I didn't get a lick while I was down there. And that's a big racket, too. Didn't get nar a lick. I was just like somebody in jail and couldn't get out. That's all. Couldn't go free. I was free there, you know. But man, we had a band there. What you talking about. Ow wee! And I—they didn't start it until I got there. I said, "I believe y'all was praying for me to come down here." I swear to God, the man said heard more talk of me than a little. [Laughs.]

Did you compose "I Believe I'm Fixin' to Die" before you go to prison?

No, after I got out, after I got out. "Fixin' To Die," yeah, after I got out. Sometime I be out I try to play it, but I can't sing it like I want to, and I hardly ever fool with it, you know. A lot of songs, I can't. Anytime I can't master anything, I, uh, best to don't fool with it. 'Cause then my voice was really good. Think about thirty years ago or better and now, you know, got to be, so now, I play now what I can handle with my voice. See, that's the way I do.

Sounds awful good to me.

[Laughs.] Well, it still sounds good to the peoples. If it didn't, they wouldn't have me going, you know. But like I say, you can't take a A-model or a T-model and make it a '72 car out of it. You just can't do it. It can't play with these speeds you got now, you know. [Laughter.]

Yeah. We sure do thank you a lot.

Well, I thank you all. I enjoyed myself. If y'all ever see any work you can get for me I'd appreciate it. . . . Everyone at the school, you know. Like I say, I've been out there twice. I was out there, I believe, last time and I broke a string. I never quit. I fixed the string and steady talking over it. Just kept it going, just kept it going.

White suffered from late-onset diabetes in the last years of his life. While on a concert tour in 1976, he suffered a stroke in Massachusetts; several more were to follow. Booker T. Washington White died of cancer of the pancreas in Memphis on February 26, 1977. He is buried at the New Park Cemetery in Memphis.

Rabbit Foot Diva

2 I Am the Baby of Beale Street
Lillie Mae Glover, a.k.a.

Big Memphis Ma Rainey

Lillie Mae Hardison was born in 1906 in the Middle Tennessee town Columbia. When she was still quite young her father, a sanctified preacher, moved her family to Nashville. It was from Nashville, at the age of fourteen, that she ran off with a traveling medicine show. Earlier she had apprenticed with her siblings, singing gospel in her father's church.

In the 1920s, Hardison settled in Memphis and married cook Willie Glover. At this time she was already known as "Baby Ma Rainey" because of the similarity of her singing to that of the great blueswoman. From the late 1920s until Urban Renewal forced her to relocate, Glover was a fundamental part of the Beale Street scene. She was a Beale Street institution and involved in the entertainment, vice, and hoodoo businesses that thrived on the Main Street of black Memphis. She was invariably described by her contemporaries as a tough woman.

When we interviewed Glover in May of 1972, she was feeling old, dejected, and lonesome. She had recently been forced to relocate from her apartment near Beale Street to a federal housing project on Lauderdale. She had been very ill and had given up show business as well as her other entrepreneurial enterprises. When Margaret McKee and Fred Chisenhall talked to her the next year, Glover was more upbeat. After our visit with Glover, we spread the word that she could still sing, and local promoters Harry Godwin and Steve LaVere began booking her for shows locally and on the traveling Memphis Blues Caravan.

After the re-creation of Beale Street as a resort for middle-class tourists, Glover once again became a fixture on Beale. Performing for this kind of audience was old hat for Glover, who was a veteran of white-only shows on the old Beale Street as well as other all-white venues, such as West Memphis's Cotton Club.

On the new Beale Street, Glover often performed with Prince Gabe and the Millionaires, with whom she recorded two songs ("Stormy Monday" and "Every Day I Have the Blues") on an album produced for the blues tourism market, *Memories of Beale Street: Prince Gabe and the Millionaires with the Original Memphis Sound* (Toad LP 001). Blues journalist Jim O'Neal described Glover on the new Beale as: "slow-moving but quick witted and still sassy at 73, she knows how to keep the crowd applauding and laughing" (1978, 29). Heart surgery in the late 1970s slowed her down, but she returned to Beale Street and to performing. Writing in 1985, the year of Glover's death, Hortense J. Spillers observed that "Lillie Mae Glover 'hangs out' well with Memphians half her age and carries a tune as pure as any that they have ever heard" (1985, 111).

[Glover sings "Haunted House Blues."] Okay, what was the name of that song?

"Haunted House Blues." And let me see, that a "Haunted House Blues" and this one ———— so far back.

"Haunted House Blues" was recorded by Bessie Smith in New York City in 1924 and released on the Columbia label.

[Glover sings collection of traditional verses.] What was the name of that one?

Just the old original blues. . . . Yes, old original blues.

Could we ask you a few questions?

Mm-huh.

Where were you born?

Nineteen six . . . in Columbia, Tennessee.

How long did you stay in Columbia?

Well, I was quite a kid, we moved to Nashville, Tennessee. That was when I was young. I run off from Nashville, but I was fourteen years old. Joined the medicine show.

Which one was that? Do you remember?

Yes, Simpson's Medicine Show.

Was there any other performers?

Yes, there were plenty of performers there. . . . Well, this one was named Simpsons and the head man was named Simpson and he had this medicine show. I can't remember the others because it was so long ago. I was a young girl. And my mama, see, they was all church people. They came and got me off of the stage, see. And at that time, you know, I quite young. I didn't know anything ———— because I was raised up in church. My father was the pastor. And I's raised up in church so, you know, they got me away from there. They. [Pauses.]

According to Michael Bane, Glover ran off with a Tom Simpson and he taught her the business (1982). She told McKee and Chisenhall in 1973 that it was Jim Hayden (1981).

Is that when you started singing in church?

Wow, yes, when I started singing. I'm a two sisters and two brothers outside of myself. There was five of us. There was fourteen of us all together, but five of us sing in a quartet-like, in church. That's where we were raised up at. Christian church. So when I got big enough to run, my mama got sick and died when I was fourteen years old. I run off from home. And I joined up with another medicine show. And this fellow was named Jim Hayden. I never will forget him. He taught me what I knew. I used to sit out and watch him. I was supposed to work ————. I started to sing the blues first then I looked at the girls on the show. They was dancing. I wanted to be a chorus girl. So I started working chorus. Then this Jim Hayden, he would blow trumpet and he would double back in the olio—he had to do the olio as the comedian. They called it the olio then. And he doubled back as the comedian. I challenged him one day. I said, "Why don't you let me be the comedian?" I slipped in a box of checkedy dress—great big ole red checks, red and green checks. I never will forget it. And I bought this dress. [Phone rings.] That's about the lady. Go and answer right quick. And so I made these checks pass. I got me some panties, had bought some great big ole panties, and I had put green ribbon and red ribbon. So I had dressed myself up and I had a white cap, an old white shirt, and I had an old bow tie, and I done this unbeknownst to him. I looked at myself and I blackened my face and made myself a comedian. And I wanted to ask him to let me be a comedian. So I didn't ask him that day. The next day I say, "I can do what you doing," 'cause I can tell those jokes. He said, "You don't know nothing about telling jokes." I said, "Oh yes, I do." He said, "Well, I'm going to let you try it tomorrow night." I said, "Yes?" He said, "Yeah. See how you come out, I'm going to let you open the olio." I said, "Good." So that next night, he had me open the olio and I come on and I tore the place up. Great big ole tent. So he told me, he says, "Well, after this you don't work the choruses no more, you're not in the chorus no more." He said, "You have stepped up a little." [Laughter.] So he had want me to do the blues and the jokes. And I'd always tear the house down. They didn't know whether I was girl or boy. [Laughter.] They always wonder who I was. Someone say she was a girl. Some say she was a boy. They didn't know what I was. So I kept on and I got in vaudeville, and then I just go from one show. I used to be on carnival, too. Used to be, and then I used to be with Rabbit Foot years ago.

The olio was a survival of the white, blackface minstrel shows of the antebellum era. Robert C. Toll described olio as the variety section that made up the second part of the show. It included comedy and a wide variety of novelty acts. Toll included in his list of this "miscellaneous" section "song and dance men, acrobats, men playing combs, porcupine quills, or glasses, and any number of other novelties." The olio also allowed the crew time to set up the closing act behind the curtains (1974, 55).

With Rabbit Foot?

Yes, Mr. Wolcott say he never had a blues singer on his show—I had a voice then that could sing—the mike got out of fix—and I sang without the mike and you could hear me all over the place. [Laughter.] Had a voice then. And so, then, I went from carnival show, I worked with Jerry Brady, I worked with Great Southern Shows, and I worked with, oh, Wallace's Show, I worked with—well, I don't know—the Amusement Company Show, and I worked with ———— and then I started to working with the Babblin' Babies. I've always been a star of each show, but I never did, I don't know, I never just wanted to, to just get away, to get out. I don't know if I was scared or what, but I was always good everywhere I went. I always got credit for it. So I'd always stop the show. A lot of [laughs], a lot of teams, and they used to have teams and they would always want to go in 'head of me. All of them want to go in 'head of me because I'd stop the show. Always was good with whatever I started with, so they'd say "Let me get on first 'cause you can't get on when she hits on there." So, I have a friend who lives up the street now, she used to be with Wolcott's Rabbit show. . . .

She told Margaret McKee and Fred Chisenhall also of her work with the Bronze Mannequins, Georgia Minstrels, Harlem in Havana, and Vampin' Baby shows (1981, 148). Rabbit's Foot Company was organized in 1900 by African American Pat Chappelle. After Chappelle's death in 1911, the show was purchased by a white man, F. S. Wolcott. Wolcott's Rabbit's Foot operated "until well into the 1940s" (Sampson 1980, 60–61). Rabbit's Foot and Silas Green From New Orleans Show were two of the more prestigious and long running of the African American minstrel companies.

Who else was on the Rabbit Foot show while you were? Do you remember who?

There was Daisy Kennedy, this Thelma James—she was on there—and, uh, I can't remember. . . . No, I don't. Because it was so far back. I don't remember. I can't 'call their names. I remember one was named Happy Satchel. I never will forget that, Happy Satchel. You know they had some crazy names, you know. And so, like today, you can tell people what my real name is. So, at this time I cannot, I'm not able to work anymore. So, I know I'll never be able to work anymore. The doctors tell me I'll never be able to work no more. No kind of work. And so, it kind of gets me down. But as they say today, There's no business like show business. That's right, I've had some good days, I've had some bad days. I know the times when we didn't make a ———. [Phone rings and Glover drops mike. Screams] Oh, my! [Laughs.] And so, as I say, . . . I still say show business, no business like show business. I still love it. I want to sing again but I know I'll never make it. So I just have to give it up. . . . But I enjoyed myself singing when I did. And it's like ——— I wild about him. I'm crazy about Flip Wilson, Redd Fox—I'm wild about him. And Carol Burnette I wouldn't take nothing for. [Laughs.] She's nuts like I am. I used to be a terrible comedian, understand, so Carol Burnette is just it, you see. And Martha Raye is another feature of mine. I'm going to call. And so, I'm going to have to give show business up now because there's no more for me. The old lady's done got up in age. So, I've got to sixty-five years old, so far. And I hope I get older. So there's nothing for me to do but sit around and look the ole ——— these singers are coming in. But I wish that they'd do more singing than they do jumping. [Laughs.] You can't hardly hear what they singing, you don't know what they singing about today. All they do is start to whooping and hollering. They take one word, and they'll find any place, and they just start whooping and a hollering, and you have to go through like that. [Laughs.]

[Emphatically] I wish they'd do more singing than they would hollering! 'Cause they scare people to death hollering. I love singing. They call themselves singing, they just scare people to death. But I do love to hear good singing. Happen to been, I went out here to see a band here one Friday night a week ago. Mark Steinberg, fellow use to work for me. He's, he's, uh, saxophone player. He's got a gang of other musicians, use to work together, and a lot of them used to work for me. So he called me and said, "Let's go out and paint the town." We went out and heard a good band. It was just four of them; and it was organ, sax, him on sax, and a bass. And they played the real stuff like we used to, you know. Li, uh-huh. And didn't have all that shouting and whooping and hollering and going on, but they sing, they sing the real stuff. And then you could get some real songs, you know. 'Cause they don't, I have, since uh, I guess back here when I working, back in nineteen and seventy, I was working. I asked the boys to play the blues, and I had carried them over here to Blytheville, Arkansas. And I had a blues singer with me, but I always carry a blues singer with me. But I had this boy; I said to see to the boys out there and ask them, you know, get them out there and see about them playing the blues. They came in there and tells me they didn't know how to play no blues. I say [loudly], "You don't play no blues, and I'm paying you twenty dollars a night?" [Laughs.] "Come again to school." [Laughs.] You don't know, and they did not know the blues, just the old original blues, mm, mm, mm. Say they know something like James Brown or something like that. I said, "James Brown ain't the onliest man that ever sung, honey." I said, "Y'all got to learn something outside of James Brown."

Do you like James Brown?

Oh yeah, I'm wild about a lot of James Brown's numbers, but still, you know, lot of place you go to, they don't go for James Brown. They like to play these dances. I's playing these dances at the time. Why you got paid makes you feel about old people there don't know nothing about James Brown and Tom Jones and all of them, you see, they look for the blues, see. And so, they can't jump. [Laughs.] And so, I just, I says the world just coming to you. You don't know the blues. So this guy, he said, "Mama, I'll get out there." They all call me "Mama." When they don't call me "Ma," they call me "Mama." So, he said, "I'll get out there, make them ———, I'll make them play the blues for you." See. I say, "Yeah" 'cause I got to do something, you know. All these people here, they ain't going to let me go without singing the blues. I don't care where I go. I can walk into a place now and they know I'm sick. "Well, I know you going to do a number, I just want a little number; it won't hurt. It won't kill you if you just do one number." There I am, I'm stuck, I got to do one number. "Well, well, you know, so-and-so just come in. They didn't hear it and they and I . . . " [Laughter.] And then I'll have to do another number and before I know anything I'm just wound up. And so I just, . . . I don't know, it gets the best of me. I just sit around home, here, and it gets the best of me sometimes. I have my little crying spells. I look at the shows and then I say, "Oh, I've got to get out of this. I'm not going to die until my time comes no how. I've got to get out of this." Yeah, so I got to get out of this so I's just get up and get out, see. Have a nice time and come on back. I don't be having that nice a time because I be mostly be scared to death these days, you know. They wants to fight these days and I ain't even can walk. [Laughs.]

You first started playing in the church?

Yes.

Then you started playing the blues?

Yes.

Well, where did you learn to play the blues?

I just picked it up.

Did any of these other singers have an influence on you?

No, no, no, no. I just picked it up and when I started, everybody wanted to hire me. I was good. And that's—now, I'm not the original, old Ma Rainey. I'm the next. I'm the baby.

Why did they call you "Memphis Ma Rainey"?

Because I had a voice like hers. I started to singing for Ma Rainey in Birmingham, Alabama, working our show for . . . the Frolic Theater in Birmingham, Alabama. They started to call me—Kelly Beatty, I use to work for him—he started to call me "Baby Ma Rainey." See, we's in there, it was cold, you know, the carnival shows closed down, and he's in there offering a show and so he gives me that name, Baby Ma Rainey. . . . Baby Ma Rainey. So it stuck. . . . Now it's "Memphis Ma Rainey."

Sheldon Harris states that Ma Rainey played the Frolic in Birmingham in 1925 (1979). Chris Albertson, in his biography of Bessie Smith, describes Bessie's visit to see Ma Rainey during her 1925 appearance at the Frolic (1972).

Did you like the original Ma Rainey?

Yes, I was crazy about old Ma Rainey. She didn't know how to pay nobody, but I stuck her show up there until she paid me. . . . [Laughs.] But I was wild about her.

Did you sing a lot of her songs?

Oh, yes, yes, yes. She had me doing a whole lot of her songs. [Laughter.] Because she stayed about high all the time, you know. Yeah, she stayed high, and so I'd have to do her songs. And after I started to learn her songs, why, a lot of times, wouldn't be anything—she wouldn't be feeling bad or nothing—she'd just go on and let me sing. And then I and Bessie Smith, we used to get, she used to come and hear her. Yeah, I'm Bessie's good—was good friends. And we used to sing down here at the Old Chicago House. . . . Yeah, we used to sing together down at the Old Chicago House.

Beale Street?

Yeah, around from there.

McKee and Chisenhall describe the Chicago House as "a back-alley cafe where she [Bessie Smith] could get her favorite food, pig's feet." They quote Glover as saying, "It wasn't nothing but a dump, but we'd go around and have a jam session, see if we could out-sing the other. Lots of times we'd sneak off in the daytime and go to those clubs and drink. Bessie was drinking pretty heavy then" (1981, 149). Glover told these Memphis journalists that she first met Bessie Smith on the road and that she would visit her when Smith played the Palace in Memphis.

Were you ever on a medicine show with Ma Rainey, or you just play with her there at the theater?

No, just played with her there at theater. I never was on a medicine show with her. No.

Do you know Mrs. Van Hunt that used to sing with Bessie? Lives in Memphis now.

Yes, I know her and her daughter both. Charlene. Yes, I know her. I heard them sing, but I was little bit beyond them. [Laughs.] You know ———— everyone peek at me, you know. A little bit over them, understand. I know they nice people.... No, I never did, I just traveled with different shows, understand me. They ... yes, they featured me.... Yes, featured me. Featured me as the great blues singer, understand? The Baby Ma Rainey, see? Now, I never traveled. I went out for myself. I was great—got to be great.

Mrs. Van Zula Carter Hunt, originally from Somerville, Tennessee, traveled with the minstrel shows in the 1920s and 1930s. She was active in Memphis until the mid-1940s. For more on Hunt, see the Little Laura Dukes chapter. Sweet Charlene Peeples, Van Hunt's daughter, had been active locally as a club singer since the late 1940s. Both recorded for Adelphi Records in 1969–70 and are included on that label's two-volume LP *The Memphis Blues Again* (LaVere n.d.; Dixon, Godrich, and Rye 1997).

Did you ever make any records?

Yes, I made one with Sun Recordings Company. Made one. At, uh, that's been a good while back, and I cut my contract with them. Uh, there's was old Baby Ma something. Now, this guy.... Two songs, you know. I don't know the other side, what the other side was. I disremember, but the side what we were talking about, ... there's some guy in Nashville got hold of this record or something, and I been trying to get, I trying to do a little something. Something I'm trying to catch up with.... There's another lady going in my name is Lillie Mae Glover. My original name, see. And she's—I heard she was using this record, you understand. I'm the original; I'm the baby to old Ma Rainey! It's not another. It's a lot of them that calls themselves, but I'm the original to old Ma Rainey. I'm the Baby Ma Rainey.

In 1953, Lillie Mae Glover recorded "Call Me Anything, but Call Me" and "No Means No" for Sun Records in Memphis. She was accompanied by the Onzie Horne Combo (vibes, guitar, piano, bass, drums), which on this date included the fabulous guitarist Pat Hare. The record (Sun 184) was released as by "Big Memphis Ma Rainey with the Onzie Horne Combo" (Escott and Hawkins 1975; Leadbitter and Slaven 1968).

Did she call you that, too?

Yes! ... Yes, she called me Baby Ma Rainey, yeah. Couldn't tell me anything, you know. I know she was great, you know. [Laughs.] And I could go in the place of her. Why, there wasn't nothing you could tell me. [Laughs.] There wasn't a thing you could tell me.

Well, when you were on the minstrel shows and making records and all this, did you have some people playing behind you? Didn't you?

No, because all of them are dead, near about. I knows all of them are dead because I hadn't heard from none of them. Pork Chops, original Pork Chops. He was a comedian, though. He didn't play ———. Now, this Jim Hayden, as I was telling you about . . . yes, he played the trombone and trumpet. He was trumpet and trombone. And this other ———. Oh, Frank. What this guy's name? Frank, something, he's out of Nashville. I forget his name. And I forget, I forget this other guy's name in Nashville. They were living here. I hardly remember about four or five years ago. I don't know if they still living or not. And mostly all the old timers is gone. . . . In those days you didn't have to have nothing but a piano. Piano, trumpet, you didn't hardly have to have no bass in those days. A saxophone—maybe you'd have two saxophones—piano, trumpet, and a trombone, but sometimes you'd have a guitar. But such as bass, they didn't have any.

When did you come here to Memphis?

I came here to Memphis in '28.

Were you still going on the medicine shows while you were living in Memphis?

No, I stopped going on the medicine shows. I joined up with vaudeville shows then. I was with the Vampin' Babies. I followed the Vampin' Babies and I been with Wagner's Show. I've been with [mumbles] Tommy Green from New Orleans, Tommy Green from New Orleans. Yes. And, uh my goodness. [Laughs.] It finally came true. And I've been with so many vaudeville shows and things, I can't place them. 'Cause my remembrance is very short now these days, but I have been with many a one. . . . On Beale Street? . . . I am the Baby of Beale Street! They love me, they love me on Beale Street. I used to work at Palace. I worked at, uh, they call it Club Handy, yeah, lately, but it used to be the Citizen's Club. And I've had those places packed so that the polices used to have to pick up my money. Yes, to keep the people from getting it, they'd watch it so well. ——— and the police would have to pick up my money. I'm well known here and I'm well thought of. And last colored show was here at the New Daisy, was a Midnight Ramble. I, Bones, and Rufus, we all used to work together. Bones, Rufus, and I. So we done a show. The last vaudeville show was done at the New Daisy with me, Bones, and Rufus.

Glover is probably referring to Silas Green rather than Tommy Green from New Orleans. It was one of the larger and better-known minstrel shows. Silas Green from New Orleans Show toured the southern states from 1904 up to the mid-1950s, when Athens, Georgia, businessman Wilbur Jones, the show's last owner, closed it down (Sampson 1980, 100; Hay 1979).

William Worley in *Beale St.: Crossroads of American Music* includes a photograph of Glover singing at Club Handy at a private performance arranged for Congressman George Grider in the 1950s (1998, 42).

Now what was Bones's real name?

His name is Robert Couch. . . . He's a comedian and a dancer. Uh-huh.

And Rufus sings?

He try to sing, but he just, he plays like he singing; he can't sing. Oh! You talking about Rufus! Rufus sings! I was thinking about Bones. Yeah. Rufus sings; Rufus is a singer. Yeah, he's famous. But, uh, we was together, he wasn't doing much singing, he was just dancing. That was years back. He's kind of up in age with me. He's no baby, you know. . . . Yeah, yeah. I used to do all those Midnight Rambles. I and Bones and Rufus, and, uh, at the Palace. Yeah. Did all them.

The Rufus referred to is Rufus Thomas, the rhythm and blues and soul singer who recorded for Sun and Stax records in Memphis, worked as a WDIA DJ, and was generally prominent in the Memphis entertainment world. According to WDIA historian Louis Cantor, Rufus "worked originally with a man named Robert Couch, identifiable to Memphis audiences as Bones. For years, Rufus and Bones delighted followers doing various comedy routines, including a variation of the old blackface minstrel show, complete with straight man, interlocutor, and burnt cork on the face. . . . The minstrel routine was soon dropped, but Rufus and Bones remained a fixture of black entertainment for over a decade on Amateur Night at the Palace Theater on Beale Street or just about anywhere there was a crowd waiting to be amused" (1992, 94–95).

Did you ever work with W. C. Handy?

No, no.

Did you ever meet him?

Yes, I expect. I met a fair lot of old blues singers. I met Ethel Waters. I met Ethel in Terre Haute, Indiana, when I was young. Yeah. I admire her so much, and everybody say we look alike. We feature alike. Little children, they get after their mothers, "Come look at Big Ma Rainey." Their mothers say, "That's not Ma Rainey." They just cried, "Oh yes, it is, oh yes, it is." [Laughs.] Looks like they had a fit. And so, uh, so ——— 'cause she's changed. It's a wonderful thing for us all to change. I do hope someday I'm going back to church, before I leave here. [Laughs.] But at the time, I don't think that there's no use going back to church if you don't mean nothing. Just be what you is. So I still would like to end up there. At my age, I just, what at the time now, I just don't look like I just could give it up. I like to go night clubbing. As I say, you don't die until you turn thumbs. Now, I used to work over here for the Cotton Club. I worked over there seven years. It's a white night club over there, and I worked at Danny's Club. I used to do shows and have a band, too, over there. And I was over there seven years and I just look at those people, those old people. They never give up, you know. They just can drag, but they be up there dancing and singing. So I don't think it's no use of you just giving up now. A lot of times, I be awful sick up in here. I be real sick, but I don't give up. I lay here a while, I shake my head. Oh, let me get up and get out of here now. Sometimes I get out on the steps there, and if it's raining, why, I just sit there at the window and look. Lot of people, they come by, say "Glad to see you. Don't hardly ever see you anymore." I'm well known, you know. And look like just everyone glad to see me. It's a wonderful thing, you know. But I don't have any kin people here. I don't have no kin people here at all. My peoples in ———— and Nashville, Tennessee. I used to think that I live here and look like I'm loved by people and everything. I don't stay at home where I belong at. [Laughs.] I just live here in these three room and I think I do pretty well. I try to make it comfortable as I can, you know. And so, I make out. I get on this phone and talk to people, and call me, good to see that I'm getting along. So, it's wonderful to know peoples who love something about you, cares that much about you, you know. 'Cause when you're sick, look like the whole world gives you up, lots of times. But it's kind of how you carry yourself. It's the way you carry yourself, see. And so, I guess if I'd been an ole meanie. . . . I've always helped everybody. I've even had the law to tell people, "You go see Ma Rainey. She'll give you a place to stay." I used to run a rooming houses on Lambert and I had five rooming houses, running them for a fellow down there. And I used to give people food [and] rooms to stay free until they gets hold of something.

Ethel Waters (1896–1977), a Pennsylvania native and popular performer of "classic" blues, stage productions, and Hollywood films, worked, later in life, with evangelist Billy Graham's Crusades.

According to Bane, Glover "'rented rooms' for a little extra money. The rooms were rented to girls for an hour or however long business would take, and on a good night she could clear two or three hundred dollars" (1982, 67).

Guitarist Rick Ireland described the 1950s West Memphis club scene that featured live black music for white audiences: "These were pretty rowdy crowds. Real heavy-duty, sure-enough, truck-driving rednecks—beer-drinking, truck-driving rednecks. Danny's Club was down the street, and they had chicken wire around the bandstand so the beer bottles wouldn't hit the musicians when the fights broke out. At the Cotton Club, they were a little more subtle" (Gordon 1995, 49).

Right now I can set out there and somebody come along, I say, "Well, what you going to do? You just going to let me sit here and starve to death?" And they'll say, "Old woman, you know you just kidding." I say ———. They give a dollar or two dollars or something. [Laughs.] So, that's the reason, now, I cried a lot when I's moved out here from Beale Street. I loved Beale Street because, in a way, you know, I was just originated there on Beale Street and I thought I was moving away from everybody when I moved out here, you see. And I used to, when I found out that I had to move from Beale Street, I used to sit there on Hernando, at the Harlem House, and I cried. I had my little dog—he got killed. And I had to let a lady have him when I moved over here. And that just hurt me to the heart. But I used to sit there and talk to my dog, and he looked like he understood me. I said, "Nobody but I and you. You got to take care of Mama now, not just sit and cry." I said, "Ain't nobody passed along now, honey." [Laughs.] I was used to the people passing; everybody knew me, would holler at me and talk to me, see. And that just kind of got me down. So, here about, it's been about three months ago, a girl told me across the driveway, my dog was dead. I loved that dog. They said when I would call over the phone, the lady would put him up to the phone and I'd talk to him and he shake his head, she said just like he knowed what I was talking about. And he would even bark, yes. He heard my voice, he'd bark. And when they bringed the dog to see me, they stop up the street to see where he was and he just tear up, he just be flying, coming here. And I'd be setting up here and sometimes the door would be open, he jump up in here and kiss me. Oh, I say, "It's Mama's baby," and he would just have a fit! So, this girl told me, she said—some kind of a lady, I told you, she scared to tell your face—she found out they left the gate open and he got out. She wants you to know he's dead. Because I told you I'd been awful sick, and which I had been awful sick about three weeks, and she heard the doctor say don't let anything upset me, you know. And she don't want you to know it. And so I told Boyd I had a dream. I told her a story. I said, "I had a dream about my dog" and I say, "I know he's dead." She said, "You don't know that." I said, "You couldn't help it" because she was crazy about him, too. She liked dogs and so she said, "Well, yes, he's dead. I couldn't help it." I said, "I know you couldn't help it, so don't feel hard about it." So she said, "Irene told you." I said, "She did not." I said, "I just dreamed about it." So she said, "Oh yes, she did." I say, "No." So I told her, I said, "No, I just dreamed about it." So she said, "Yes, yeah, I told Irene to don't tell you because, she said she wouldn't tell you because you was in awful shape, and I told your head dresser not to tell you." She said, "She knowed she wasn't going to tell you, crazy as you was about that dog." [Laughs.] And so, but Irene told me about the dog. She said, "I rather for you to know it, you know, than to be calling out there and asking about him and asking to speak to him." I ask to speak to him just like he was a human. I say, "Could I speak to my child?" [Laughs.] And she'd put him up to the phone and he'd bark at me, "Whoop! Whoop!" [Laughs.] But I'd say, "You still Mama's child, ain't you cake ————." So, I'd say a lot of times, I had been sick down there in Hernando, where I lived at, and that dog would take his head and lay it on my breast. He take his head and do it like he say, "I'm with you." Understand? . . . And I'd talk to him, I'd say, "You all I got. Mama's got no one here but you," and, I don't know, I just felt that dog was just all of it, you know. So, I say, I never. . . . That makes three dogs I've had. Which dogs I never. . . . When you get crazy about something, you can't keep it. If it's a kid, you crazy about that kid, something happen to it. So I'll never have another dog. No way, because I guess I'll be here until I die because the rent is cheap.

They say they going to pay me up. I want them to pay me up so I can have curtains and draperies and curtains. . . . I likes the jazzy-looking machine. [Laughs.] I just don't give up, and so I never have been in a place where I had to pay twenty-five dollars rent for light and gas, you know. So I thinks it's great for old people like us, you know. It's wonderful place. And so, of course, I have all these little bills piles upon me, but I make it through all open and paid for me. So I says the Lord's in the plan, but I get along as well as I do, something comes along to help me. Sometimes look like things is pretty tight, but I make it somehow or another on one hundred and thirty-seven [dollars]. That's all I get, that's all my allow. They want you to, I have to pay fifty-four dollars for a girl to come in here and clean up. Ain't that pitiful? That's really pitiful. And they don't want you to have anything but food and a place to stay; you don't have to have no clothes. They don't care whether you any clothes or not. How you get them clean or what. It don't make any difference. Just food and a place to stay, somebody to clean up for you. So I thank them for that. I make out the rest of the way. [Laughs.]

Did you ever use to sing with the old jug bands, string bands, and things?

Yes, I have. . . . Yes, I used to work with Dewey.

Dewey Corley, born in 1898 in Halley, Arkansas, moved to Memphis in 1916. Corley played harmonica, jug, kazoo, piano, and washtub bass, and was an active player in the Memphis jug band scene from the 1920s on. Recordings of Corley were made and released on a number of labels in the 1960s and 1970s, including Adelphi, Arhoolie, Rounder, and Albatross. Corley died in Memphis on April 15, 1974.

Uh-huh, and then I used to work with Son Brimmer, you remember? You heard of Son Brimmon? . . . I worked with Son Brimmon and then I worked with . . .

Son Brimmon, or Brimmer, was another name used by Will Shade (1898–1966), the guitar and harmonica player who organized the Memphis Jug Band in the 1920s and wrote many of their songs. For more information on Shade, see the Little Laura Dukes chapter.

Yeah, then I worked with this other Son, Blind Son. Oh, what's his name? I knew him well. And what's this other little woman's name? What's her name?

Little Laura Dukes?

That's right. We've worked together. Yes, we have. . . . Yes, she did pretty well, uh-huh.

Did you ever work with Gus Cannon?

Yes, uh-huh. Yes, yeah. I know him well. He just don't know where I live at or he'd come to see me. He, uh, I worked with him and Laura Dukes. We used to work on the *Delta Queen*. . . . Yeah, we used to go down the Mississippi River. Worked on the *Delta Queen*. ——— used to work together, worked the *Delta Queen*. We was lonesome souls together, yeah. Laura Dukes is as old as I am. She's around my age. She's little light, she's tiny, she's a tiny thing to be as old as she is, uh-huh. I ask her; she says, "I'm not quite as old as you is, Ma." I say, "I imagine you're not." [Laughs.] "I swear, you might not be as old as I am, but you been here a long time." [Laughs.] I like to kid her, you know.

Did you ever work with Memphis Minnie?

Yes, yeah. She's in some sort of.... Yeah, I want to go see her, too. If she's still living.... She's out there at some sort of home. Yeah.... Yes, she had a stroke. I've got to go see her because she used to come see me all the time when I lived on Linden. Anywhere she know I was, she'd come see me, yeah. Yeah, I know Memphis Minnie. I know quite a lot, a lot of blues singers, but I've forgotten them, you know. Like Sara Martin. You know Sara Martin? . . . Yeah, I knowed her way back yonder. Since I was a girl and I started to singing, but I'd meet all those.... Old fellow named Jim Hayden. I don't know whether he's living or not, but he used to carry me around and make me acquainted. We'd go to town to town and we'd meet a lot of them. See, I played shows in Effingham, Illinois, when they didn't like colored people. Red Bay, Alabama, they didn't like.... Yeah, all those old places and things. So.

An exceptional guitarist and vocalist, Memphis Minnie (1897–1973) was born Lizzie Douglas in Algiers, Louisiana, and died in Memphis. Memphis Minnie, one of the greatest and most influential of blues performers, recorded from the 1920s to the 1950s. Her last days were spent at Jell Nursing Home in Memphis. Minnie frequently played with the members of the Memphis Jug Band and recorded with them for Victor in 1930. For more information on Memphis Minnie, see the Little Laura Dukes chapter.

Sara Martin (1884–1955), a native of Louisville, Kentucky, was a superior singer of "classic" blues.

Perhaps it was to Effingham that Glover referred when she told Bane, "We'd go to places where they'd never seen a colored person before. I remember once in Illinois, when we rolled into this little town, they thought we was no-tailed bears! Lawd, can you believe that? No-tailed bears!" (1982, 66). The no-tailed bear image for blacks appearing in all-white communities has also been reported by John C. Campbell (1921, 95) for the southern mountains.

Did you ever play around Georgia?

Rome, Rome, Georgia. I played Rome, Georgia. Now, Louisiana, I used to play Lake Charles, Monroe, Bear Straw ———. Oh, so many places I've played in Louisiana. . . . No, I don't know exactly. Seems like I have played Atlanta. I believe I have because it ain't too far from Rome, I don't think. No. And I believe I played it. There's so many places that I have some friends who get after me about. Hey, we sit down and talk, start talking about old times, you know, and uh, "You remember when we played ———?" "No, I never did play there." "Oh yeah, you did, you just done forgot now," you know. [Laughs.] "You know you played there." . . . No, no. See, I been sick. My remembrance ain't nothing. Sorry, I'm trying to remember here, just little things I do around here, you know. And I remember, not this far back.

Based on a 1951 article in *Melody Maker* that reported Big Bill Broonzy's claim that he had seen Ma Rainey in Atlanta in 1945 (the original Ma Rainey died in 1939), Sandra Lieb speculated that Broonzy may have actually seen Lillie Mae Glover, the Baby Ma Rainey (1981; Schuler et al. 1951).

Yeah, I played Texas. . . . Met Mary Lou Crosby, met . . . Ida Cox—me and Ida Cox has done some numbers here at the Palace. . . . Uh-huh. Right down there at the Palace Theater. Yeah, old Ida. [Laughs.] I used to tease her, she such a wise about her, "Well, stop singing, now all you talking." [Laughs.] She'd cuss me out, I swear, she'd cuss me out about the talking. So, there's quite a few of them. . . . I think St. Louis, too. I played around St. Louis. I think played the Franklin, the ———— and Deluxe, and then I played a lot of those clubs, but those were the theaters I played in. Vampin' Babies. I come up with . . . And we had a great show; they went crazy over it. They just went crazy over it. And they said, "Is she a woman or a man?" And then some of the boys got back there, was messing with me, they found out [laughter] I was a woman. They came 'round, "She's a woman! She's a woman! She's a woman!" And so, I never will forget that was an old blues tune, "It was early one Monday morning, I was on my way to school." I sang that in St. Louis with ———— hanging down my back with a little ole hat on with a streamer on it. And my hair, I had real long hair then. I had it combed down and I had—I used to wear red drawers with the white trimming around it. I done see'd some up here at the police station. And those red drawers with the white trimming around it. And my dress was short then. And I was singing—I come through the stage—I was singing "Early one Monday morning I was on my way to school, that was the morning I broke my mama's rule." [Laughs.] And so, that's one of Ma Rainey's old-time numbers, too. And when I come on doing—it was an old number— I used to be a dancer, too. I used to teach dancing—now I can't walk. Ain't that pitiful. [Laughs.] I used to a great dancer. I could dance ————. I used to take there, "Oh, so-and-so doing such-and-such a thing, she can't beat me." That's it. In those days, see, you trying to outdo the other one. You go on and learn, see, the hard [way]. You had to learn the hard. They think today . . . in those days you had to work. See? These girls think that when you learn how to do the Twist it's all of it now. That's no show business; you have to dance. Twist ain't nothing—anybody can do the Twist. And I tease them sometimes, get up and do the Black Bottom, you know, and they just die laughing, be laughing.

Ida Cox (1896–1967), a native of the north Georgia town Toccoa, was one of the greatest of the "classic" blues singers. She was also one of the genre's outstanding songwriters.

What's the Black Bottom?

That's a dance they call the Black Bottom. Ma Rainey originated that, the Black Bottom. The Black Bottom, and uh, tip over you do ———— step over your back, backing your toe up, you know, you twist and go on. They call it something, they call it something now. They call it, I believe, they say Scratch in the Gravel or the Sand, yeah, the Sand. I say, well, we been doing the same all our lives. That's what it is, they call the Black Bottom the Sand, they step in the Sand, you know, and they call that the Sand, and I say we've been doing that all our lives. I'll show you. It's two girls live up the street, you know. They are old, you know, chorus workers, and we laugh sometimes about, you know. She's says she's trying to rehearse a show for—I believe it's uh, mmmm, I use to work for the same show—but she's going back on it now and she's rehearsing some girls. Her name is Annie Jean Barnett. She's rehearsing some girls and she's talking about how stiff they was and so she was talking to me about it, liking to break the girls' legs about this Knock-Knock, when they come out. We was going some place—I believe it was Hot Springs—and this Knock-Knock, I wanted to curse this Mop-Mop. I had them three days to work with. At this time, I would curse a lot. Okay, it was hard on you, we had to work you, you know. And that was those steps, I'm telling you. "What's you—what's wrong with you?" "I don't know," "Can't you do nothing wrong?" I'd haul off and hit [her] across the beak. "Bitch! Bitch!" [Laughs.] "Mop, mop, mop, might of been of sleep if I knowed you wouldn't have it done by this time," "Can we relax now?" "Alright, sit over there. I'll cook a pot of pig feet." I was living on Fourth Street, down there over Rothschild grocery store. I had an iron stove. I'd cook a pot of pig feet so when they'd get hungry at night, why, I'd give them sandwiches. I'd work them so hard, I give them sandwiches. I said, because we'd have to go when they're hot. [Laughs.] And I'd give them sandwiches, and I never will forget Betty Evans—she's in St. Louis today. She called me here about a couple of months ago. A lot of the old timers, they find out where I'm at and they call me, you know. And so, one's named Daisy Killabrew, and Daisy, oh, she was good. She worked with a rope—we had a rope, course, you know, and you had to do it. You worked then. But now days they don't know nothing but the Twist. You can do the Twist, and you got it. Oh, she can dance, she can dance. She's a regular gumshoe. [Laughs.] Now, she ain't dancing. She's act like that . . .

Back when you worked, did you just sing the blues or did you sing ballads and other types of songs?

Yes, yes. . . . Now, [sings] "woke up this morning, [speaks] my baby is gone." And then I used to sing "wonder what became of Sally, my old gal." And [sings/hums] "yes, sir, that's my baby. No, sir." [Laughs.] And the "Do Da Blues," I used to do, uh, the "Do Da Blues" and [hums] "some day, sweetheart, you're going to be tied" and "Sugar Babe." "Sugar Blues," did the "Sugar Blues." [Sings quietly to herself.] The "Sugar Blues," uh-huh. . . . Uh-huh. [Sings "Sugar Blues." Laughs.] I guess I know some of it. [Laughs.]

"Sugar Blues" was a standard with the blues women of the 1920s. Sara Martin, for instance, recorded a version at her first recording session in New York City for Okeh in 1922.

Would you think up most of your songs or did you pick them up from other people?

No, I pick them up. . . . Guys like, what's his name, that composed it. You know. I used to know. Did; I used to know all of them, you see. Ty McCoy. . . . And you see I used to be all up in the social clubs, the [Y-B?] Club, and to this woman up there, she used to give me all these clubs, so I got work to do. And I worked these clubs and I worked these hotels and I worked all these old white old places and I worked this white club, the ——— Club. . . . Well, I got to go with rock 'n' roll and the same type thing. I can do rock 'n' roll. . . . Oh yeah. I can do the Twist to death. [Laughs. Laughter.] . . . Well, now, I used to do "Rock me, baby, won't you rock me all night long." And it's [hums] "Every Day I Have the Blues." I did that. And did the "Dog," "Walking the Dog." Oh yes. "I Got My Mojo Working," and I don't know. I used to do a whole lot of them. . . . Yes, I'm a blues singer. Blues [Laughs, then sings softly.] Someday soon I ———. I used to love that song. . . .

"Every Day I Have the Blues" was recorded by Memphis Slim in 1948 and subsequently recorded by many other artists, including Lowell Fulsom, Joe Williams, B. B. King, Elmore James, Brownie McGhee, and James Brown.

"Rock Me, Mama" was recorded by Big Arthur Crudup in 1945. Lil' Son Jackson, Muddy Waters, B. B. King, Slim Harpo, and Otis Redding were among the many who followed suit.

"The Dog" and "Walking the Dog" were hits for Rufus Thomas on Stax Records in 1963.

"Got My Mojo Working" is usually associated with Muddy Waters, who recorded several versions of the song beginning in 1957.

[Sings] Someday, sweetheart . . . [Phone rings. After call, she sings the song.] Someday, sweetheart, you going to be sorry. . . . [Laughs.] I was kind of hazy on that one. [Laughs.] There's another song I want to sing. [Sings softly to herself, then sings "Every Day I Have the Blues." Laughs.]

All right! That was very beautiful. Where did you learn that song?

B.B.

Did you learn that song from a record or did you learn that from him?

Learned it from a record. I'm the one who kept B.B.—he'll tell you— kept him going. He used to tell me. We used to meet at, after our gigs, at the Hamburger Heaven on Beale Street. And in the mornings around 3:30 and 4 o'clock. So he says, "Ma, I'm near about ready to give it up. I ain't making no money." He says, "What you think about it?" I said, "Don't give it up; you're good." I say, "Someday you'll amount to something." He said, "You reckon I will, Ma?" I said, "I know you will." So he said, "All right, I'm going to try it." So now he plays. Anytime he comes in town, he finds me. "I never will forget my Mama." And he'll tell anybody, "This is what's kept me up today; this is what got me don't give up and I wouldn't give up." And, yeah, so he always finds me somewhere to do something. Oh yeah, yes, yes, he's wild about me. And I bakes him cakes, a lots of. I had a godbaby used to work with B.B., Bessie Harris, and, uh, I can't find her. Don't know where she's staying or what. But her, uh, they would always fight over the cakes. I'd bake them and send them to different towns. . . . All Bessie would want. . . . She'd, uh, "These are my cakes, Mama." I'd say, "No." I would call them and tell them, "Don't start having none of those cakes; they got names on them." [Laughs.] They got names on them, and of B.B., he—my god—and . . . Bobby. Bobby, he's a 'preciator of mine, too. . . . Yeah, uh-huh, yeah. Bobby Bland . . . he's a 'preciator. All the blues singers, . . . they think I'm a wonderful thing. Yeah, they do and so. I was with Bobby here, when he was here before. Had a nice time. I was sleeping on the daybed in the house. I didn't know he knowed I was in the house. I called myself sleeping there. Because I'm not allowed to drink because I've been sick, you know. And so, I had not knowed but he told me, he said, "Baby's got to stand up." He wanted me to do it. I'm not going to do it. I just can't do it. Everybody was just screaming and hollering, "Yeah, make her do it, make her do it." I should know, I can't do it. I'm sorry. I told him that I just couldn't make it. He said, "You got to come back here and stay with me until [laughs] until the thing's over with." And so I just stayed back there and talked with him and everything. And Junior Parker, he was a 'preciator of mine. We all be coming, we come up the hard way, you see. And they's really good blues singers. The late Junior Parker was good blues singer. . . . Yes, he was.

Herman "Junior" Parker (1932–71) was born in Mississippi and raised in Arkansas. A talented singer and harmonica player, Parker recorded many great postwar blues songs for the Sun and Duke labels. A cover of his song "Mystery Train" was an early hit for Elvis Presley in 1954.

And I tell you another 'preciator of mine. He died. ———— What was his name? Oh, you remember. ———— I tell you, he and Earl Forrest used to work together. Earl Forrest is a blues singer. Earl Forrest—he's out here on Maury—Toast of the Town. He's got a place out there. . . . Yeah, uh-huh.

Earl Forrest, a drummer, was one of the original Beale Streeters, which included B. B. King, Bobby Bland, and Johnny Ace.

Fellow was named Johnny, Johnny. . . . They was a great big singer. You know when you spin the pistol, what do you call that?

When you spin the pistol?

Yeah, until you set, you know . . . Russian roulette. He killed hisself with Russian roulette. This blues singer did. And his name is Johnny something. I forget his name. Johnny, Johnny, Johnny, yes. He was a great blues singer, yes.

"Johnny Ace" Alexander (1929–54) was a smooth-voiced rhythm-and-blues crooner who was especially popular with teen audiences. He died playing Russian roulette in Houston, Texas. James M. Salem's critically acclaimed biography of Alexander, *The Late Great Johnny Ace and the Transition from R&B to Rock 'n' Roll,* was published by the University of Illinois Press in 1999.

What, did he do that on stage one night, when he was singing?

No, it was back of the stage. [Phone rings. Muffled speech.] Shake a hand, shake a hand.

Do you know "Shake a Hand, Shake a Hand"?

Uh-huh.

What type blues now does Earl Forrest play?

Now, he's not doing any kind of blues now. He's just running this club. A club, nightclub . . . and cafe, but he's not doing the blues. ———— blues singer. He's . . . [a] piano player. He tried to play a little piano. Yeah, uh-huh. Something like that. But this Johnny Ace was great. . . . Yeah. Johnny Ace is great. I just remembered "Shake a Hand." I made many a dollar off "Shake a Hand." Ah, I better not forget it.

Do you remember any of the other of Johnny Ace's songs?

No. I don't.

You talked a minute ago about how you used to sing "I Got My Mojo Working. . . ." Did you ever know Muddy Waters?

Sleep in a hollow log. [Laughs.] I say drink muddy water and sleep in a hollow log.

Do you know the song that came from?

No, I don't. I never did sing that. . . . Yeah, yeah. I'm going to drink muddy water and sleep in a hollow log. That's a part of it.

Or stay in Atlanta and be your dirty dog.

Yeah, something like that. Yeah, uh-huh. . . . I'll tell you another one, "See See Rider." [Sings three verses of "See See Rider," including verse about drinking muddy water.] I don't know the rest of it now. [Laughs.] I used to do that, too.

Mojo is from voodoo, isn't it?

Yes. [Sings "I Got My Mojo Working" to herself, practically inaudibly, then starts to sing louder.] I can't think of it.

All right, back in your days of traveling around and playing here in Memphis and all, did you come in contact with voodoo and conjure and all?

No, oh no. I'm just like on those shows, you know. ———— but I never came in contact with voodoo, no. I wish I would. [Laughter.] I never. . . . Now, I was a manager to be with the [pauses] when I got off the show, I played clubs, you know, see. We had clubs to play the ———— and we had clubs to play, and we'd work those clubs. We'd be so tired, we had to go home, you know. . . . And then they get up and play cards, you know, until time to go to work. And then, a lot of times, when they'd be so tired, you know, going back to work, it look like . . . In Dallas, Dallas, Texas, I used to work that fair. Dallas, Texas, I played that fair for five years. . . . At state fair, I worked that fair for five years. And working so hard, you know, that your tongue would be hanging out of your mouth, you know. [Laughs.] You'd be so glad to go to bed when you got a bed that you almost ———— just as you got there, you know. So I went, I went in Texas. I've just enjoyed myself, you know. I can say I—those were my biggest days, when I could work. There's nothing to me no more. [Laughs.] In a way, nothing to me, but I'm not going to give up. Nothing to me.

A year later, Glover recounted to McKee and Chisenhall her many experiences as a merchant of mojos and other conjure services (1981).

Did you ever meet Blind Lemon Jefferson, Lightnin' Hopkins, or Huddie Lead-belly?

Sam "Lightnin'" Hopkins (1912–82) was the famous Texas guitarist/vocalist who recorded prolifically for both the "race" market and, later, for the folk revival one.

Huddie "Leadbelly" Leadbetter (1888–1949) was the celebrated blues/folk musician, self-styled "King of the Twelve String" guitar, and former convict in Louisiana and Texas.

Yes, I met Lightnin' Hopkins. . . . No, I met, I met this—oh, what's his name, my God? He's an old blues singer. He plays the guitar and the guitar . . . Bukka! . . . Yes, he lives in Memphis, yeah. He's another one that comes to see me when he knowed where I lived at, but when I moved off of Beale, you know, they lost me, and they didn't all the old blues singers, they had come to see me. All come to see. I lost a lot of them when I moved off of Beale Street. They don't—you don't see no old timers now, you know. You don't hardly ever find no old timers, and when you do meet one you just have a fit. I see people across the street a lot of times I know and the old timers. I say, "How are you?" "I don't know who you are, but come here just a minute." And they just a looking. "I know you face, honey." And they get close to me. "Ain't you, you, uh. . . ?" [Laughs.] I say, "Yeah, that's me." Uh-huh. I say, "You know there are so many different ones, got so many different wigs, you don't know who they are now," you know. [Laughter.] "This is me, this is Ma," I say. "I just got a new wig on, ——— Ma Rainey" ———. Just like sometimes, I go to the market and they just have a fit. People see me in there . . . I go down there to Lebanny Church. I have to ride a cab—they say I can't do no walking or standing up on my feet ever again. And they stand there, "Is that you?" "Yeah, its me!" [Laughs.] "I heard you was dead." "No, I'm still here." Said that they had heard two or three times that I was dead. And, I don't know, it's just one of those things.

Well, when you were singing in Dallas, did you ever hear the song "Deep Ellum," the Deep Ellum Blues about Elm Street?

I've heard of "Deep Ellum." I don't know if I heard it in Texas, now. I don't know where I heard that, but I heard it. . . . No, I never sang it. And, uh, this ——— out of Texas, let me show you. She's a blues singer—oh, what's her name? She was working with James Brown awhile. . . . No. She was, she— what's her name? Oh, she dances and sings. But I'm the one who brought her to Memphis. She had a—she was a singer—she had a great voice, but she didn't know how to keep time, and I showed her how to keep time. And I don't hear of her now, but she sings great, she sings good, she . . . I don't know what she. I don't know. I could find out from my friends, my younger friend. I cook for her. [Noise at door.] Now, what is that? Hold on. [Sings "A Good Man Is Hard to Find." Hollers out door at neighbor.] ——— That's one of Bessie's.

"A Good Man Is Hard to Find," credited to E. Green, was a popular song with the blueswomen of the 1920s and 1930s. Bessie Smith recorded her version in 1927.

Do you know a lot of Bessie's songs?

No.

Did you know "Kitchen Man"?

Uh-huh. I used to know that back ———. [Sings inaudibly to herself. Hollers out door at neighbor.] Now, this ain't no old blues; this is a late blues. I forget who. [Sings "Stormy Monday." Hollers out door.] My breath is getting kind of short now. Kind of getting me down. I told you that I can't do too much now in this life. . . . No. I had to . . . [Sings "Woke Up This Morning, My Baby Was Gone."] I have to give it up. I can't do no more, y'all. . . . Yeah, I heard of Jimmie Rogers but I never did see him, you know. I met Clyde McCoy at the Crescent Theater. Day and night ——— and he'd come on. . . . Big bands and things, yeah. [Referring to the camera] Put that thing back. ———, oh, I have had my fun if, as they say, never get well no more, I've had my fun. [Laughs. Phone rings.]

Memphis Ma Rainey died in 1985, but her passing received little notice in the press, not even in the blues specialty periodicals.

Nightlight

3 Come On and Be Fair with a Black Man

Tommy Gary Blows His Harp

Tommy Gary was born and raised some fifty miles northeast of Memphis, in Brownsville, Tennessee, sometime before 1920. He died in Memphis in 1975. His story has much in common with that of Hammie Nixon. They were apparently about the same age, and both became expert harmonica players, met Sleepy John Estes when they were about eleven or twelve years old, and traveled with Estes and accompanied him.

Why Nixon became Estes's most frequent accompanist and closest friend and Gary disappeared into obscurity can only be guessed. Certainly by the 1970s, Nixon was the more amiable and coherent of the two men. Gary was bitter and sometimes confused (or at least confusing), as can be seen in the following interview. Though we probed Gary about other musicians from the Brownsville area, including harmonica players, he did not mention Nixon.

Gary was a significant player in the important Brownsville/Jackson blues scene. Some of the blues's most accomplished and influential musicians cut their musical teeth in the area, many of them actively working with blues pioneer, guitarist Willie "Hambone" Newbern. Henry "Little Wolf" Palmer, a fine harmonica player himself and nephew of Willie Newbern, remembered Gary as an outstanding musician. Palmer recalled that he learned to blow harp by "following" Gary. Gary and Estes would often visit Palmer's mother's house in Memphis and his aunt's in Brownsville. In exchange for the hospitality, the musicians would frequently play music for their hosts, giving the teenaged Palmer an opportunity to pick up pointers in the art of harmonica playing from the older Gary.

Palmer would follow Gary and Estes to the fish fries and "frolics" where

they performed. Gary would sometimes let the teenager blow a few pieces
before sending him home, where he would get a whipping for slipping out
after dark. Palmer also remembers Gary as the only musician, other than himself, who could "reach" the fourth position on the harmonica. (Like "crossharp," or second position, the third and fourth positions involve playing the
harmonica in a key different from that to which it is tuned. Playing in the set
key is referred to as playing "straight.") Like Nixon and many other harmonica players of that generation, Gary was known for his showmanship—he
could play the harmonica with his nose and in his jaw and could play several
harmonicas simultaneously.

Tommy Gary remains an obscure figure in the blues. He got less attention
("assisted by harmonica player Tommy Garry" [sic]) than the young white
blues revivalist musician Michael Stewart ("a young student of traditional
Negro blues whose sensitive support indicates handily the depth of his studies and his understanding of the traditions in which Estes' music is based") in
the liner notes to Blue Thumb's *Memphis Swamp Jam*. Of the various blues
biographical sources—these have been proliferating at a remarkable rate in
recent years—only Austin Sonnier's often inaccurate and egregiously selective *A Guide to the Blues: History, Who's Who, Research Sources* (1994) includes
an entry for Tommy Gary. It is based on his Fred Hay's *Living Blues* obituary
and perpetuates Hay's misspelling of Son Bonds name as Borum.

In the spring of 1972, Gary lived alone in a small house only a few feet from
the street and from the houses on either side. His residence at 2271 Hunter
Street was in north Memphis, near the Hollywood neighborhood. We brought
beer, but Gary insisted on whiskey, so Bill left to purchase a bottle.

I want to get my guitar anyway.

[Neighbor woman yelling from next door] Stay away from this front door!

Y'all going to get a great piece out of this. I don't blame you. [Neighbor
woman yelling in background. Gary blows a note on harp.] Now, which one
of these [microphones] works?

Both of these are working, either one you want.

[Microphone noise as Gary moves mike around.] It's little, but I'll try. [Gary
blows several choruses.] Blues, man, that's all I know how to play, the blues,
but I just need somebody else. [Gary blows for a while.] See there?

That's sounding pretty good.

Huh? . . . I supposed to have another loud speaker, but you doing the best you can.

Did that song have a name to it?

No, but I tell you what you would have to do. I'll plays, I'll play rhythmic, I play rhythmatics of blues in the disposition. You can just be wise enough to learn in the ear. First that tune and learnt that song. See? Put what you want to, to it, but you got to first catch that tune.

Right.

I just wish to [louder] God, boy, you had a guitar player here with you. . . . I don't know of no one nowhere. Let me see. Ot uh. [Pause.] I set y'all down as a fine man, right, that y'all find a guitar player to play with me. Okay, I can play this, but playing it's too hard by myself. [Tape recorder turned off, then on again when Bill returns.] [To Bill] Just come on in, Slim. [Gary chuckles as Bill shows him a whiskey bottle.] What you got in that bottle?

Where you want me, just leave his here?

It won't do no good for y'all. . . . Yes, yes, yes.

[Gary gives us some of the beer we brought.] Thank you. [Cans pop.]

Waiting won't do y'all. If y'all hadn't called me, I don't want no damn bottle. [Louder] Guitar player!

We called up, you know, Bo-Pete Flemings. . . .

Uh-huh.

. . . over in West Memphis?

Uh-huh.

Called him up; he got to work. Called up . . . Big Lucky Carter and we called up Will Dawson. . . . Who else did we call up? We called up . . .

Look a here. Look, wait, wait a minute. I just thought of a dude. Big Lucky. Y'all ever heard of him?

Guitarist Levester "Big Lucky" Carter was born in Weir in Choctaw County, Mississippi, in 1920. In the 1950s, Carter, by now living in Memphis, worked with his cousin Ed Kirby (Prince Gabe) in a band that often played for white audiences. They recorded for Sun, 606, and Savoy—many of these sides remain unissued. In 1965, Carter fronted Kirby's band, the Millionaires, on a Westside single and in 1968 for a Bandstand USA single. In 1969, Carter recorded six songs for Willie Mitchel at Hi Records, resulting in two M.O.C. singles and six songs on the Hi blues anthology LP *River Town Blues*. English blues writer Bob Groom stated in 1986 that "In 1970 Big Lucky was hot locally, with two M.O.C. 45s and six tracks on the well-received *River Town Blues* LP anthology. . . . The Hi records could have been his big breakthrough—the potential was there" (1986/1987, 12). By the late 1990s, Carter and his band had become a staple on the blues festival circuit and were again making records. In 1972, we spoke with Carter both by phone and in person on the neighborhood street corner where he and his friends gathered, both in the company of Gary and without him. Carter did not seem at all interested in backing Gary for this interview.

Bo-Pete Flemings, a guitarist who had studied with Joe Willie Wilkins, lived at 700 South Seventh Street in West Memphis in 1972. He often worked with another Wilkins protégé, harmonica player Son Blakes.

Will Dawson lived at 19 South Willett in 1972.

Yeah, we called him up and he wasn't around. Wasn't anybody around. Wasn't anybody there. We called him up yesterday afternoon. . . . And yesterday night, too. Yeah.

I'm going to tell y'all something, mans. . . . I learned y'all's personality very well, and y'all are going to put a lot of hurt on me today. In my condition, I got to take all this load by, uh, upon myself, by myself, and so I'm going to try it. Well, now listen. I want y'all to come on and be fair with a black man. Y'all the white man. There is a question of the validity of time at they trying to make thing different, what I don't think they ever be different. But listen, will y'all come on and just be frank and tell the truth? Y'all know one thing? . . . I'm going to tell you what it is. You record making right here. I know it. I know! I know what I'm talking about! I know what I'm talking about!

Uh, Mr. Gary, you trust Steve [LaVere], don't you?

Huh?

You trust Steve, don't you?

Very good.

Well, you can ask Steve and he'll tell you we aren't making a record here. We're just making this tape and we're going to take it to class and play it and we're going to study it and all but we're not going to make any records off of it. . . . Like you say, I guess we could take it down to the recording company—I don't know anything about that—and they could make a record.

Well, I know about it. . . . I know about it. You can take, you can take this shit. I know what I'm talking about. You can take these shit what I play or what I speak and take it to the, a recording company and get my name and put it on it here, and shit, man, you a millionaire.

Well, we really aren't planning on doing that. This is just for the class.

Well, now, I, I, I'm not disputing that. I, I'm not disputing y'all . . . but that's the same shit I played ——— up yonder in Washington and I made records three times and they had me sit in there and they had the same shit, y'all.

Well, we really, that's not what we're going to do with it.

I'm not disputing y'all. I ain't got no more to say about that. 'Cause y'all know what y'all are doing, but I will say this much: same thing. You can cut records on that very thing there. You can cut records right on that. I wish to hell I had one at home. You say what they cost, man?

This here?

Yeah.

A tape recorder.

I know it is. . . . What they cost?

What kind is it? It's an Ampex.

I'm talking about what that cost. . . . [Louder] What that cost? Cost?

I don't know. . . . See, we borrow the equipment to come out and do this with.

Well, I'll ask y'all a question, 'cause I'm sick but I'm not sure. Come on drive around the block—just to drive but to look—and the last house there along as, you can put the stuff in your, and if you don't want it you can leave it here. I think I know a guy I can't think of . . . yeah. It's 9:23 now. And I'm known all over Memphis. . . . I'm not trying to be funny or smart or nothing. I'm an honest, fair colored man. I don't try to have no funny doing. I like y'all dudes;

y'all, y'all dudes acts very nice . . . acts kind of cool. I watches people very good. And so let's just go 'round here, just a few minutes. We won't be gone just a few minutes. And if I can't get nobody, well, I got to come on back and try to do something by my damn self. [We turn off the tape recorder and the three of us drive around the neighborhood looking for Big Lucky without success, then return to Gary's house.] And I want something from you.

You want something from me?

I do.

Would you mind telling us when and where you were born?

What? . . . I was born in Browns, Tennessee.

Browns, Brownsville?

Yeah.

And when was that?

It's been quite a good while ago, but my . . .

You say you are fifty-eight years now, right?

I'm fifty-eight years old now. . . . Mm-huh, yes. And y'all can then reduct from that. See? . . . And this dude [referring to Fred] here, he's, szzz, I don't know, he's a kind of tough fellow here. [Car horn and sound of cars on street in front of Gary's house.]

So, did you start playing harmonica when you were eleven years, did you say?

Yes, I been playing the harmonica ever since I was ten or eleven years old.

Uh-huh. Did anyone else in your family play any music?

No. . . . I learned it by myself.

By yourself? Did you just pick up the harmonica one day and just start working on it?

Well, I'm going to tell you something in there. . . . I know the old man by name of Louis Rogers . . . and he sold me a harp one evening . . . and for a nickel. And I can play the same song now that I learned that evening.

Did he teach you that song?

What? . . . No, no, listen, listen! Now, that here was a gift to me! Listen. What I mean is, see, wherever is a person talented in life, a —————— will be given to him. . . . I can play the same song today that I knowed then.

What's the name of the song?

[Groans.] Now, wait now, I'm ain't going to tell you. Wait, now, I's studies about it. See y'alls got to remind with me. . . . The song was "Pretty Woman."

"Pretty Woman."

Yeah, "be down in the ground." That's the first that I ever have learnt to play.

And was it a blues song?

Yes, yes.

And you can still play it today?

What?

You can still play it today?

Oh, sure I can.

Well, as you were coming along learning to play harmonica, was there any certain style you learned to play it in, that you preferred to any other style?

One, yes, I know quite a different style.

Yeah. Did you pick up a special style from anybody or just learned it on your own?

No, I didn't pick up nothing from nobody. . . . Huh?

Did you say that you left home when you were around twelve or something like that?

Mmm, eleven or twelve years old.

Where did you go?

I don't know, out in the world, man. [Hollers at car with loud muffler as it drives by.] If you's got him to talk with someone, I can talk with him. Blind John Estes?

Sleepy John Adam Estes (1899–1977) will always be associated with his hometown of Brownsville because of the popularity of his composition "Brownsville Blues." Guitarist, distinctive vocalist, and outstanding blues composer, Estes first recorded in Memphis in 1929. He last recorded in the mid-1970s. Estes, Yank Rachel, John Lee "Sonny Boy" Williamson, Charlie Pickett, Son Bonds, Hammie Nixon, and Willie "Hambone" Newbern were among those musicians who developed an active blues scene east of Memphis in the Brownsville-Jackson area. Estes was a star of the blues revival of the 1960s and 1970s, by which time he was completely blind and usually led around and accompanied by harmonica player (and Estes's son-in-law) Hammie Nixon.

. . . Y'all know who I'm talking about then?

Well, I've heard of him. Yes, we've listened to his records, too.

Yes, yes, well, listen, listen, listen. I'm going to tell you something I do know. And I'm not going to lie to you for, man, nothing, or else I got not to lie to you for nothing. For I used to go to church, what I used to, enough to take care of myself. . . . Listen. I left home with John Estes when I was between eleven and twelve years old. Listen. . . . And this is true. I'm not lying to you. I have blowed, I can blow now, if I get down hard enough on a harp, I can pull the reeds out of a harp and spit them on the floor.

Henry "Little Wolf" Palmer, in conversations with Hay, confirmed Gary's claims that he could suck the reeds right out of a harmonica.

That's doing good. That's a lot of blowing.

Huh? . . . Well, I can do that, and you can call John Estes up and ask him did he know Tommy Gary and ask him can he play a harmonica. This all I want you to do and you to do. . . . Because is, they's just this one thing that is got to be said, and I —— believe it and I can't see into it and I'm a got to tell you and him, too. They's something else behind this [pause], because you listen, man! Look! Look! Look! I'm a too old a man. I've been playing music all of my life. And you, ain't nobody in the world going to come up to me and going try to show me some. I show time or period. And ought I play you two? Ought I play you one? Something wrong! There's something wrong now, you can believe me or not if you want to hear, but there's something wrong. But now I, [pause] I rates a man like this. I'm a [purer?] man. I've got three ways that I look at any man. I don't care who they is. [Pause.] This dudes here, he's got more of a qualification of knowledge of experience of what, that is he trying to put out a few wise than this dude is. But this dude, after he get started, well, he got a lot to say. See, what I been into that kind of junk. And what's worse thing about it, if you bring a mind, I can prove it. I can bust this motherfucking mike over ———.

Well, I believe that.

But there's one thing about it. I'm going to tell you more special than I do him [pauses], but I wants you to think over it. I can't give my talent away throughout this country forever for other people to make money off of it and I don't get nothing. I, uh . . .

Well, I told you, Mr. Gary, we aren't going to make any money off of this. We are doing it only so we can learn and we have already given you all the money we've got. And that's all I can tell you because that's all the truth that there is.

What, you not going to pay? Mister! Mister! Mister! I'm going to tell you something here. Don't you know that you couldn't drive this car from one where you rode it from down here through this city and don't have no money? No!

That cost all the money that we had.

Listen, man! Listen! . . . Wait! Wait! Wait! Wait! . . . Listen. . . . You and him over here can't tell me nothing about these things here. I have done made records behind these things three times. . . . And listen, let me tell you something. Okay, I can, uh [pauses], I know how. . . . [Slurs words, imitates harp sound.] Wo, wo, wo, wo, wo. Well, I can do it. I mean I can do it. Well, let, shit, y'all not going to help me none. See, you give up probably or more a dollar of something like that, but no, man, that ain't shit. [Stands up.] That ain't shit. [Walks to other side of room with back to us.] A dollar not going to carry, to go for it no more.

We turned off the tape recorder and left, then returned several days later with Bob Eagle.

In Brownsville, Tennessee . . . the twenty-ninths day of December . . . That's my hometown.

You just made it in the year, didn't you?

[Laughs.] That's right, that's right. . . . Well, I say.

What year was that?

I'm telling you the truth, I done forgot what year it was.

Well, do you know how old you are now?

Yeah, I'm fifty-eight now.

According to Steve LaVere's liner notes to Aldelphi LP 1010S *Memphis Blues Again, Vol. 2,* Gary was born January 9, 1919. If Gary was fifty-eight years old in May 1972, he would have been born in January 1914 or December 1913. If Gary had been born in January 1919, he would have been only fifty-three at the time of this interview. If born in December 1919, he would have been fifty-two. The Memphis *Commercial Appeal* reported Gary's age at the time of his death as sixty-six years. Henry Palmer, who was fifty-six years old at the time of Gary's death in the summer of 1975, remembered Gary as being a grown man when Palmer was still in his teens (Hay 1975, 5).

. . . Yeah. . . . [Yelling to someone outside] Come on in, come on in, Henry.

[Henry] How y'all?

How you doing?

Well, come on, come on.

[Henry] I was looking on the corner, if you think you want it, come on over to my house this morning. I'm ——— to get here, if you think . . .

I appreciate that, Henry, I sure appreciate that. Yeah, here.

[Henry] ——— I call them.

Yeah, here would be the best.

[Henry] Alright. [Henry leaves. Children play in the yard and on Gary's porch.]

[Pointing to a child] There's another one over in there.

He's an aggravation, ain't he? . . . [Laughs.] That boy is something else. I'm telling you. That boy at the other place, me and Aunt Grace was there in Brownsville, was brought up together. . . . You know, when I left home with John, I, uh, when I was twelve years old, he was a grown man then. I've been playing harmonica ever since. And just let me say one thing about it. I, I, I, I do know how to play harmonica.

Since you were twelve years old?

Yes, sir.

Is that when you started playing harmonica?

Yes, sir, when I was twelve years old.

Who was the first person you ever saw play harmonica?

I'd know there was a friend—used to be a—of mine called Lib Rogers. . . . Louis Rogers. He had an old harp. I give him a nickel for it one Saturday evening. And I learned how to play one song that Saturday evening. I never, I never will forget the name of the song. . . . "I Heard a Rumblin'." . . . That's it.

Did he help you learn to play that first song?

No, he ain't, he didn't help me out, help me to play nothing. . . . That's right.

Had you heard that before? Like on records?

Yeah, I used to hear him play it. You know what I mean?

"I Heard a Mighty Rumblin'" sung unaccompanied by Willie Young was recorded by the Library of Congress at Parchman State Penitentiary in Mississippi in 1933. The Library also recorded Fred Lee Fox in Jacksonville or Cross City, Florida, in 1939 or 1940 telling a story called "I Heard a Mighty Rumblin' at the Water Trough."

. . . I'm pretty apt at learning things . . . such as cutting hair and playing harmonica. Well, I can do that. . . . I sure can do that.

So, you said that you left home the next year?

I left home when I was twelve years old. . . . Uh-huh. . . . I sure did. . . . Huh?

Were you home when you saw Louis Rogers?

Yeah, yeah, I sure was, sure was. . . . I don't know. He couldn't do nothing with no harp no way. He tried, you know, like a lot of dudes do. . . . I don't know

what 'come of him. He died or whatever, I don't know. I ain't seen him in quite
a many ages. I don't know what happened to him.

Where did you go when you left home?

I took up then after that, I took up with John Adam Estes. And we walked
every stitch of the way down here.

You walked all the way to Memphis?

Walked every step of the way down here. Sure did.

Hammie Nixon said of Estes, "If I'd have let him, he would have walked to Memphis! He'd walk
that 60 miles if I'd just follow" (Lornell 1975, 18).

What did you do when you came to Memphis?

Nothing but played music every day and night. I had a booksack full of harps
that I had blowed the keys out of.

Man!

[Chuckles.] That's true, man. I ain't lying. . . . Yeah. John'll tell you about me.

Did you play with any others?

I played with many guys in my life, many, many. I've played with John more
than anybody else. . . . more used to him. I know I knows his playing pretty
good. . . .

You ever make any records with John?

John? . . . Near about three years ago, me and John made some records with
that same guy I telling y'all about. . . . Sure did.

Gary [spelled Garry] and white guitarist Mike Stewart accompanied Estes for a recording session
at Memphis's Ardent Recording Studio on June 9, 1969. This session was supervised by Arhoolie
Records' Chris Strachwitz with the assistance of John Fahey and Bill Barth. Two of the five songs
from this session, "Need More Blues" and "President Kennedy Stayed Away Too Long," were
issued on Blue Thumb 6000 (double LP), *Memphis Swamp Jam.* In June 1970, at the Peabody
Hotel in Memphis, Gary and Backwards Sam Firk (Mike Stewart) accompanied Estes on his standard "Drop Down Mama." This recording was released on Adelphi Records 1010S, *The Memphis
Blues Again, Vol. 2.*

What about recording when you was very young? You do any of that?

I didn't, I didn't do any recording then. I tried to get John and us in that. He's kind of like a dude who wants to play for nothing all the time. I don't like that. Playing music is a hard job. . . . It's not easy.

I heard that you had an opportunity to record with John Estes but you turned it down [a] long time ago.

I sure did. You sure heard the truth.

What record company was that?

I don't know. John going up in Chicago then . . . and the man come here twice after me, man. Told me that a guy playing with, told me he didn't want him but he'd take me.

Who was the guy playing with him that he didn't want?

The guy that was playing with me then was named Son Bonds. He dead. . . . He played guitar. . . . He played guitar. He played guitar.

Guitarist Son Bonds was born March 18, 1909, in Brownsville. Paul Oliver speculates that he was both kin to and learned guitar from the older Willie "Hambone" Newbern. When Bonds was in his early twenties, he partnered up with harmonica/jug player Hammie Nixon (1908–84). Nixon and Bonds played for change on the streets and hoboed as far away as Chicago. In September 1934, the duo recorded ten songs for Decca in Chicago. They were labeled on Decca and Champion releases as "Brownsville Son Bonds" and on Decca as "Brother Son Bonds" (for religious songs) and "Hammie and Son." In the liner notes of *Son Bonds with Sleepy John Estes and Hammie Nixon (1934–1941),* Paul Oliver wrote that the "titles that Son Bonds and Hammie Nixon made over the span of a few days in September that year show them to be well integrated with Hammie's accomplished harp wailing in support of Son's rural singing." Bonds recorded again for Decca in New York City in April 1938—two songs accompanied by John Estes on guitar. In September 1941, Bonds recorded three additional songs, accompanied by Estes and Raymond Thomas on imitation (tub) bass, in Chicago for the Bluebird label. Also at that session, Bonds recorded six songs with Estes and Thomas (the group was labeled "The Delta Boys") and accompanied Estes on three songs released under Estes's name. Bonds eventually married and settled down in Dyersburg, Tennessee, where he was shot to death on August 31, 1947. According to Oliver, Bonds was thirty-eight years old at the time of his death.

Did you ever play any other instrument besides harmonica?

Never did. I wish I could learn to play guitar. If I know how to play guitar like I do harp, I swear, I wouldn't be here, I wouldn't be here in the South today.

Did you stay here in Memphis? . . .

I been— . . . Oh no, I left from here. We didn't stay in no one place long. We was, you know . . . just everywhere. . . . We'd been all up in Chicago, Detroit, and everywhere else. But we—what it is I'm trying to say, if I just had a thought and used myself like it was supposed to been, I'd of been a man to-day. . . . Yes, sir, I'd of been a man today.

Well, when did you come here to Memphis to settle down?

I been here in Memphis about six or seven years.

According to the *Living Blues* obituary for Gary, "After his first wife died in 1943, Tommy hoboed around for several years before returning to Memphis. Once in Memphis, he worked for Hartwell Brothers for a number of years, before retiring" (Hay 1975, 6–7).

. . . Uh-huh. Sure have. And if I had a good guitar player with me today and had steady work to do, I'd do just what I used to do with a harp. Right this evening.

How would you describe the difference between the way John Estes plays and sings the blues and the way other people do it?

Well, I tell you the truth, you talking where there are some deep facts now. Now, John is really good. John is really good in his way of doing—but now I wouldn't want it to get back to him because me and John is real good friends. Johns thinks a lot of me and I thinks a lot of John, but John just naturally ain't no guitar player. . . . He really ain't no guitar player and that's the truth. . . . John used to, John used to be real good. Tell you what carried him: John had a good name—well, what I mean his name done carried him—now his voice done got kind of bad now, you know. John's voice not much good now. . . . But he used to be a man, brother.

He used to have a real good voice?

Whew! That John Adam Estes used to be somebody! I ain't lying to you! The first record he ever made was in '29. Right down here at the Auditorium. 1929. . . . Sure was. . . . Sure was.

In Estes's own words, here's how he became a recording artist: "Well, it was the guy that recorded the 'Kansas City Blues,' Jim Jackson. We were coming down the street, me and Yank Rachell. He said 'Boys, that was a mighty good piece you sang on the street the other day. You can really sings. I can tell you how to make some money.' Yank said, 'John, we can go 'round ourselves. We don't need him to carry us.' I went around to the Ellis Auditorium and we talked to Mr. R. S. Peer of New York City. He told us, 'Boy,' he was recording two or three other boys there, they'd hit two pieces in about an hour. 'We got some more boys here but I want to see you before you go. I want you to come back late in the afternoon so I can hear what you can do.' We went back then and we recorded" (Lornell 1975, 14).

Look, do you know, could you say the difference between the way John sings and the way other people sing?

Yeah, I can tell a whole lot of difference in them. You take Albert King . . . and B. B. King. . . . Uh, and Muddy Water and all them dudes. And them grown children can natural dig in the blues. I tell you someone else can sing, can sing, can sing pretty good, too—ole Big Lucky. . . . Yes, sir, ole Big Lucky can sing pretty good. John, he's—I like him, but I just don't know—he, poor fellow, he just out of tune. That's all to it about it. . . . John's old man. . . . Huh?

Just gotten too old?

I don't know what to say. I don't believe John is as old as Blind Lemon was. Because his voice just hadn't broken so bad. . . . John sound like he crying. I wish I had a record player; I got one of me and John records right there now.

Uh-huh. Did you ever see Blind Lemon?

No, I never met him, I never see him.

Just heard his records?

I heard his records a lot of times.

For more on Blind Lemon Jefferson, see the Furry Lewis chapter.

You ever see Blind Blake or Blind Willie McTell?

No, I sure didn't, I did never did see them. Ole Lucky, he be around in a little bit. He told me that he'd come right around just before we stepped in the car. Didn't he? He said he'd be right on, he'd be right on.

For more on Blind Blake and Blind Willie McTell, see the Joe Willie Wilkins chapter.

Do you remember any of the other people that you played with around, with John or. . . ?

Around here?

Well, around anywhere.

Well, I know some guys up in Brownsville, man, I'm telling you the truth, I know a dude up in Brownsville by the name of Eddie Pink. He's a left-hand guy. . . . Yeah.

Eddie Pink?

Boy, let me tell you something [chuckles], that Negro can go, brother! . . . Yeah, he still live up there in Brownsville. He can go! He a left-handed player. . . . Huh?

Do you know what street he lives on?

I know he lives out there in the rural somewhere. I could find him for you. That's my home up there in Brownsville. . . . I was born up there in Brownsville, Tennessee.

Do you know anybody else that plays up there? Or sings?

Well, not right now. I haven't been up there in quite a good long while, you know.

What about when you left there?

Oh, when I left from there, there was quite a few guys 'round there could play. . . Let me see. Yank Rachel was, well, Yank hadn't left from down there before I left. But let me see, I know several guys, I can't think of their names right now, but that Eddie Pink, he was [white?]. I don't know of no recording he ever did. . . . But if a man was going to record some record, it would pay him to put himself to some trouble to get him. . . . Say he can go, boy. I ain't lying. He can go. He left-handed guitar player and he can sing. Boy, he can natural-born horn in. Make no mistake about it.

James "Yank" Rachel (1910–97), a Brownsville native, played both guitar and mandolin. As a youth, he worked with the older Willie "Hambone" Newbern and later with Homesick James Williamson. Rachel formed the Three J's Jug Band with John Estes and pianist Jab Jones, and it was with them that he first recorded in 1929. Rachel continued to record, with and without Estes, as featured performer and frequently as sideman until 1941. Rachel moved to St. Louis in 1940, later returned to Brownsville, where he got married, but left again for St. Louis before settling in Indianapolis in 1957 (James 1997, 54–55). He recorded again, for Delmark, in 1964 and made a number of recordings and public appearances in the last three decades of his life.

What does he do for a living?

I don't know what he do for a living. I don't know what he do now. You know, things have change so much. You take a man from Brownsville, now. . . . It's not too many people from up there in Brownsville now. . . . So I don't know. But I sure would love to get in touch with John and talk with him some and see what he has got on his mind. John's stone flat blind. . . . Yes, he's flat blind. He's a good, he's a good fellow. . . . But just one thing about John: I not going to tell nothing, but everybody that has told John told me, too, but I know it— I can outplay John. . . . I really can outplay him. Always could.

Do you sing yourself?

I don't do no singing . . . do no good. Sometimes I get kind of high and sing, high. I do know how to sing.

But you have sung every once in a while?

Yeah, I have, I have sung but I don't think too much of the prices of it. . . . I get too, I get kind of high, I can sing my ass off, man. [Laughs. Laughter.]

This guy who they wanted you to replace, Son Bonds, did you hear how he died?

Yeah, he was sent out a killer. . . . He was at a dance one night and somebody shot him, somebody shot him. He [shouldered?] with them. . . . That was in Dyersburg. . . . That was in Dyersburg, Tennessee. . . . That was in Dyersburg, Tennessee. . . .

Hammie Nixon gave this account of Son Bonds's death: "He got killed around the same time that Sonny Boy got killed. Sonny Boy got killed in Chicago, Son got killed in Dyersburg. A fellow shot him, he thought he was shooting somebody else. Son was sitting on his porch. This guy wore them great thick glasses and had got into it with the guy who lived next door to Son. It was way about 12:00 at night and he thought it was the boy who lived next door" (Lornell 1975, 15).

Nixon told Francis Smith a decade earlier "that Son Bonds was shot on the porch of his house in Dyersburg, Tenn., in 1948. Hammie's story was that Bonds had been shot by a man with 'thick pebble-lensed glasses' who mistook Bonds for the man next door." Estes, "while confirming the shooting, had a different version involving a woman and a plot to get Bonds' insurance money" (1971, 236–37).

Uh-huh. I don't know how I'm going to tell you. I'm going to try to get in touch with some of these dudes. Y'all should do it, too. And let's work up something. It worth it. . . . It worth it. I know what I'm talking about it. I went to Washington last summer with Steve and them. Well, they paid us pretty good, beared all the expenses and everything. . . . Well, I got back here. Over two hundred and eighty some dollars. Well, I didn't mind that. . . . You know what I mean.

Gary performed with Estes and Rachel at the American Folklife Festival in Washington, D.C. in the summer of 1970.

I wouldn't mind that either.

I didn't mind that, I didn't mind that at all, at all. That was alright. . . . That's alright. That's alright. I wouldn't mind working, twenty more hours of work. They was real nice. I know met a bunch of white people, so nice, as young people up there, before in my life. . . . That's the truth, they real nice people. . . . They really treat you nice. I like nice, nice people anyway.

Did you know another guy 'round there who played with those guys, guitar player named Charlie Pickett?

Oh man, did I know him! Where he at now?

Not much is known about guitarist Charlie Pickett. Sheldon Harris reported that he was Estes's cousin (1979). Hammie Nixon had him performing in a group with Estes, Nixon, and others on the streets of Chicago in the 1930s and 1940s. Nixon told Kip Lornell in 1975, "He started preaching in St. Louis, been living in St. Louis for a couple of years. I think he's preaching in Los Angeles now" (1975, 19). In August 1937, Pickett recorded four songs, accompanied by himself on guitar and on two cuts by Lee Brown on piano, and on one of these by Hammie Nixon on harmonica. These four songs were released on Decca. About one of these songs, "Let Me Squeeze Your Lemon," Nixon said, "I never will forget the first time he started playing that song, how he sung a something like, 'When I got home, another nigger kicking in my stall.' The bossman told him don't say that no more!" (Lornell 1975, 19). Pickett also accompanied Estes on his 1937 and 1938 Decca sessions in New York City and possibly pianist Lee Green's 1937 Decca session in the same city.

Well, that's him there.

That's the one. . . . He's the first dude that ever made that. . . . A good guitar player, too. . . . He could flat play some. . . . Yeah. He can still play guitar now, right? He was really good. . . . ——— find a dude by the name of Tim Wilkins? . . . I used to plays with him. . . . He's a minister now, and me and him did some numbers up there in Washington. . . . Yeah, me and him did some numbers. He played all spirituals.

Tim Wilkins (1896–1987), in later life known as Reverend Robert Wilkins, was a Mississippi-born guitarist who moved to Memphis in 1915. He was an integral part of the prewar Memphis blues and later recorded as a gospel singer. "Prodigal Son," a gospel remake of one of Wilkins's recorded blues songs, was made famous by the Rolling Stones.

Was that just a couple of years ago?

Oh, that was just, that was last summer. . . .Uh-huh, sure was, sure was.

Did you play with him before that ever?

Oh, man, I used to play with him every night down here.

In Memphis?

Sure did. Me and him and a guy by the name Leroy [Shenaw?]. He a little bitty dark fellow, but he dead now.

I believe he's in Chicago, isn't he?

That's why, that's where he went to.

Yeah. But he died?

I heard that he dead. Is he dead? . . . Tim told me was dead. . . . Mmm.

According to Francis Smith, Hammie Nixon did not know Robert (Tim) Wilkins but did know a guitarist, "a man with a name something like Leroy Shennauld (this is my aural spelling and probably highly inaccurate—as Hammie said it, it was pronounced more like Shenno, but with an implied final D)" (1971, 237). The above quote is from *Nothing but the Blues* (Leadbitter 1971), a collection of short articles previously published in *Blues Unlimited*. In the index to this volume, the entry for this musician is "Shinault, Leroy."

How long ago were you playing with him?

That's been quite a good while since I played with them guys. I turn, what I mean, uh, I turn, I turn, I quit playing things worthwhile until here about two or three years ago, John come down here and wanted me to go with him and make some records. Come after me one Sunday evening, and me and him got up that Monday morning, we left, went out here and got a cab, and went on out yonder to that man's place. This man's place was out here . . . was out here. And this other man's place was over here. . . . And so, boy, let me tell you the truth. I don't know. That man had a nice place out yonder.

Yeah, he was renting it for the time being.

Say, he was? . . . Well, it's a nice place. Well, a little further from where we went to his house one night. We stayed there until dark. I don't know, it was about twelve or one o'clock. He had a nice getup there, too. And he had some of every, all kinds of instruments in there and everything. And wasn't nobody there but me and John, me and John. Man, that man like to play me to death.

These men must have been Gene Rosenthal and his brother-in-law Michael Stewart. They came to Memphis in 1969 and 1970 to record blues musicians for Rosenthal's Adelphi label.

[Laughs.] When you were coming along, were there a lot of other good harmonica players in Memphis?

I have met a lots of them, but I'm going to tell you the truth and I ain't going to tell you no lie about nothing because, you know, I mean, it don't prosper me to just jump up and tell you a lie to be telling you a lie. . . . Raise my hand to God, I ain't never had no man to beat me playing no harp. . . . That's true. Ask John, ask John Adam Estes about it. John know my life. John Estes knows my life! . . . . And I'm fifty-eight years old now. I ain't lying to you. I remember. . . . Who?

Remember any of the other harp players?

I don't know, I [mumbles Willie Smith? Lemon? Larmon?]. . . . There's a guy —he ain't over there now but he been here with me this evening—try to tell me about guys playing harp, and playing music, that Albert King—. . . is, was B. B. King—B. B. King took out that trumpet he rather play—they got a thing they play for—uh, uh, convention . . . and all them stars that down there, and B.B. was the onliest man walk, to walk up there and got a way. Albert King can go, boy, he really can go. . . . Ain't no joke about, Albert King can go. . . . He really can go. . . . But B. B. King, I tell you the truth, that joker can rock. . . . He proudly can rock. So just for the blues, I don't know, I a bluesman. I can't play spiritual songs. I know spiritual songs—me and John made a lot of them, right down here in this town, made a whole lots of them. . . . "Nearer So God to You" and all that. I just couldn't begin [voice rises dramatically in pitch] . . . How can I put out a record on religion? He don't come this way, didn't come this way ——— now. Steve have a bunch of them records. I didn't know Steve had none of them until . . .

What records are these?

From when . . . me and John made a world of records. I bet you me and John made over a hundred and some records here.

This would have been the Adelphi session.

When was that?

About three years ago. Man, ain't heard none of them on the ———. . . . I wonder where they to.

They just haven't put them out yet.

Is that what it is? . . . I don't understand it. Well, y'all got a lighter on y'all or y'all got a match?

No, I don't, no.

Man, I be glad when this son of a big joke, big joker come in here. Now, I tell you, we get back to this now. Lucky, he's a very nice guy, he's a nice cooperating guy, but y'all are going to have to give him a little something. . . . You shouldn't have to do that. [Softly] Now he can play, and you will play. We'll sit down, plenty of time. Tell him how it is, tell him much as you can afford. [Voice rises dramatically in pitch] I don't mind going along with y'all. I told you the other day, didn't I? . . . Him and him really talks nice, and you do, too. I don't mind going along with a person who acts nice with me. I declare I don't. I go out, I go ahead with them. . . . I don't mind it. [Long pause, then sighs.]

Did you ever play with anybody besides a guitar player? I mean, did you ever play with a . . .

A piano player?

Piano player or anything.

Oh man, yeah. . . . I don't know. I'll be frank, tell you the truth. I don't know who they were. I'll tell you what, this man who we went to make them records, who stay out here. We went down there one Sunday night, and he was a colored guy, an albino, look like a white man, he was . . .

Piano Red?

. . . Think something like that they call him. But boy, that joker could play that, you know. . . . Me and him and John got together and we like to lay it all the way through, but I don't know, some way he crossed his notes, some ——— here. [At door] Y'all don't work here, let's go . . . over to this other house.

John "Piano Red" Williams (1905–82) was a large albino man who played in a rambunctious barrelhouse piano style and made awful-tasting and powerful homebrew. Williams, a native of Germantown, Tennessee, hoboed all over the country in his youth. He played with Barber Parker's Silver Kings from Tunica, Mississippi; Woodrow Adams; Joe Willie Wilkins; Joe Hill Louis; and others in the 1950s. His first recordings appeared on Blue Thumb's *Memphis Swamp Jam* and Adelphi's *Memphis Blues Again* set. Other recordings later appeared on European labels Flyright, Albatross, Ornament, and L&R. He opened the show for the Memphis Blues Caravan in the 1970s and later toured Europe. Profiled in Margaret McKee and Fred Chisenhall's *Beale Black and Blue* in 1981, Williams was a great raconteur. Some of the stories with which he entertained his friends were hilarious, if of questionable veracity. (For example, he claimed that he copulated with Memphis Minnie after she had been paralyzed by a stroke. He also told this tale: As a child, sitting on a church pew next to his mother, his erect penis started troubling him by poking out of his short pants. To remedy this situation he slipped out into the field next to the church and had sex with a cow. During the consummation, the cow defecated on Williams's pants, causing him great embarrassment on his return to the church service.)

   Cousin Randy (as Joe Willie Wilkins called Williams) was on the phone with Wilkins's widow, Carrie, when an intruder broke into Williams's house in early February 1982. Memphis police found Williams beaten to death on February 5, 1982.

[Gary blows harp.] That was really good.

Huh?

What was the name of that song?

Put a name on its your own self.

Ha, ha, ha, ha. Did you make that one up?

Yeah, uh-huh. That's not nothing, nothing I know of. I just made that up.

Would you play that first song you ever learned?

Yeah, I think I know it. Yeah, I think I know it. Let me see. I'm going to play this here song here about "My Baby Don't Stand No Cheating," you know. How do you like that?

The popular blues standard "My Babe" was recorded by harmonica great Little Walter Jacobs for the Chess brothers' Checker label in Chicago in 1955.

. . . Huh? . . . [Gary plays.]

Mmm, that's good. . . . Where did you first learn that song?

Huh? . . . I've been knowing it for years. That's an old song.

Do you remember where you'd learned it from? A record?

Uh-huh, from a record . . . I'm going to play y'all a church song. This is, let's see [blows note], this sucker here is short, ain't it [referring to mike cord]?

I'll move the machine over.

That's good. [Blows "When I Lay My Burden Down" and, in quick succession, with only brief harmonica flourishes serving as change-ups, two additional, distinct melodies.]

Tommy Gary died July 31, 1975. According to the obituary in the *Commercial Appeal,* he was "survived by his second wife, Mrs. Ollie Gary, four daughters, two stepsons, three sisters, two brothers, seven grandchildren, and three great-grandchildren" (Hay 1975, 6).

Furry's Dice

4 When You Through Talking about Your Brick House, Come See Furry's Frame

Furry Lewis at Seventy-three

In his later years, Walter "Furry" Lewis (1899–1981) was Memphis's best-known bluesman. He had opened for the Rolling Stones, appeared on the *Tonight Show,* played a small part in the movie *W.W. and the Dixie Dance Kings* with actor Burt Reynolds, and had been portrayed in a children's book (Surge 1969) and the Joni Mitchell song "Furry Sings the Blues."

Lewis had seen plenty of hard times growing into his celebrated old age. His father deserted the family before he was born in Greenwood, Mississippi, in 1899. When Lewis was still young, his mother brought him and his sisters to Memphis. Catching a free ride on a train through Illinois in either 1916 or 1917, Lewis's foot slipped and he lost a leg. From 1922 to 1966, unable to support himself with his music, Lewis worked for the City of Memphis as a street sweeper and garbage man. When Lewis sang "been down so long, looks like up to me" (a line from his song "I Will Turn Your Money Green," borrowed by Richard Farina for the title of his famous novel), he meant it.

Lewis was an active part of the Memphis blues scene as it developed in the early twentieth century. He had known W. C. Handy and had played with the jug bands as well as nearly every blues musician who had spent any time in the vicinity. Lewis had traveled for a number of years with a medicine show, and his performance style with the guitar twirling, clowning, and humorous stories was a legacy of these traveling ventures.

Recording in the late 1920s for the Victor and Vocalion labels, Lewis did not record again until after Sam Charters visited him in Memphis in 1959. Charters recorded an album with Lewis for Folkways in 1959 and two more LPs for Prestige in 1961. Subsequently, Lewis made a number of recordings for various labels. Indeed, British writer Bob Groom wrote that Lewis's "return has been one of the most satisfying of the [blues] revival" (1971, 49). After his 1975 appearance in the movie *W.W. and the Dixie Dance Kings*—a role first offered to and declined by Nashville harmonica wizard Deford Bailey (Morton and Wolfe 1991, 161)—new audiences discovered Lewis, ironically, at a time when his skills as a musician were rapidly deteriorating because of his advancing age.

As a younger man, Lewis had been an accomplished and innovative guitarist who skillfully crafted original and traditional ideas into wonderful and memorable songs. Lewis successfully integrated the peculiar and vigorous musical sounds of the rural Delta of his birth with the more uniform and sophisticated urban music of the city. In the liner notes of *Shake 'Em On Down*, Pete Welding wrote that Lewis's music, "engagingly direct and sincere, typifies the best that the Memphis blues has to offer. If any single performer can be said to stand as the living embodiment of the Memphis blues, a performer in whose music can be found the full span of that urban-rural polarity, that man is surely Furry Lewis." Lewis was an influence on countless younger Memphis musicians of both races, on later-day country bluesmen of the Piedmont region (Pearson 1990), on Appalachian old-time music (Wolfe 1993, 242), and even on modern soul singers like Bobby Womack—who made a statement to that effect when he introduced Lewis to an audience at Nashville's Vanderbilt University in the early 1970s—and rock 'n' rollers like Jimi Hendrix.

In the 1960s and 1970s, Lewis's apartment became a pilgrimage site for many visitors to Memphis, from anonymous blues fans to world famous celebrities. The front room of Lewis's two-room duplex on Mosby Street, where we interviewed Lewis in 1972, has been described by a number of writers. Margaret McKee and Fred Chisenhall's description is typical: "A double bed, a couch, one chair, a dog bed, a veneered dresser, and an amplifier stuffed the dimly lighted living room-bedroom. . . . Tacked on the walls were a number of blues posters, a calendar, a hand-printed note saying 'Lord help me keep my nose out of other peoples business,' and pictures of Martin Luther King, Jr., and John F. and Robert Kennedy. Other photographs and clippings traced his recent blues excursions" (1981, 104). Bruce Cook added that "He spends a lot of time on that bed, which, oddly enough, is stuck up against the wall next to the front door of his house on Mosby Street. . . . He spends most of the day with his leg off, hopping around the room when he has to, and waving the stump about without embarrassment" (1973, 116).

McKee and Chisenhall observed that Lewis greeted the famous and the obscure with the same courtesy and friendliness. This was indeed the case. When Allen Ginsberg came to town to make an appearance at Southwestern at Memphis (now Rhodes College), he wanted to see Lewis. Ginsberg's wealthy host requested we bring Lewis to his house so that Ginsberg could meet him. When I explained the situation to Lewis, he said, "Well, since I'm more famous than he is, he should come see me." I asked Lewis what made him think he was more famous than the poet. He replied, "Well, he's heard of me and I ain't never heard of him, so I must be more famous. Right?" I called Ginsberg's host to report Lewis's reaction; apparently Ginsberg appreciated the logic of Lewis's statement, and they announced that they were on their way to Mosby Street.

Stanley Booth, who had been sitting amused on Lewis's couch throughout our conversation and phone calls, quickly departed before Ginsberg, his host, and his host's entourage arrived. Lewis greeted Ginsberg, as he did everyone, from his bed with his artificial leg removed. (Lane Wilkins described a visit to Lewis's Beale Street neighborhood apartment with her grandfather Robert Wilkins in 1963. Lewis was sitting on the porch and Wilkins had to go inside to locate Lewis's leg for him [1995].) I'm not sure Lewis ever knew which of the party was Ginsberg. After a night of playing, talking, and drinking, Ginsberg and his party departed. Ginsberg reportedly said that Lewis was the most Zen musician he'd ever encountered. The next day Ginsberg chanted new songs/ poems about Furry Lewis at the college. He proclaimed that the school should make Lewis head of its music department.

Steve and Linda LaVere and Bob Eagle joined us in the spring of 1972 for the Furry Lewis interview. Several neighbor women were visiting Lewis when we arrived at his apartment, and they stayed to watch and listen to Lewis perform. Earlier, when Lewis had agreed to the interview, he had stipulated that he would not play or sing when the tape recorder was present. He had good reason to be cautious; it had not been long since a tape of his music, made casually at his home, had been used on a commercial record without his permission and from which he had received no compensation.

[Women chatter in the corner of the front room and on the front porch and street.] What's that toast you said a moment ago now? It wasn't that one about Nixon, but there's another one you said over in Arkansas. It was real good. . . . Who's going to buy two more when these two go? How does that go? That's good!

Well, ——— had certain, certain, I'm going to hold the bottle up when I say it. . . . That glass all right. No, no, the glass all right. Let me hold your glass. I had a little pig. Eva. [Eva and friends quiet down. Furry holds up his whiskey glass.]

> I had a little pig, I fed him off of cheese,
> He got so fat till he couldn't see his knees.
> That's the best ole pig my pa had on the farm,
> Now who going to buy some more of this when all this gone?

[Laughter.]

Thomas Talley collected a similar verse in Middle Tennessee in the 1910s:
> I had a liddle pig,
> I fed 'im on slop;
> He got so fat
> Dat he almos' pop (1991, 135).

Robert Gordon includes a slightly different version that he collected from Lewis in *It Came from Memphis* (1995, 200).

Damn!

I give [snorts]. . . . Ut oh, you ought to be ashamed of that gas stuff. You going have to kill me? You ain't got no business drinking unless you going to put some in my glass. Never mind, I got some. [Wheezes, laughs.] All right now, what want, y'all going to start to doing here?

Okay, Furry, can you tell us when you were born and where you were born?

Well, I was born in Greenwood, Mississippi, down in the Delta . . . in eighteen and ninety-three. . . . That's my birthday. March 6, 1893.

Sam Charters located Lewis in Memphis in 1959 and made his "rediscovery" recording for Folkways. In his 1959 book, *The Country Blues*, Charters states that Lewis was born March 6, 1900 (1975, 103). Good ole boy gonzo journalist Stanley Booth reported in his 1969 *Playboy* profile of Lewis that Jerry Finberg, a white boy who had been learning guitar from Lewis, had done some research at Lewis's old school and determined that his birth date was March 6, 1893 (1991, 25, 27). In his 1977 book, *Sweet as the Showers of Rain,* Charters, while not mentioning Booth's article, repeats the story of Finberg's discovery. (In fact, Charters quotes Booth's article several times without citing it and even attributes quotes from Booth to Swedish researcher Bengt Olsson.) Charters accepts the 1893 date as accurate; he wrote, "Occasionally Furry himself will forget and give other dates, but this seems to be the correct one" (1977, 50–51). Steve LaVere, through interviews with Lewis's elder sister and research in federal and municipal records, has established beyond doubt that Lewis was born as Walter Lewis Jr. to Victoria Jackson in Greenwood, Mississippi, on March 6, 1899 (1993). Therefore, Lewis's age at the time of this interview was 73 years.

[Eva] But where was you raised at, baby? [Furry indicates with gestures that his guests should be quiet while the tape is rolling.]

That's all right, Furry, that's all right. . . . Where were you raised at, Furry? [Laughter.]

Where was I raised? . . . Well, they started raise me in Mississippi. . . . But the reason why they didn't raise me in Mississippi, the rope broke!

Ahhhh! [Laughter.] How long did you stay in Mississippi?

I stayed there, I was six years old since I been here in Memphis. . . . I was six years old when they brought me to Memphis. I've been right here in Memphis seventy-three years.

This is the usual story that Lewis told to interviewers. Bengt Olsson, however, reported that Lewis claimed to live in Greenwood until his teens and that he ran away from home at the age of thirteen to follow entertainer Jim Jackson (1970, 76).

Hey, Furry, who brought you to Memphis? You never have said. Was it your folks?

My mother and father, mother did. Yeah. . . . Yeah, my stepfather. Yeah, because my mother and real father separated before I was born. I never seen my daddy in my life. . . . No. My mother married again and I had a stepfather, and he used to give us a nickel ev-v-vry Christmas Eve night and steal that nickel. And wake up, and it got Christmas morning, he whup us for losing it. He done stole it. [Laughter.]

So, when you come here to Memphis, did you stay with anybody?

Stayed with my mother and my father and my auntie. That's my mother's sister. We live. . . . Yeah. We lived then on Brinkley Avenue. That's what they call Decatur Street now. That was Brinkley Avenue. 319. We lived there forty-seven years in one house.

Lewis's cousin, Beaula Mae Fritz, told William Thomas that Lewis lived with his mother, Victoria, and two sisters named Winnie and Lettie. "Furry's mother worked as a cook in a white man's house. I remember her coming home in the evening with a pan of leftovers from the table. That's what they ate. I get the shivers thinking about it" (1981).

When did you start learning how to play guitar?

Well, when I first started to learn how to play the guitar, that was shortly after I got here. I was about seven or eight years old. And I come up with W. C. Handy. Me and W. C. Handy started to playing on Beale Street, you know. They had a place on Beale Street, all night house, they call Pee Wee's. . . . And all the musicians used to hang around there, and get together [sound of glasses clinking] and hang there, and so that place never closed up, 'cause when they first opened that place, they had a key and put a string around it and put it around a jack rabbit's neck and they never did catch the rabbit to get the key and they never could close up. [Laughter.]

Lewis often told the story of how W. C. Handy and tavern owner Cham Fields gave him his first real guitar. It was a Martin that Lewis played for many years. "They brought it out to my mother's and I was so proud to get it, I cried for a week" (Booth 1991, 29).

Did anyone help you learn to play the guitar?

It's no one never help me learn to play anything. And but the way I always did, if I go around and see you play, I just watch your hands and kind of see where you put your hands on it and I keep that sound.

[Eva] Do you want a beer?

And I keep that sound with me and then I go home and play it.

[Eva, same time as Furry] I ain't . . .

Come in, Musley.

[Musley, entering front door] Uh-huh, I come to bring you this paper. Look like the paper boy wasn't going to leave me no paper.

Yeah, what happened?

[Musley] And I sent to the corner and bought me a paper. Now, I got two.

Well, I declare before God!

[Musley] And he come by, right now.

Thank you. Uh-huh.

[Musley] And I didn't need, didn't need two of them at home.

And I do. I'm so glad you come. Now, listen. If he left, if he left you two, why didn't you let me have the two?

[Musley] You crazy!

[Furry guffaws. Laughter.] Come on in, Gert.

[Musley] No, I'm going on back home.

I see you in the morning. Call me.

[Man from Hot Mama's nightclub enters during the exchange with Musley] I'll come over tomorrow when Lee is talking to you, right? And just talk instead of talking everything now. And, uh . . .

This is the guy from Hot Mama's, Furry.

This man may have been referring to the late Lee Baker, a local rock guitarist, who was Lewis's friend and sometime accompanist. Hot Mama's was a nightclub on Lamar Avenue that often featured local blues performers.

Well, you say you come in. Come on, come on and set on the bed.

[Man] I'm supposed to be cooking now.

Now, I understand, give me [tape recorder turned off] . . . I don't know where I was at.

I don't know where we was.

I was in the bed. [Laughter.]

Furry, you were telling us about how you used to watch the guitar players play the guitar. Then you'd go home and try to, you know, play the same, do the same thing they did.

I sure did, but now, I'll tell you, if I go somewhere and look at a person's hands, and hear where, and hear him play and make a different tune, different sound, and this and that, I couldn't go home and do that right away, 'cause, but I kept that in my head. Sometimes just take my fingers, run down, down on one string, get the whole song out of one string. Run up and down, stop it at different places till it sound good and until I got so I could use the other five. [Laughter.] See, that's the thing on the guitar. Uh-huh. That's for real, I'm not, I'm not jiving you there.

Well, who were these people you used to watch?

Ohhhh, I used to watch this fellow they call Blind Joe. I used to watch W. C. Handy, where I got my start at. That's where I got my start. I used to watch Jim Jackson. I used to watch Willie Polk. I used to watch James Manus. I used to watch Son Brimus. . . . Yes, Son Brimmer, I watched all them pieces. And then, it got so then that I commence to playing with Mamie Smith, Bessie Smith, Texas Alexander, and Blind Lemon Jefferson in Chicago and New York.

Jim Jackson (1890–1937) was a performer of blues, minstrel, and popular songs in the medicine shows of the early twentieth century and on the streets of his adopted hometown, Memphis. Jackson was something of a mentor for Lewis, and Lewis accompanied Jackson in 1927 to Chicago, where they both made their first records for Vocalion. Jackson's debut record, *Jim Jackson's Kansas City Blues,* was one of the best-selling blues records of the 1920s.

Willie Polk is a mystery. Stanley Booth quotes Lewis describing an early band in which he played that included a Willie Polk on fiddle (1991). Olsson quotes Lewis as saying, "And there was a fellow they called 'Funny Willie,' but his name was Willie Pope; he used to dance and sing" (1970, 76). Charlie Polk, a jug blower, recorded with the Memphis Jug Band.

James Manus is unknown. He is almost certainly the same individual that McKee and Chisenhall refer to as James Maynor (1981).

Son Brimmer, a.k.a. Will Shade (1898–1966), was a Memphis born guitarist and harp blower who was an organizer and star of the Memphis Jug Band. The Memphis Jug Band, which recorded more than 75 sides for Victor and Okeh from 1927 to 1934, had a fluctuating lineup but always included Shade.

Mamie Smith (1883–1946) was a black vaudeville singer whose recording of "Crazy Blues" in 1920 was such a success that the "race" record market was developed by the industry.

Bessie Smith (1894–1937) was a great and influential blues singer.

Alger "Texas" Alexander (ca. 1880–ca. 1955) was one of the first generation of blues singers. Alexander did not play an instrument himself, but he sang in a beautiful and archaic style which owed much to earlier forms, especially the field holler. His singing was recorded, backed by others, including Lonnie Johnson, King Oliver, and the Mississippi Sheiks. He last recorded in 1950. Alexander was reportedly a cousin of Lightnin' Hopkins.

Blind Lemon Jefferson (1897–1929) was one of the best-selling blues singers of the 1920s. His brilliant guitar playing, exceptional poetry, and haunting, moaning vocals have made him, quite possibly, the most influential of all recorded musicians on the development of the blues genre.

You played with all them?

I, with every one of them.

Would you tell us how you met Blind Lemon Jefferson and what you played with him and all?

Yes, I met him just like I would do now. Like you all want me, y'all probably want me to come to the school to play. I would go there to play and I would meet somewhere else and somebody else come in there, too, from [a] different state. They come in and play and we'd get acquainted one another like that. Now, I didn't know all, him all that well. Now, like he live in Chicago and I live here in Memphis. They give a big thing there in Chicago and I'd go and he'd be there. . . . You know, all the musicians get together.

Did you meet him when you went up there to record in 1928?

The correct year for this recording date was 1927.

That's exactly what it was. . . . Any more questions? Huh?

I've heard there's quite an unusual story about your first guitar. Could you tell us about that?

Why, certainly. The first guitar that I had, I made it myself. Because, quite naturally, it couldn't been no guitar if I made it, but I could make some tunes with it. I taken a cigar box and tacked it down, where you couldn't open it, and I cut a little hole in there, in the middle of it, just like a guitar. Then I taken another guitar and got me a strip off of it like that and tacked it on there like the guitar neck. And I got screen wire, just like you get off your screen door or screen window. . . . And I had some nails and I nailed them in there, in the neck part like you was tuning it, and the nails bent in there and bent them. And then when you bent them like that, it tuned it. Don't you think it won't. Yeah, that's where I learnt.

Similar accounts of Lewis's homemade guitar are reported in McKee and Chisenhall (1981), Olsson (1970), and Booth (1991). In these different accounts, only the material used for the neck (board, beaverboard, and two-by-four, respectively) varies.

Could you tell us how or when was it you first started playing professionally, first started getting paid for your professional playing?

Oh, well, I wouldn't just, I couldn't just say. That's a little too far back; because it's been so long, I couldn't exactly remember.

Do you remember about how old you were?

Ah, no, I was about twenty-one or -two years old.

Was that when you started going on minstrel shows?

Oh yes, on medicine shows, yes, mmm, I was on medicine show.

Could you tell us some of the medicine shows you were on?

Well, I never was on but just one, but I stayed on there so long they thought I owned it.

Which was that?

Dr. Miller. . . . Uh-huh. We sold Jack Rabbit syrup. We sold corn salve. And we sold, like they got now aspirins, but they was the best aspirins in the world, you know. That's what they say on the doctor show, and they wasn't no better than the rest of them. But they was selling them, you see, some corn salve ———— sore your corn is. Doctor could come up there and put it on top of your corn and stand on your feet. You couldn't hurt, you couldn't hurt, you couldn't hear, hurt then. . . . Well, you go home that night and everybody kill you. See, that do long enough for us to get away from there. [Laughter.] You know I'm telling the truth, man! [Laughter.] Yes I is, I swear I'm telling the truth! [Laughter.]

Samuel Charters reports that Lewis worked with Jim Jackson, Will Shade, and Gus Cannon for Dr. Willie Lewis's Show (1975, 103). Cook also reports it as "the Dr. Willie Lewis Show"

(1973, 119). McKee and Chisenhall quote Lewis as saying he worked for "Dr. Benson's doctor show" (1981, 106). Lewis described for these Memphis journalists how they used a flatbed truck for a stage and how they would dress up and use lamp black on their faces for the comedy routines.

Who were the other performers on the show?

Huh? . . . Yeah, them the same ones I said, yeah. . . . Well, just like I tell you, Willie Polk, James Manus, Son Brimmer, Dewey Corley, Earl Bell. That's some of them on that picture right behind you. Right there.

For more on Dewey Corley, see the Memphis Ma Rainey chapter.

Earl Bell (1914–77) was a guitarist originally from Hernando, Mississippi. Bell traveled widely but had settled down in Memphis by the mid-1950s. In the 1960s and 1970s, he frequently told audiences and interviewers that he had helped Robert Johnson write "Terraplane Blues." Steve LaVere in his obituary for Bell states that Bell eventually admitted that this claim was false (1978, 31). Bell appeared on the Adelphi label's *Memphis Blues Again* set.

Did Blind Joe make any records?

Blind Joe?

Blind Joe.

[Eva] Joe!

Oh yeah, he was blind, yeah. . . . They wasn't making no records then. . . . No, uh-huh. Blind Joe, that's where I really see him sit down now, like I take my guitar and put it in my arms like here and pick it. He played it with a barlow knife and laid it flat across his lap. . . . Yeah, yeah.

What, like that?

Absolutely. . . . Absolutely, yeah.

Like a steel guitar?

Yeah.

What happened to him?

Oh, he died with the black tongue. [Laughs.] . . . No, he died, I was just teas'. I was having fun because don't nobody die of the black tongue but a dog. I was just having a little fun. [Laughter.] . . . Nobody die of that but a dog.

What is it?

Oh, just what they call it, die with the black tongue. [Laughter.]

Were there any white performers on the show?

Humph. No, no. Just a colored cast.

Well, how long did you work with the show?

Well, I work there for just, I work there regular, I guess, about fifteen or twenty years ————. And I just got tired of that and I just. . . . Too much traveling for me, in them days. . . . Sometimes I'd fill in, just like somebody be on there was sick or something or probably quit, but he'd find me and get me in there, and I'd go on make it probably a week or two more like that.

Well, what would you do after you finished with the minstrel shows? Did you come back here?

Oh yes, I come back home.

And did you play with any groups here in Memphis at that time?

W.C., oh yeah, no, I played with W. C. Handy and all the rest of them because I was playing with Handy before I started on the medicine show.

So you went back and played with him again?

Yeah, uh-huh. Just like the same thing. I want to, I wouldn't call myself professional when I first started with Handy, but I used to be up there at the music place with him and I got so I could play just as good as anybody else and I just joined his band.

Stanley Booth refers to Lewis as "a protege of W. C. Handy" (1991, 24). Lewis told Olsson, "I was not a regular—if a guitar player couldn't come or got sick or something, I'd fill his place" (1970, 76). He told McKee and Chisenhall, "I never did have just a regular job with Handy, but I played more than some of the regulars did 'cause they's off all the time and every other night I filled in for one of 'em" (1981, 105). David Evans wrote in a *Living Blues* obituary, "[Lewis's] guitar playing was too idiosyncratic to fit easily into a jug band sound, and his work for Handy was probably nothing more than as a fill-in guitarist in one of Handy's fill-in bands" (1982, 55). Lewis was obviously proud of his association with Handy and often spoke of it during interviews and other performances. It is curious that Charters does not even mention Lewis's connection to Handy.

Was Handy playing trumpet or guitar?

Trumpet! I never know Handy to play a guitar in my life. No. If anybody told you that, I'd like to see them. Uh-huh.

Handy, a famous band leader, music publisher, record label owner, and popularizer of the blues, was a cornet or trumpet player. It is with a trumpet that he is portrayed in the statue in the park bearing his name on Beale Street. Handy did record, accompanying himself on guitar, for the Library of Congress in 1938 (Rust 1978).

When you were playing with Blind Lemon, were . . .

Blind Lemon Jefferson? . . . In New York, yes.

How did you play with him? Were you using the bottleneck?

Bottleneck . . . bottleneck. He, uh, I'd lead sometimes and he complements behind, sometimes he lead and I complements, but when you complements you don't need no bottleneck, you just need that [holds up hands]. Four fingers and two thumbs, then you got to go way down here sometimes. Yeah, to make it sound. But I know that. Uh-huh.

Did you have any problems playing his style of music?

No, no, uh-huh.

Did you have someone else playing with you on your first records?

No. Yeah. . . . Landis Waldin and Charlie Jackson. Both of them's dead now.

In the liner notes of *Furry Lewis in His Prime, 1927–1928,* Stephen Calt, following Olsson, states that Landers or Landis Walton was a guitarist from Greenwood, Mississippi, who accompanied Lewis on his 1927 trip to Chicago to record. Lewis told Olsson, "He played guitar like I did" (1970, 76). Charlie Jackson is an unknown.

Landis Waldin?

Landis Waldon!

What did he play?

He played guitar like I did.

Uh-huh. Did you know him before you made the records?

Well, sure. Sure I knowed him before I made the records 'cause we all made records together.

Was he from around here?

Yeah, from right around here in Memphis. . . . I knowed him before he made the record, now. And the first record we recorded in, on Wabash Street in Chicago, there in the Brunswick-Blake Building. That's where they make pool tables and pinball machines. . . . On Wabash.

Olsson quotes Lewis as saying the "Brunswick Black [i.e., Balke] building in Chicago" (1970, 76). Lewis recorded for the Vocalion label owned by the Brunswick-Balke-Collender Company of Chicago (Dixon and Godrich 1970).

And that was in 1928?

It was actually 1927.

Oh, a little later than that.

And what about Charlie Jackson? What did he play?

Well, Charlie Jackson blow a harp and a kazoo. You know, one of the things you put in your mouth like that. He played a kazoo; something you call it like that.

Where was Charlie from?

Right here. . . . Mm huh, I don't know where he at now. He died. I don't know whether he going to heaven or not. [Laughter.]

Didn't he play something else on those records?

I'm's the onliest one that I know—excusing Gus Cannon, and he's a banjo player and they call him Banjo Joe. You know Gus Cannon is still living ————? And all of the mens that I have played with, forty or fifty or sixty years ago, is gone. Nobody but me and Gus. Gus about eighty-seven or something like that and I'm seventy-five. That's true.

He's eighty-seven years old?

Gus Cannon? Why, certainly. Or older.

[Eva] And he just made seventy-five?

Yes, he's eighty-five all right.

Yes, he is. Hey! . . . Now, listen, you stop that. [Laughter.] Don't put that on there. Now, I'm seventy-eight, seventy-five for real. Really seventy-five. When I tell you I was born the sixth of March in eighteen and ninety-three, way down in the Delta . . .

[Eva] Delta.

in Greenwood, [with Eva joining in] Mississippi.

Was there a mandolin player on your first records?

[Eva] Mandolin? . . .

Oh yes, used to have a little mandolin, call it, some people used to call them tater bugs. [Laughter.] One of them funny things, you know. . . . Just high up under there, you know. Did you know that ———. Well, sure, I can play that. I can play that. . . . Yeah, I can play a mandolin. Certainly.

What else can you play?

Good! I can blow a harmonium. Good! Yes, I can, yes.

What else can you play besides the guitar and mandolin?

The Dozens. [Laughter.] Alright, alright. . . . What else can I play, excusing that? . . . I can blow the harmonica . . . a little bit. Not, I'm not a . . .

The Dirty Dozens is an elaborate, often rhymed, verbal competition in which the participants insult each other's families, especially their mothers. The insults often refer to sexual aberrations or grotesque, obscene behaviors. The object is to remain cool while provoking your adversary to anger.

[Eva] Hey, Furry, play your jaw for them.

Oh. . . . Oh yeah. . . . I ain't got but about two or three teeths. [Laughter.] But sometimes what she's talking about. I can, wouldn't call it, you say, exactly a note, but a—you take your hand like this and have your teeths rattle in them.

[Beats a rhythm against jaw and teeth.] Like that. [Laughter.] Ain't got but two, but I tell you hit together. [Furry guffaws, all laugh.] Do that, Evelyn. . . . No thanks, she ain't got nairn but—[Laughter.] I'm sorry.

[Eva] I figure you was going to get out on me!

Well, look. [Laughs.]

[Eva] I'm going to go home and . . . [Furry laughs so loud he drowns out what Eva is saying. Laughter.]

Any more questions?

Furry, on your first record you said there was a mandolin player. What was his name?

Mandolin playing? . . . Jim Jackson.

That was Jim Jackson playing the mandolin?

Yeah, uh-huh. He play the mandolin and man, he play a guitar. Now, Jim Jackson the first one whatever I know put out "I'm going to move to Kansas City, baby, where they don't allow you." Uh-huh. That's real, you know the thing, Steve. If I'm not telling the truth now I hope God will kill me, that's just right, exact.

Well, you told me one time that was Charlie Jackson played the mandolin with you.

Jim Jackson! But Charlie Jackson could play a mandolin, too. But he didn't play the mandolin on the first record I made, you see. . . . Yeah, just like if, you . . .

Calt also reports that Charlie Jackson played the mandolin accompaniment on Lewis's first records (Calt n.d.). The fourth edition of *Blues and Gospel Records 1890–1943* lists the personnel accompanying Lewis as Landers Waller, guitar; Charles Johnson, mandolin; and unknown speaker (Dixon, Godrich, and Rye 1997, 539).

How did you come to make those records? How did they approach you to make those records?

How do they did which?

Approach you. . . . How did they come and ask you to do them?

Well, I tell you who that was. They's a man they call Jack Kapp. He dead.

Did he live here in Memphis?

No, no. Live in Chicago. Well, you see, Chicago people or probably any-where they hear about—Memphis used to be famous for the blues, you un-derstand, used to be real famous. . . . And peoples from far off somewhere would hear about that and they'd come here and find you and get you to-gether on it. Jack Kapp, he's dead. That's where I made at the Brunswick-Blake Building.

Jack Kapp had worked as Columbia's Chicago representative before heading Brunswick-Balke-Collender Company's Race Record Division. In 1934, Kapp took over the new U.S. company started by the British Decca label (Dixon and Godrich 1970, 33,77).

Did someone else tell him about you?

Now that's, uh, a little bit, a little something I don't know. Somebody must of have told him because he didn't know about me and he come away from Chicago to find me here in Memphis.

[Eva, softly] Oh, yes. Yes.

Did he write to you or did he come down?

Oh, he just come down. He didn't do no writing because he didn't know where to write at. . . . Say which?

Did he carry you back there with anyone else or by yourself?

Oh, there's a bunch of us. . . . It like you, right now, like you go to Missis-sippi and get Fred McDonald [i.e., McDowell], get John, get Mississippi John Hurt before he died, you get Frank Stokes before he died and all like that. You just get, just a bunch of us and give us, you know, a little anything then. 'Cause I remember the time you used to be able to get two loaves of bread for a nickel, but the devil of it was where you going to get the nickel. [Laughter.]

Mississippi Fred McDowell (1904–72), a local hill country and Delta musician and share-cropper, was "discovered" by Alan Lomax in 1959. In the 1960s, McDowell was extensively recorded and appeared often at folk, blues, and rock shows. McKee and Chisenhall describe his funeral and a eulogy that Lewis delivered there (1981, 112–13). For more on McDowell, see the Boose Taylor chapter.

Mississippi John Hurt (1893–1966), a favorite of folk music audiences, had a second career as musician after his "rediscovery" by Tom "Fang" Hoskins in 1963. He initially recorded in 1928 but did not make records again until the 1960s. He was a soft-spoken and humble man whose delightful music was characterized by influential finger-picking guitar work and smooth, easy vocals. Stanley Booth took Lewis to Hurt's funeral and wrote an essay about the experience. Booth quotes Lewis as saying, "But he was sho ugly. I swear 'fore God he was" (1991, 39).

Frank Stokes (1888–1955) was a guitarist, a wonderful vocalist, and the composer/compiler of exceptional songs. He was one of the earliest Memphis bluesmen and was a tremendous influence on the local music scene. He recorded solo and with his friend Dan Sane as the Beale Street Sheiks.

You remember who else was with you on that first trip?

Just what I said. That's all, that's all.

Who else got brought up?

That's on the trip with us? That's all. . . . Because we got where we just played. We performed as a jug band. Yeah, I was in the Memphis Jug Band.

Didn't you make that first trip with Jim Jackson and Gus Cannon?

That's what I said. . . . I said that just now. And. . . . Uh-huh.

Who was Ham Lewis?

Ham Lewis?

Yeah, there was a fellow used to play jug named Ham Lewis. And it's not the Ham we know now, but it's another fellow.

They call him Hammie Nixon.

No, it wasn't him.

Booth quotes Lewis describing a little band he had in the early days that included "a boy named Ham" on jug (1991, 30). Olsson mentions a Ham who blew jug as an associate of Lewis's in Greenwood (1970, 76). A Hambone Lewis did blow jug on recordings made by Noah Lewis, Kaiser Clifton, and the Memphis Jug Band in 1930. Lewis told Booth that Ham left Memphis during the Great Depression: "The boy we called Ham, from our band, he left, and nobody ever knew what became of him" (1991, 31).

For more on Hammie Nixon, see the Tommy Gary chapter.

Well, I don't know. . . . Well, I tell you. The reason why I say such as that. It's more than one of anything. It's had more than one jug band. . . . Just like when we was on the doctor show, some travel east, some travel west, and some travel north, and some travel south. They didn't all go the same way. And so they had the different jug bands. And some plays on the other jug bands, I didn't know. . . . But all I know is them who I'm with. And I know them perfect.

Where did you travel?

We traveled in Arkansas. . . . We in Arkansas. . . . Yeah, with the jug band.

How long were you with the jug band?

Oh, well, just come on down to the fact, I'm kind of with it now, 'cause some of those boys play yet. Earl Bell and all of the rest of them, we get together now and kind of perform another one. We play, last time I remember, the last play we had, I can't remember the name of Arkansas, but we played there at that big ole factory where they make Singer sewing machines. I can't think of that part of Arkansas to save my life. They make Singer sewing machines there. . . . What?

Remember that story you told me about making shirts? Out of . . .

Oh yeah. I didn't do that, my brother done that. Don't put that on me, now. . . . What did I tell you? My brother, he didn't have no job, and he was staying with me. I told him if he didn't get no job, I was going to put him out. And so he said, "I can't find no job." Well, I said, "I'll find you one." I looked in the paper the next morning but seen no job in there but tailor, where they make clothes. I went to him and said, "Now, I got a good job," but I said, "You can't do that because that where they make clothes, that's a tailor." I said, "Well, come on." I taken my brother to the tailor shop and they hired him. And after they hired him, me and my brother started out the door and the man come back and he said, "Come here a minute." He said, "There's one thing I forgot to ask you. You says you a good tailor. I'm going to ask you one question." He say, "What is that?" He say, "How many yards do it take to make a shirt?" He say, "I don't know how many yards it takes to make a shirt but, hell, I got three shirts out of one yard last night. [Laughs. Laughter. Furry sputters.] Alright now, shit. [Laughter.]

Furry, can you remember the first person you ever heard singing the blues?

Naw, I really can't. Uh-huh. [Gravely] I really can't. Because it, uh, it been, it been, people been singing the blues ever since the world, and I know I've heard people singing the blues when I was six years old or a little bit younger, but I didn't know who they was and don't know anything like that there. That's one deep question you asked me there. I really can't. . . . The first person I ever heard, no, I can not. Huh?

Did anyone else in your family play any musical instruments or sing?

Well, I tell you, just like I pick a guitar, my daddy used to pick, too, but he didn't pick guitar, he picked pockets. 'Cause there's more money in pockets than they is in guitars. [Laughter.] No, just [snorts]. . . . [Quietly to interviewers] It right now, see, you got a whole lot of stuff.

What gave you the idea to take up music?

Beg your pardon?

What made you decide to start playing music?

To start? . . . I just love it!

Did you, any special reason why you started?

Noooo! No special reason. I never had a music teacher, I never had nobody, I just don't know. I could hear you play same right here then, and if I lived across the street, I'd go across the street and get my guitar and get that sound. I play funny than anybody do now, than anybody else. You never seen nobody play the guitar bottle style like I do. I don't care who he is. Uh-huh. Because I got the first ———— I've been to many places and I've run upon some hard propositions, but I ain't seen nobody yet play in my style. Have you, Steve? . . . Nooo. Course it's funny me, that be the latest style. [Laughs.]

Furry, did you ever listen to someone singing the blues when you were young and decided that that's the way you wanted to sing?

Well, I tell you. Yes, I have, and then, no, I ain't. [Laughter.] I have and I ain't. Well, now. . . . I have listened to people and I really like to hear them sing the blues and go on like that and then come on back again and I say "oh no." If I was to sing the blues and different things, I want a style then that—you might say I just don't want to play surfing music. It's all such as that, you know, it's the way your mind run in music now. Um huh. Just like, I can get my guitar and I can say, "I'm going to play you so and so and so and so." And I get the guitar and everything and I say, "Well, no, I'm going to play you something else." Then I play you something I don't say I'm going to play you in front. It would be that way to you, you could hear me play now. You may say, "Well, I don't like Furry's style." Well, you get your own style and play it then. Well, that's the way you do like that. Now that's straight oil from the can. You know that's like a man was carrying me to a town, and on our way to town he have five punctures, four on the ground and one in the spare. And, I mean, they all come on at once, it's like in Shanghai. It pop so loud, and he say, "I've got to take my car through inspection." So he was going to take his car through inspection and he got about as far from the inspection bureau as he is Poplar Street. And the man seen him coming and got out there and done that way. "Can't come in here." He got out of the car and he came in here. He went to him and ask, "How come I can't come in here and get my car inspected?" You know what he told him? "Your right light high and your left light low. Your taillight's dim and your horn won't blow." [Laughs. Laughter.] I'm sorry about that. [Laughter.]

How did you develop your style, Furry?

How did I develop my own style? . . . Well, I tell you, that's just as easy as anybody could ever think anything is. I could see you doing something now just don't want to do it that; I want to do it my way. Just like you sing a song right now, I couldn't sing your song but I could make up some verses different from your, but I be, they the same tune. I can play "John Henry" right now on a guitar and you'd get up and get the guitar, you'd play "John Henry" but, you see, you ain't playing it like I did. 'Cause that's the way you know it and I play the way I know it. And so. Now you understand me?

Lewis first recorded "John Henry" for Vocalion in 1929.

What was the first song you learned?

"Near-O My God to Thee. . . ." And the first thing I learned to drink was Early Times. [Laughter.] . . . Huh?

"Nearer My God to Thee" was one of the gospel songs that Lewis regularly included in his shows in the 1970s.

What was the first blues you learned?

Oh God. . . . You know, that's a pretty hard question. Because if you started playing guitar young as I was when I started, you couldn't tell to save your life what song you first played. No. That's impossible for me to do that.

How old were you when you started?

How old I was when I started? Well, now, I couldn't say, exact say, that, but I could say about eight or nine years old. I wasn't an old man.

According to Booth, "'I was eight or nine, I believe,' [Lewis] said, 'when I got the idea I wanted to have me a guitar'" (1991, 29). Olsson quotes Lewis as saying he was "'just six years old'" when he began playing the guitar (1970, 74). "'Well, I guess I was 'bout twelve, thirteen years old, something like that, when I first started playing guitar,'" Lewis told McKee and Chisenhall in the early 1970s (1981, 105).

Did you start from the beginning playing bottleneck or did you learn that later on?

No, I didn't start at the beginning. Now, my beginning my playing guitar like that, I had a knife . . . a pocket knife, and I play with the pocket knife, but the pocket knife kept a slipping down and it kept me doing that a way, pushing it back up. . . . And I just said, I go on and make me a bottleneck just like what I showed you, she was broke. See, I was going to make a bottleneck because you can put just, uh, this far and it ain't going no farther. You ain't going to lose it that way. . . . And then again, that's the way I done.

Did you see other people playing it?

Why, certainly! If I hadn't seen nobody else do it, I wouldn't done it myself. . . . But I think I was the first one started that bottleneck because, just like I tell you from the first time, everybody would be playing with a knife.

Who was the first person you saw playing with a knife?

Blind Joe. . . . Why, certainly.

What was Joe's last name?

That's all we ever know. Blind Joe. I know he had more name than that, but I didn't know. [Laughter.] But I didn't know it; everyone call him that, you know. I wasn't nothing but just a kid. I didn't know nothing! I tell you, I wasn't nothing but a little kid, and kids in those days didn't know like children now, children now know more than me. And I didn't know that when I was a kid. Uh-huh.

In the liner notes of *Furry Lewis in His Prime, 1927–1928,* Calt gives this quote from Lewis about Blind Joe: "'I think he's from Arkansas' Furry says of him, 'See—people called him Arkansas sometimes'" (Calt n.d.).

Did Blind Joe help you learn to play with a slide at all?

That's where I learnt how to play with the bottleneck. He had that. . . . Yeah!

Or did he help you any?

No, no. He didn't help me nothing. I constantly tell you every time that . . . I see someone else do it, I go and try to do it the same way or different way. You know that's true.

Where did you first see him, Furry?

On Brinkley Avenue. . . . Right, yeah, on Brinkley Avenue, that's Decatur Street. . . . Then, too. That's Decatur Street, a man had a grocery store there they called Pete [Tilman?]. And the porch come across the sidewalk, and [you] had to come up on this step to come across to go down on the other step to go where you was going. And Decatur Street where it's now is Brinkley Avenue. And I know when Decatur Street was the city limits. And you got the block the other side of Decatur Street you was in the country. Used to pick cotton right at Parkway and Decatur. I'm the man what help build Sear Roebuck; I blowed them stumps. And playing music.

Where did you used to get molasses and bread?

Where did I get molasses and bread? . . . You call that a [brosch?]. Mister Bowles, right here at Ashland and Lane Avenues, right this way. He had a store. Had a big ole dog on the outside of the store that say "You can't get bit if you buy Mr. Bowles." Well, we was going to school. You could take, you want, groceries, they call it. They had molasses in a barrel. You know, turn the handle just like you might go get coal oil now. You turn that handle the molasses come out. We'd go get [bolo shear?] and take a loaf of bread and split right straight, just like that, and put near about a pound of butter in it and then take that bread, you know, and turn the molasses on like that; call that brosch. You know you get that from the [pause]. . . . I've seen it so tight. . . . Yes, you could. Right there at Dunlap and Poplar, used to be a watering shop where they'd water the horses and the mules, I've seen it so tight here that I had to go up the alley one day, and I seen it, it was so tight—that's when Hoover was president—I went up the alley one time and I seen a rat sitting on top of a garbage can eating an onion crying. [Neighbor woman laughs.] Yeah, he couldn't get nothing else. Yeah. [Laughter.] Alright, now you behave yourself. [Laughter.] Well, I think we've about had enough, ain't we?

When you first made records, was that before or after you first started with the medicine show?

When I first made records? . . . It was the same, it was the same time. . . . Yeah, it was the same time. But now when I get ready to make a record like that, you know, that's like a, you know, like a—you fill in in any place. Uh-huh.

Well, how did you make your records in Memphis? Who got you that record?

Here in Memphis? . . . Sam Charters.

No, no, no . . . in the old days.

Oh, way back? . . . Oh, man, I don't know. One of them was Jack Kapp. Whomsoever it was, I forget now. . . . But anybody we made it at the Peabody Hotel. Huh?

Was it Mr. Peer?

I think it was something like that. I can't think now.

Ralph Peer, a white Missouri man, developed Okeh's race and hillbilly catalogs before joining Victor in the mid-1920s. Peer is credited with having made the first southern field trip—to

Atlanta in 1923—by a recording company to record local artists. He recorded several artists on this trip to Atlanta, including blues singer Lucille Bogan. Subsequently, he made a number of trips to southern cities to record black blues, jazz, and gospel musicians, and white country musicians. Peer was especially prone to record traditional and original songs that were not copyrighted, which he could then publish through his company. Many of the great blues songs recorded by Victor and its subsidiaries in the 1920s and 1930s are owned exclusively by Peer International Corporation (Dixon and Godrich 1970; Barlow 1990). Barlow said of Peer's publishing activities, "It proved to be a profitable scam" (1990, 26). Peer was certainly not alone in cheating blues artists out of their property.

It was at the Peabody Hotel?

[Coughs.] Uh-huh. Peabody Hotel. . . . Say what?

How did he find you?

Just, just hear about, just hear about. Listen, Memphis used to be the famous place in the world for blues. . . . Memphis and New Orleans. . . . People would come here, want to find some real blues players and all like that. I didn't know him from Adam's oil cart.

Did he advertise in the paper?

What? Advertise? What you mean? . . . No, no, no. No, no, they don't do that now.

Was that before you went to Chicago or after?

Oh, that was after.

When did New Orleans get big with the blues?

Well, I tell you one thing. New Orleans always is has been famous. . . . Oh, well, not only from Chicago, some come away from here there. Memphis. Didn't come away from Chicago. Just like, now I've been going to New Orleans for years and years and years and have been playing in there like that, but when I play I come on back here, but a whole lot of people go up there but don't come back. They stay there.

When you were making records in the old days, did you play behind anyone else, as well as on your own records?

Do you mean did they all of us have records?

No. [Loud clap of thunder.]

Oh, my God! Say what? [Laughter.]

Apart from your own records, you know, apart from you own records, did you play behind anyone else as well? Second anyone?

Oh yes, I could. Complement. That's what you call it.

Did you? On the records?

Oh, did I? . . . No. . . . Always been on my own.

When was the first time you heard "Casey Jones," the song?

Oh, Lord. That's when, I guess, that's when I first started out.

"Casey Jones" originated in the black tradition and was once very popular among African Americans. By the 1920s, "Casey Jones" was more popular among white performers than black. Howard Odom and Guy Johnson observed in 1926 that "Casey Jones" was only heard occasionally among black performers in North Carolina, South Carolina, Georgia, and Tennessee (1969, 126). Furry Lewis, John Hurt, and Charles "Cow Cow" Davenport (whose versions were not issued) were the only black singers of the 1920s who recorded "Casey Jones"; even Deford Bailey's instrumental version was not released. Lewis's version has much in common with the song "Eastman" collected by Odum (see below). Paul Oliver wrote that Lewis's version also made "an oblique reference to a more obscure ballad, 'Stavin' Chain'" (1984b, 243). Lewis recorded "Kassie Jones" in two parts for Victor in August 1928. Norm Cohen includes a transcription of "Kassie Jones" and an analysis of the various versions of the song that Lewis recorded during his long career (1981). Albert Friedman also includes a transcription of "Kassie Jones." He writes that "many lines are unintelligible, others are cliches from songs about 'natu'l-bohn eas'man'—pimps" (1971, 315). Charters suggests that Ralph Peer changed the spelling from "Casey" to "Kassie" so that he could copyright Lewis's version (1977, 52).

Do you remember who you heard that from?

No, ot uh.

Furry, did you ever hear the Memphis Jug Band sing "On the Road Again?"

Sing it? . . . Memphis Jug Band? . . . Yeah. Sure. Uh-huh.

The Memphis Jug Band recorded "On the Road Again" for Victor in September 1928.

That's sort of like "Casey Jones."

That's what that is. . . . You know, that's same thing. Now, say, "On the Road Again" is "Casey Jones." Well, that's something just like a fiddle and a violin. Now, that's the same thing. Uh-huh. Yeah.

Right. What does "natural-born eastman" mean?

Well, that's just most anything. I could say, "I'm a natural-born man." You just put that in there yourself. "I'm a natural-born eastman, I'm on the road again." You could say, "I'm a natural-born man, and I'm on the road again."

Does that mean you are going east?

Nooo, I just put that name in there. I could say, "I'm a natural-born Furry, but I'm on the road again." You just, that's just a name you put in there. . . . It's not going east or west or nowhere. . . . Yeah. Just something to fill out. . . .

In 1911, Odum published a song "Eastman" that he had recorded in Lafayette County, Mississippi, from a traveling singer. It contained the lines (also found in Lewis's "Kassie Jones" and his later version of "On the Road Again"), "I got it writ on the tail o' my shirt, I'm a natu'al-bohn eastman, don't have to work." Odum defined "eastman" as a "typical character" who is "kept fat by the women among whom he is universally a favorite" (1911, 354). Odum also collected a version of "Casey Jones" in Lafayette County. Jean-Paul Levet suggests that eastman is a corruption of "easy man" or "ease man," and that he is a hustler (1992, 91). Oliver writes that eastman refers to a pimp (1984b, 245). Clarence Major, compiler of *Juba to Jive: A Dictionary of African-American Slang* (1994), defines eastman as "a pimp; a man who is supported by a woman or women" (157). His example is from Carl Van Vetchen's 1926 novel of Harlem, *Nigger Heaven*. The white singer, Jimmie Rogers, used this same couplet in his recording "Blue Yodel No. 9 (Standin' on the Corner)" accompanied by Louis Armstrong in 1930.

[Eva] I can't go home ———— behind me tonight.

Well, I sure hope it rain all night, then, so you do that. [Laughter. Laughs.] Let it rain. Come on down, rain. Hey.

[Eva] I'm going to run, Furry. I pick up these things later.

No, no.

[Eva] I'm going to run for it.

No, no, I tell you. You sleep over there and I sleep over here.

[Eva] If it rain too hard, I'm going have to sleep over here somewhere. [Laughs.]

Oh, you ain't going to get wet. Mm uh. Because I'll let you take the roof off of my house because I can get wet until you come back and bring the roof back.

[Eva] It rain on you the other day? . . . It rained on you the other day. You said I should come by and let's go home with you. "It ain't going to rain." "Oh, wee! Raining in Caroline's house! Here it is a little pool, here it is." Looking for the rain and they wasn't no rain.

Well, [thunder rumbling] that [laughs] was because a greenhorn.

[Eva] Right on! [Steve and Linda are smooching.]

I see that, look at that. Now, you see that, look at them kissing. [Laughter.] I'll be dogged.

[Eva] They hugging each other.

Steve, say, what y'all doing? [Eva laughs.] She kissing, you see'd that, didn't you! I was looking. [Furry roars with laughter.] Hey, you see it? Did you see it? . . . Oh, uh-huh. . . . [Roars again with laughter.] Lord!

Furry, what year did you leave the medicine show?

I'm trying to sense, trying to think now. Well, that's another hard pill to swallow. And it's like I 'fore said, I ain't got near the membance that I used to have. I just have to do the catch the can. Think, Steve, what year it was or nothing. But I know it's been a long time but I couldn't say it's this and that, this and that. . . . I'm trying my best to tell the whole truth about the deal we're doing here and I wanted to be straight. But I just couldn't tell what it is to save my life, because I don't know.

Well, who was president? Do you remember that? When the medicine show stopped, do you remember who was president then?

I don't know who there it was. [Pauses and thinks.] One of them Roosevelt brothers or not. You know there was Franklin and Teddy Roosevelt, and both of them were president . . . brothers. But now I don't know. I'll tell you one thing, I don't know this but I read about it, might near every president you get, gets killed if he stays there because President McKinley, not Kinney, President McKinley got killed shaking hands. You know, that's right, that's for real, that's the truth, just like you just meet a person, say, "How is that?" and the man had something, a pistol in his glove and killed you. And you ask anybody how this President [emphasizing the pronunciation] McKinley got killed, got to be an old person that tell you, though, he say got killed shaking hands. Shake hands with a man with a pistol in his glove and he shot him.

Furry, what did you do after you quit the medicine show?

I went home and ate. [Laughter.] Went home and ate that day, and the next night I went to sleep. [Laughter.] Well, I did.

Well, did you get any jobs after that playing? [Thunder clap.]

Jobs. Oh yes. I used to play for parties. I used to play around here for parties, and then see the saloons and things. This was a wide-open town. Had bars and different things here. And see, Memphis, used to go to a bar and get you a dime drink or fifteen-cent drink or such like that. I used to play around them kind of places. And then we used to serenade. Now, serenading it is, I could come to your house about, we'd all get tuned up, a bunch of us we'd all be tuned up and come to your house at one or two o'clock in the morning. And y'all be asleep and we just light right out and start to playing on your porch. Well, you know, when you're asleep like that and somebody comes on your porch and start the music like that and it sound good to you. But in them days, they will get up and the man's wife would go right in the kitchen and start to cooking. . . . Oh yeah, mm huh.

Is that why you serenade, to get food?

That was called serenading. No, we didn't serenade for the food, we'd just be out drinking and having a nice time. Now, I play in Alabama and different places and [loud thunder] I played in Alabama and different places so we had a song in Alabama, says, "The stars do the shine and the moon get the light. We Alabama people are going to walk out tonight." Now, see, that means, uh, a drunk. See, we all just get together and sometimes go there, grab a fifth and sit there all night long, right [mumbles]. It was good times then. Now, I'm just telling you what I've been through. If I ain't been through that I couldn't tell you. What I.... House rent parties? . . . No, I never did play for none, but they used to come and play for mine. [Laughs. Laughter.] I was so behind they paid the house rent for me in a week, every week, you know. I was living in a two-room house, like this s'here, and I was paying four dollars a week. Meant to say four dollars a month, a dollar a week for it. Mm huh.

Lewis told Olsson, "We'd get together and serenade around. I played by myself, but if I wanted to get together I'd get Buddy Doyle or Landis Walton. We'd get out and just have fun like that" (1970, 78). Little Buddy Doyle, a midget, was a guitar player who was active on the Memphis blues scene in the 1930s. He recorded in 1939.

Furry, who did you use to play with after you quit the show when you was playing the saloons and serenading?

After I quit the show? . . . Well, I just went for my own. . . . Went on for my own, like I'm doing now. . . . There's some cold cuts out there. Some cold cuts. Huh?

When did you start playing with the jug band?

I think you asked me that before but I just can't remember that. . . . Been so long. I think that you have brought that question to me again. And if you ever ask me again about that, I might have done thought of it. [Laughter.] . . . Huh?

Were those saloons pretty rough in those days?

Oh, was they? . . . Oh, why, certainly now! . . . Why, certainly, I've seen a whole lot of shootings, plenty of it. I've seen a whole lot of people get kill't.

[Were] you ever involved in any of those scrapes?

No, by the time I see a pistol, I always run and left there. No. I know a man shot at me once and shot at me five times. [Thunder clap.] And I was running and it was pulling to catch up with me, and when I got in the house, the bullet hit all against the door. I outrunned it. Yeah, you can do that, if you scared enough. You can outrun a bullet. Sure. [Laughter.]

What were you doing when Samuel Charters found you in 1959?

What was I doing? Working for the city. . . . Yeah.

What were you playing for then?

Different parties and different things like that and . . . Jim Jackson, Memphis Willie B., and all of us.

You played with Memphis Willie B.?

Why, certainly, Memphis Willie B. live right down there on ———— Street in [Partham?]. Yeah.

William Borum, a.k.a. Memphis Willie B., was born in Memphis in 1911. He plays guitar and harmonica and has penned a number of original songs. Borum recorded in the 1930s and again after his "rediscovery" in the early 1960s. In the early 1970s, Borum was married to a "sanctified" (Pentecostal) woman who did not approve of the blues. At that time, Borum would neither play blues nor allow himself to be interviewed about blues music. Alan Lomax, in his *The Land Where the Blues Began*, confused Borum with Willie "Highway 61" Blackwell, another Memphis/Mississippi blues artist who Lomax had recorded (1993). In 1972, Borum lived at 740 Alma Street in North Memphis.

Was Jim Jackson still alive in 1959?

No, man, Jim Jackson had been dead a long time ago. He been dead so long he near about ready to come back. [Laughter.]

When did you start working for the city?

Oh, I don't know exactly when I started working for the city, but off and on, I was there for forty-four years. I worked for the city when they didn't have nothing but mules and two-wheeled carts. They didn't even have a truck. The bossman used to ride around in a buggy. And the buggy the same color like, you see these trucks are here now. City orange. . . . It's true, I done that. Well, I think I'm going to cut out now, y'all. Now, I done think, y'all. . . . I think I done pretty good, now.

I want to ask you one more question, Furry. How did Samuel Charters find you when he come down here?

When Sam Charters found me, I was way out on Third Street, me and a fellow they call Tom [Melon?]. That's his name. We was cleaning that viaduct. You know, it like a, you see grass growing through the cracks? . . . That's what we were doing.

In Charters's version of this first meeting, he found Lewis in "a frame house on one of the North Memphis back streets" (1977, 56).

[Johnny, entering door] A man could get drowned out there.

Hi, Johnny.

[Eva] Hi, Johnny.

[Neighbor woman] Hello, Johnny.

[Johnny] Hey, y'all.

You say, you see my mailman?

[Neighbor woman] What's happening?

You can put it in your pocket.

[Eva] No, I didn't?

No, you didn't, Eva.

[Eva] I'll put in a chair down here.

No, put your money back in your pocket. Don't do that.

[Eva] I just trying to give the man his due. I'm not going to steal anything from him.

Ha, ha, ha, ha, ha. Johnny, how you coming?

[Johnny] Well, I'm all right.

How you coming?

[Johnny] Scared. You see what we got out there? Huh? You know it's dark out.

[Eva] No.

Want to sit down a minute?

[Johnny] No, no.

You got to go kicking, whooping, and hollering like that, I won't do it. Just like I got this man. But he fixing to say, "Don't drink." [Eva laughs.] And people said, "The Lord is my shepherd and I shall not want." But I will say, "The Lord is my shepherd and I got what I want." [Laughs. Laughter.]

The Lord is my shepherd and I can't see what I can get.

Alexander "Papa George" Lightfoot (1924–71), the Natchez harmonica blower and recording artist, used this line in a spoken monologue on a record that LaVere produced for the Vault label in 1969.

The Lord is my shepherd and you let this bottle alone.

[Eva] The Lord is my shepherd and I'm going home. [Furry laughs loudly.] I want to eat supper and I ain't got none.

Well, Johnny, I'm sorry for you. You got to go because Eva sure ain't going out there in that rain, and you sure going to get out of here.

[Eva] No, darling, ot uh, no, ot uh.

[Johnny] Eva going to leave here.

[Eva] Ot uh, ot uh! [To Johnny] No, I ain't been home. I ain't fixed nothing to eat, I'm don't want to fix something to eat. . . . I going to finish supper right here and keep drinking and eat my ——— all night long. Brought me a whole can of [salmon?], y'all.

Sit down, Johnny, sit over here, sit over here.

[Johnny] ——— curfew here. . . . She's going to leave here five minutes before curfew.

No, no, she ain't going to go nowhere now.

[Eva] What curfew?

[Johnny] Five minutes before eleven, Eva be stepping.

But Johnny, no Johnny, now.

[Johnny] Her curfew.

[Eva] The police not working tonight. The police not working tonight!

Johnny, this is my little place here, now, where you's here you can boss at, but I'll tell everybody in the world when you get to talking about . . .

[Johnny] But I had to keep her four to eight.

Yeah, but let me tell you. I tell everybody in the world when you through talking about your brick house, come see Furry's frame. I live here, don't I?

[Eva] I'm glad you brought my [medicine?] now.

Speak up for yourself; you want to tell it like it is.

[Eva] Right on.

Hey, you want some, Pat? Pat?

[Johnny] Pat?

[Pat] Ot uh.

[Johnny] Goddamn.

[Eva] Better not nobody allow me to drink it because I do.

[Furry laughs.] Ain't no problem. [Discussion breaks down into several different simultaneous conversations and we turn off the tape recorder.]

Lewis died of cardiac arrest at the City of Memphis Hospital on September 14, 1981. He was being treated at the hospital for burns he'd received in a recent fire at his home. Local rock musicians and Lewis's protégés, Sid Selvidge, Lee Baker, and Lindsay Butler, played at his funeral. Notice of his death received considerable media attention in Memphis and was carried by the Associated Press. Obituaries appeared in the *New York Times* (Palmer 1981), *Guitar Player* ("In Memoriam," 1981), and *Rolling Stone* (Clayton 1981), among other publications.

Based on his memory of Lewis from 1969, Terry Manning recently wrote a fitting epitaph for Furry Lewis: "He was somehow part musician, part magician, part clown, part philosopher. But he was above all else an entertainer" (Manning n.d.).

Boose Taylor

5 It Don't 'Bide a Good Man Well for You to Play Them Things

Fiddler Ernest "Boose" Taylor

In 1972, Ernest "Boose" Taylor was getting by, farming other folk's land, just as he had done his entire life. He was living in a small house with his wife, Daisy (or Daisy Mae, or Jane, or Mary Jane), and children in Shelby County, east of Memphis and near the town of Collierville. He had no phone but could, in emergencies, receive phone messages through a white neighbor.

Taylor was surprised, even shocked, when we contacted him. Outside his family, neighbors, and friends in the hill country of north-central Mississippi and the adjacent area in Tennessee, no one had heard of Boose Taylor and his music—music he had quit performing many years previous. When we played the tape of his singing and fiddling, he laughed and giggled in sheer delight, for he had never before heard himself. His friend Fred McDowell must have experienced similar feelings when Alan Lomax first recorded him in 1959.

Boose Taylor and his brothers were participants in and creators of a regional blues style described by ethnomusicologist Sylvester Oliver as the Northeast Hill Blues: "The northeast hill region is a vibrant crossroad region that is locked between two major cultural regions: the predominantly white lower Southern Appalachian Mountain region and the predominantly African-American Mississippi Delta region." Oliver wrote of both the influence of Appalachian "reels and fiddle and banjo tunes" and a "powerful African-American musical counter influence" from Memphis: "jug bands, string bands, jazz and ragtime, and blues" (1996, 400). This region's music is at the same time described as more heavily influenced by white mountain music yet retaining to a greater degree the character of West African music than does other secular music of African America.

A distinctive feature of hill country music was the survival of the fife-and-drum band. These bands created a music for which Lomax and others have claimed an African connection. As we discovered in later conversations, Taylor's first instrument was a fife he had made himself, and among his first musical experiences were those of following the popular fife-and-drum bands of the area.

But Taylor's primary instrument was the fiddle, and he was of the generation of hill country musicians to rework traditional country fiddle and banjo tunes into the new blues music. (Fellow hill country native Gus Cannon did the same for the banjo.) Other musicians of Taylor's generation changed from the older instruments to the guitar (on which Taylor was also accomplished) and "consciously or unconsciously employed fiddle and banjo tunes and techniques" in their guitar playing (S. Oliver 1996, 404). Blues researcher and entrepreneur Steve LaVere, after hearing the tape of Taylor's picking—rather than bowing—the fiddle, commented on how it sounded remarkably like a fretless banjo.

We came to the Taylor house down a dirt road at dusk after the workday was mostly over. In front of the house was a recently planted cotton field through which we crossed to find Taylor relaxing after having finished his evening meal. Daisy Taylor was doing the dishes and children were about, occupied in various activities but playing close attention to the strangers. Under a bare, hanging bulb, Taylor sat barefoot with his old fiddle as we began to talk.

Well, okay, could you tell us when you were born and where you were born?

Well, I . . . , uh [pause], I tell you that kind of hard for me to do [laughs]. I'm not sure no more about that than I am . . .

[Daisy] They say you was born about Christmas time, wasn't it?

Yeah, I was born in December.

[Daisy] They say ———— supposed to be cooking cakes, I would say that it must of been on Christmas Eve or on Christmas.

Or a day or two before Christmas.

[Daisy] Or a day or two before Christmas one.

And, uh, I was born in . . . , uh [pause] Marshall County.

Was that in Tennessee?

No.

[Daisy] It was back up here.

That's up here. In, uh, si, sip, Mississippi. . . . In Mississippi, yes. [Fingering fiddle strings] Back up, back up, well, I say, southeast, southeast.

Marshall County in north-central Mississippi is still the center of blues activity in the north Mississippi hill country. The African American music of this area has been extensively documented in Sylvester W. Oliver Jr.'s 1996 dissertation for the University of Memphis.

Well, do you have any idea how old you are now?

I'm sixty-five years old. . . . Mm huh. Sure is.

Could you tell us how you started playing the fiddle? When did you start playing?

Yes, sir, I can tell you all about how I did it. . . . Well, the way I started playing that, playing fiddle, I heard another man play one and I . . .

[Daisy same time as Boose] ———— a man if you would go to school.

I didn't go to school.

[Daisy] Now, I talking 'bout Baby Brother. I told him no sneaking—what he going to school for? You don't see nothing to eat in here.

[Plucking fiddle strings] I heard another fellow play up there . . . and I told that fellow, I say, "I sure want me one of them there things, I didn't, didn't know where to." I said, "I want one of them there things." I said, "I want." I said, "If I never know how to play it, I just want it. . . ." [Rubs rust off fiddle strings.] He said, "Well, he's playing so good and the thing was sounding so good." And the first time I'd ever had see one. Well, I was a big fellow, I was a big ole boy, I was just about a grown man, I tell you. . . . And this fellow played it and so I told him—he wouldn't let me look at it; I was wanting to put it in my hand but he wouldn't let me look at it. He, I reckon he thought it was too precious and he, I told him, "I'm going to get me one." He said, "Well, if you get one you got to be shown, you got to go to school and learn how to play." I said,

"Well, I may have to do that but I'm going to get me one if I have to study so hard where I got a song." . . . He didn't let me sees his and so I was working, I was working wages for a fellow.

[Daisy referring to microphone] I imagine he not going to be talking with your voice toward that.

Oh yeah, that what you want? . . . And I was working for wages for a man and his wife. I told her I want a violin . . . and she said . . . [to son] Tell him you excused. Step over that wire. . . . And she say, "Alright, I order you one." I say, "Yes, ma'am, I just want one. I can't, I want to learn how to play, try to, to play something on it." She say, "Alright." So she ordered it. She ordered me one. [To Daisy] There he is. . . . She ordered me one. She say, "Ernest . . . " Say, "I can't, I going try to learn to play it myself after it come." It come. She ordered it and it come. . . . I couldn't even tune it up. I didn't know how to tune it up. So, my brother—at that time he living—he could play a guitar. . . . And I carried it, I carried it this house, carried it down there to they, his house. I told him, "I can't tune this thing here." He tuned it up. He tuned up, he tuned up and played the first piece on it and hand it to me and told me, said, "Well, I couldn't play it because I leave home if I play this thing." So he just handed it back to me; he never did try to play it no more. He took it, he tuned it up for me and never had none in his hand, but he played guitar so he knowed how it go. And he played a perfect little tune on it and handed it back to me. "Well," he said, "if I had to play this thing, I'd leave my home. I wouldn't stay here." And so he handed it back to me, and so he didn't borrow, he didn't never play it no more. So, I sawed around, sawed around, tried to play around and scooing it, and scoo-to, scooting and going on. And so some fellows came to my house that could play guitar. So they were old fellows and they could play guitar so I get my fiddle, I say, "I'm going to try to do something with y'all, I'm just going to ———." And so I get with them and I got with them, fiddle going with them. So I come to try a little piece along with them, just trying to play, and done pretty good. And so, that fellow then, that fellow, they finally left then I just took it on my own roost then. Somehow just come home, tried to play me a piece, and learned how to try to play me a piece like that. I don't play no fiddle like people do play 'em. Peoples, some peoples play the fiddle by, you know, uh, uh, another way. . . . I learned another way to play. My brother like guitar, like he, just like a, if I falling, he could, he picked me up. See? . . . That's where I learnt it, see. So I didn't play it like these fellows. I's seen some fellows play some pieces and they played, they didn't play me, but when I was playing, anything, anybody else, anybody playing on guitar. I played, I played, I played the rhythm. I didn't care where it was, I picked it up and I played with 'em. Well, that's the way I learnt, that's the way I learnt. Now, some people learnt how to play a violin, they can't play but two or three pieces and they will sing that, and but that's all. . . . But I play with a guitar all the time, and I play a song, I play the song, I play a song like I sing a song, now, that's the way I play. I play just like I sing it, now. I always did do it, you know. And sometimes I sing. Maybe my brother in his lifetime, he'd sing a verse and I'd sing a verse. That's the way we used to play it, you see. And when he didn't sing and I didn't sing we made our guitar and fiddle say what us supposed to say, see. So peoples knowed exactly how, how it went. That's the way, that's the way, us played. . . . That's the way us played all the time. . . . Peoples would be glad to hear us anytime! Anytime we went out. They'd say, "They Taylor boys are going to play at such and such place." Man, you couldn't stir them with a stick.

Where did y'all used to go?

Oh, we went different places. I went to Red Banks, Mississippi, and, uh, different places. We went to, uh . . .

[Daisy] Went down to [La Martin?].

Oh yeah, all way up in there and we went, we went to . . .

[Daisy] I'm not sure.

We went to another place where Richard stay. Richard stay, I can't 'call the name. We're here, go over yonder to Hickory Valley, all up in there and that's what. We went all up in Hickory Valley playing. We'd go all up there. Anywhere, anywhere peoples. . . .

Hickory Valley is east of Collierville in Hardeman County, Tennessee.

[Daisy] Didn't y'all play at . . .

Send for us, they'd call, they'd get us word and, and so . . .

[Daisy] Didn't y'all play up here at this picnic?

What picnic?

[Daisy] Rossville, the road down there at Wade Newton's.

Rossville is due east of Collierville and west of Hickory Valley, in Fayette County, Tennessee.

Yeah. I played over there, see I played at that picnic myself. I think my brother was uh, since he dead, I think played some up there at the picnic. The ———— picnic and uh, we played different for all down in here. McIntyre, we used to play McIntyre. We used to play all down in Tyro. We used to play for the laws in Tyros there. We used to play for them; theys pitch us quarters and everything just. . . . Us used to play for them.

The McIntyre community is in Marshall County, Mississippi. The Tyro community is in Tate County, Mississippi. Vernon Lane Wharton wrote in 1947 that "the monotony and the poverty of their daily lives seem to have intensified the delight of the Negroes in social gatherings. They have come together by hundreds or even thousands during the summer season for picnics and barbeques" (269). He describes, based on newspaper accounts in the Jackson, Mississippi, papers, picnics that took place in the summers of 1874–79 with their ball games, music, dancing, and drums. Similar descriptions have been made by Lomax and Mitchell for hill country picnics in the 1950s–1970s. Even for the 1990s, Oliver describes three-day affairs with baseball games, vendors, and lots of music. Oliver (1996), Lomax (1993), and George Mitchell (1971) describe these marathon parties in quite sensuous, even erotic, terms. Lomax was even asked to turn off the cameras when things got too hot at a picnic in 1978 (342).

These rural African American picnics, once common in Mississippi, are still vital in the hill country, where they often feature the African sounding fife-and-drum bands. Lomax describes the dancing as African and compares the contemporary hill country picnic with the outdoor celebrations of the first African American pioneers of the Mississippi Delta.

Sir?

Where did y'all used to play? At dances or. . . ?

Play for dances? . . . Well, that's something, man. We'd play at dances, we'd got up dance all night. We'd played dance pieces. Man, we played pieces; they'll pay us to play a dance piece, and we played that piece and we play, we play that piece and peoples would jump all night, long as us would play that piece. We'd let them jump a looong time! [Laughter.] We play, we play way over for record, you know. . . . We let them jump a looong time.

What was you brother's name? [Daisy coughs.]

He was name Richard. . . . Richard Taylor.

Do you remember the name of that first person that you heard playing the fiddle?

[Daisy] What?

The first fellow . . . that I heard playing the fiddle? He name Chaney. . . . Yeah, he name Chaney Bailey. That was Chaney Bailey played the. . . . What the, yeah, that was Chaney Bailey. Chaney Bailey was his name.

[Daisy] Chaney Bell.

Chaney Bell, uh-huh, well, he living in Arkansas, he played over here at the Victoria, Mississippi, where I heard him.

The Victoria community is in Marshall County, Mississippi.

How long did you stay in Mississippi?

Oh, that's where I was, I was raised in Mississippi. . . . I've been in Tennessee for 'round about, let's see, for about thirty, well, close to thirty-five years, I know.

Thirty-five years? Have you been here all that time?

Yes, in Tennessee, here. I wasn't living right here but just say in Tennessee. . . . Yes, in Tennessee. . . . I been, I was raised in Mississippi, in Red Banks, Mississippi, uh-huh.

Red Banks was also the home of Memphis banjo player Gus Cannon.

What were the names of those songs you used to play when you first started playing the fiddle?

Well, I played a song about "Drop Down Mama and Let Your Daddy See" and I played "Too Many Mornings," and, uh, I can't think of it now, I played some more. And uh, I don't know.

"Drop Down Mama," a blues standard, was first recorded by Sleepy John Estes (from nearby Brownsville, Tennessee) in 1935. It was also recorded by Mississippian Tommy McClennan in 1940. "Drop Down Mama" was a favorite of Rossville native Fred McDowell, who told Pete Welding that he had learned the song from Vandy McKenna in Rossville (Welding 1971, 146).

[Daisy] Didn't y'all play the "Boogie Woogie"?

[Laughs.] "Boogie," yeah, the "Boogie Woogie" [laughs]. I played the "Boogie Woogie." I played the song about "Run Here, Baby, Let Me Smell Your Hand." I played so many, I don't know, I just can't think of them. I can't think them all up. We played so many.

[Daisy] You had one ole song that you used to play about going to what?

[Singing softly to himself: "Little girl."]

[Daisy] Get me a sack of greens or something, keep that pot a popping.

Oh yeah. Well, I played that, I played that, I didn't play that with my fiddle, I didn't play that, I played that with guitar and I played fiddle with my hands on that. I didn't put no bow. . . . Oh, I played so many songs and then we turn around and play so many church songs. . . . Played so many church songs.

Where? Did you play them at the churches?

We didn't, us didn't play in the church, but we played them for old folks. . . . Just like we been out a party and meet some Christian old folks who coming on by, uh, that Sunday morning. We'd been out all night, coming on that Sunday morning, we be going about playing some songs, so, uh, "Play us some hymns or some church songs." We come by there and play them songs, and play them some songs. Make them happy, now. Done had the devil all night, now. Just come by to make them folks happy. Make them happy, we play them church songs, so make them happy. [Sounds of Daisy doing dishes.] They was quite, they'd be, they love to hear us play them things. So, I got a first cousin, he's a preacher, he laugh at us, he joked us, "Oh, you ole boys are part of the devil." We told him, said, "Well, yeah, we play pretty blues, but" we said, "we was born to astriculate." He was in the car with us and he said, "Y'all ought to throw them ole things away." He was a preacher. Preacher, now. And so I, we said, "Well, alright." Said, "We going to make you happy going down the road not be no blues, you ain't going to play no blues. You old boy play blues. No more of them here." I said, "That's alright, we going to make you happy." So me and my brother seen that went to playing church songs, sounded good to him, he went to singing. And he sung all the [moments?] we played [the takes?] out there to the picnic. And he said, "Ooh, y'all boys ought to go to church, y'all ought to carry them things and play them in the church, as good as y'all play." Said, "Boy, y'all ought to play, y'all ought to carry them things and play them."

I said, "Well, we didn't go in the church and play them but we could." He said, "You's sure, y'all sure ought to carry them to church and play them and let peoples hear y'all, the way y'all play. I didn't think y'all could do this. I thought y'all ought to throw them away, but y'all supposed to keep them, the way y'all play church songs. Boy, y'all got it bad." [Laughter.] So he bragged on us from then on. He did brag on. He said, well, us play church songs better than anybody he heard, you knowing playing on such things as that. So I use to mix little ole fiddle; I talk the church songs. [Quietly, muttering] Oh, my God, I tell you truth here.

You said you played the guitar, too? Right?

A little bit. I never could do much with a guitar. I played that old piece what Daisy spoke of. I used to play an old piece like that well. That's all I could play on it, I know; couldn't play nothing else. But I mean, you know, like nobody else. That's an old piece my daddy learnt me when I was a boy. 'Cause, now, he played it and I learned it and I just keep it up all the time. 'Cause it's an old piece. . . . He played pretty well.

Did he play anything besides the guitar?

No, sir. He didn't play nothing else, nothing but, he'd get a guitar. He play for us children and he play that. He'd keep an old guitar 'round there and he play that. Play that sometimes and he'd play that old song, and so I never forgot it. I kept it up. You know, I come up and play something and I learn it myself. What he learnt that piece. That's the only piece I learnt. I learnt my brother. I never could play no guitar, I learnt my brother, though, I learnt him, but ———— play the fiddle. I learn him how to play such as to it. I couldn't play but I could chord it and he learnt me that.

Mm huh. Did anybody else in your family play anything?

Oh yes. I got a sister that play a guitar but she's sanctified, she plays sanctified, she plays church songs. . . . She live in Memphis . . . in South Memphis. Yes, sir. . . . She's named Martha, Martha Howard. . . . She play the, though, she played it, though.

[Daisy] She sure can play them church songs.

Martha Howard was a member of the Church of God in Christ, the Memphis-based, African American, charismatic denomination of which former bluesman Robert Wilkins was also a member. Howard's son and Taylor's nephew, Fred Howard, was a member of the famous and venerable Spirit of Memphis gospel group during the height of its commercial popularity in the early 1950s (Lornell 1995, 98).

She play, kind of, well . . . I got a little ole nephew—he tries to play. He ain't so much but he think he play. [Daisy chuckles.] He play guitar. He out there try to play. He, I didn't, he was old enough to do much. Some piece he play pretty good, and he love to try to *play*.

Does he live in Memphis?

Yes, living up the road.

[Daisy] He don't live over in no Memphis.

I say he's living up the road here.

[Daisy] He sure do ———.

I guess it ain't no Memphis.

What's his name?

Hilton, Hilton Taylor. . . . Hilton Taylor. . . . Here he are right up . . . Says he which, say he which? . . . He live there, uh, hit the highway.

[Daisy] Up there above city near about.

No.

[Daisy] Ain't he?

No. He stay right over here, you know [kids all chime in].

[Daisy] Oh yeah, that's right.

Right over here by this old [Nibia?] grocery store.

[Daisy] Right over here by Mary Sue's.

Right on, right after you hit the highway, go up, up there. It's a little, it's a some silos, just like them two silos out the door. . . . It come in right by them and right on and his house right down below them signs. It's a dairy barn, have been a dairy barn. 'Tain't none there now, they done tore it down. . . . And he live right down below that dairy barn. Right, oh, I say, go down there. . . . It'd be, well, it wouldn't be two miles. . . . It wouldn't be quite two miles. Just go cross here, now, he wouldn't be quite two miles. [Daisy grunts.]

[Child] Two miles down there.

Oh yeah, you go down to the corner and go up to the highway. . . .

[Child] ———— barn down there.

It would be, I'd say, it would be a little better than a mile. Go across here walking, then it would be a mile. [Picks fiddle strings.]

Would you mind playing us a song now?

Let me see if I can play y'all a song now. . . . [Laughs, tunes fiddle, bows fiddle, returns to tuning it, bows some, resins up bow, begins to play tune.] . . . Put some more resin on that thing. That ain't take care of the resin. [Rubs resin on strings.]

[Daisy] You ain't played it in so long.

Rust, it was rusted. [Continues to rub resin on strings.]

[Daisy] Well, it ain't got no strings on it, can't play . . .

I know ain't got no strings in the car. I ought, that ought to do it. [Boose plays.] . . . Let me put some more resin on that thing. [Resins bow.] This thing don't sound good to me. Maybe I get more resin on it. It about wore out, I reckon. Bow about twenty-five years old or more. [Laughs.]

[Child] How 'bout them strings?

Bow is sprung. I don't know this bow. And when I bought it, I bought it secondhand. Thought this fiddle ————, you know. Done wore out. [Boose plays a few minutes.] It don't sound good! [Retunes.]

[Adult Voice from doorway] ————.

[Daisy answering] No. I don't believe, maybe. [While Boose continues to tune his fiddle and try his bow, among Daisy, the children, and the person at the door there ensues a mostly inaudible conversation about going to a neighbor's house and taking somebody something to eat. Boose begins to play and then stops.]

It don't sound right. Got to get close to you; don't sound the mike. . . . [Boose plays and sings "Drop Down Mama," including a verse not usually performed.]

> Come here baby let me smell your hand,
> Smell just like it been on another man.

She don't sound good. She don't. [Retunes.] She's dead.

Taylor's bowing was quite heavy, and he sang in a shout similar to that of Fred McDowell, producing an effect dominated by the rhythm and recalling Alan Lomax's comments about fellow hill country musician Sid Hemphill's fiddling: "[He] bowed so heavily the fiddle sounded almost like a drum." His voice "was bold and sure, in the harsh, shouty tones of a truly African singer" (1993, 315–16). Lomax concluded that this style was the same as the newly arrived African's when he first picked up this European instrument in the slave quarters.

She's dead.

[Voice] She's dead.

[Daisy] She sounds pretty well to not be having no new strings on her in about eight years.

[Quits fiddling.] About when? Twenty-five, thirteen, it's been about twenty-five years since I took the man's strings.

[Daisy] I thought you put something on there when [Jocene? Joe?] play.

Yeah, but that's been a long. No! Girl, I don't know when I ever bought new strings for this thing. . . . [Retunes, quits tuning, starts bowing.]

[Daisy] You know you used to play a song about a ———. No, a ———.

[Quits bowing.] I done forgot my song now. [Boose laughs, then Daisy laughs.] It's been a long time since I've pulled this thing out. Huh?

[Voice] You don't know how to fool with it.

[Rubbing the strings] I may try to again, I done forgot, you know, I done . . .

[Voice] You don't know how to fool with it now, do you?

Think I which?

[Voice] You don't know how to fool with it now, do you?

No, no. [Bows a little.] See, that old string don't sound. I don't know, wore out, but it used to sound better than that, used to sound good. Wore out, rusting, everything. [Retunes, plays fiddle, pats foot on wood floor, sings.]

> Well, it's three o'clock in the morning, I didn't even close my eyes, [repeat]
> I'm going to find my little ole baby, and ain't going to worry me what I'm
>   going to do.
> Come running here, baby, let me smell your hand, [repeat]
> Well, it's smelling like it's been on, well, been on another man.

[Laughs.] I swear. [Laughing.] It don't, it don't 'bide a man well for you to play them things. I tell you the truth. [Laughs.]

[Daisy] Yeah, I hear what's you saying. I know what you're saying.

Where did you learn that song?

Oh, we just, that's a song we didn't . . . That's a song we learned ourselves. We made up and sang it. . . . We made up that, we made that song and made, uh, we just carried it and made it on out ourselves.

You and your brother?

Me and my brother. . . .\

Did you have a name for it?

We just made it a old corn field song, that's old, old, picked up song. That's what we called it. And folks went, folks went a hollering, "Hey, play that song about c'mon, baby, let me smell your hand." [Laughter.] That's what they say all the time. [Boose laughs. Laughter.]

[Daisy] That was the thing.

They holler, "That's a new one—run here, baby, let me smell you hand." They make a joke with me now all the time. He see me, say, "Hey, fellow, can you play that song now what you used to sing about 'run here, baby, let me smell you hand'?" Boy, I'm telling you the truth. [Laughter.] And they joke with me now and laugh about it. "No," I say, "I done quit." I say, "I used to could play it." He say, "I bet you can play it now." I say, "Well, if I fool with it." Now, if I fool with this thing I could play good. See, I don't fool with it, I don't fool with it. I don't, I ain't, man, I don't know when I had this thing in my hands. It'll be back in here, and I forgets it in there. And me and my brother, we could sing, we could sing some things. Man, we could sing to our music. We sing . . .

[Daisy] I imagine that you and John L. could get together now.

Oh yeah. . . . I could perform now with a guitar, I could go on, go on, go on and play with a guitar. Now I could play. I can't hit a lick by myself.

[Daisy simultaneously with Boose] Because he could play, he could really pick a guitar. Anything that he, any record that he hear, he could really play it.

Uh-huh. I could just go on with a guitar now. That's what . . .

[Daisy] I like to hear him play.

If somebody come up here with a guitar now, I'd tune that thing and this thing, we might just come up and sound good. [Laughs.] . . . And man, I just as well, we'd come up playing.

[Daisy] And John L., he could really play an electric guitar.

Have you ever heard of a man named Buck, got six fingers and he plays the guitar?

Have, have which? . . . On both?

Yeah, he grew up around this area somewheres.

[Daisy]——— his hands.

I don't believe, I can't remember. Buck, but . . .

[Daisy] Well, what's the last part of his name?

We don't know.

You say he play the guitar? . . . And his name Buck, got six fingers.

[Voice] Who now, uh, I believe I've heard of a man you talking about, live out at the fairgrounds. . . . Yeah, that one up and one of them that play and I know he had he six fingers. I forget the man's name. I know him if I see him but I done forgot his name.

Do you know where he lives?

[Voice] No, I don't know where he lives at. He be in Collierville the time I see him. But I know him, though, I just can't 'call his name.

I may, I might know this fellow, but I just can't place him. But I may, but I may know him.

Do you know anybody else that plays any music around here?

Well, no more than John Eldridge and Claudale.

[Daisy] Darnell can really play that ——— anything ———. He play good, though.

He beat out, he sure play it, oh Darnell.

[Daisy] What are you talking about!

I learned him how!

[Daisy] Any record that he hear come out Seaburg or radio.

The Seaburg (sometimes called "seabird") jukebox was often found in rural cafés and juke joints.

I learned him how. [Laughs.] I learned him. I learned Darnell. Bought Darnell the first guitar right here.

[Daisy] "Let me see that guitar" and he pick it up and played the fool out of it. He really can play.

I raised him. . . . Yeah, I raised him, I raised him. I raised him. I raised that boy.

[Voice] He just live right up the road here.

Where? Right here?

[Voice] No, up there on the highway . . .

Right up the road. Yeah.

Do you know anybody else who plays any music around Collierville? . . .

[Voice] Yeah, I know big fat Cousin White over there, married [Amy Led-tower?], what your Ma calls it daughter. . . . You know who I'm talking about, don't you, cuz? Step, he real fat. He be playing ——. I forget that boy's name.

He play, oh, talking about George Union?

[Voice] Yeah, that what I'm talking about.

Yeah, yeah. George Union . . . George Union. Yeah . . . George Union, yeah, George Union play . . . he play good! . . . George play good. Uh-huh.

What type of music does he play?

Oh, whatever.

[Daisy] Play blues.

I don't go up there with them boys and play.

[Daisy] Some have a bass, fiddle and things, y'all; sounds good to me.

Do you know anybody else around here that plays the fiddle?

No, I don't know nobody else that play the fiddle at all.

Or harmonica, or anything else?

Well, I know some boys, but they in, they in Mississippi. . . . They, them my cousins. Well, David Todd and one of them named John Lee Whitelow.

Where in Mississippi do they live?

They live over here at west side of Red Banks. . . . Yeah . . . We say, play up there, housepaint up there. We used to, uh, would go over here, would go through by Casey—no, not Casey, Tracey. Go up the road there, you can turn and go through Casey. . . . Well, it's right on across there, right on, they on this side, the bottom. —— on the side of Casey, Mississippi, there. . . . Casey, Mississippi, would be, we call it Red Banks. . . .

The Casey community is in Benton County, Mississippi, east of Marshall County and adjacent to Tennessee.

Now, I was told that you knew some stuff about Payne family, Alex Payne.

Payne family? . . . Talking about Raymond Payne? . . . Raymond Payne. He dead, though, ain't he? Yeah.

Sylvester Oliver states that, according to musician Leeandrew "Cotton" Howell, Raymond Payne came from Hudsonville in Marshall County, Mississippi, as did Fred McDowell (1996, 410). McDowell told Bruce Cook, "That Raymond Payne, he was the one who taught me. It's too bad he didn't have time to record" (1973, 83). Jeff Titon wrote that Payne never made records "because he was afraid other singers might 'steal' his songs" (1977, 48). " 'If you'd walk into the room when Raymond was playing,' Fred recalled, 'he'd right away put the guitar down so you couldn't see what he was doing. Then he'd make some kind of excuse—"I'm tired now" or "my fingers hurt" ' " (Pomposello 1990, 36).

What was his father's name?

His father's name? Cal Payne.

[Daisy] Cal Payne.

And what was his mother's name?

I can't, I don't know. . . . Do you know, Mary Jane? Did you know his mother? I don't know his mother.

[Daisy] It's been so long.

Oh, talking about Raymond's . . .

[Daisy] Raymond's mother.

Raymond's mother? . . . Name not Lizzie, but Lizzie's sister.

[Daisy] Talking about [Mar?].

Martin.

[Daisy] Wasn't Lizzie Martin, was it?

Yes, Lizzie was a Martin but she had a sister. Lizzie wasn't his mother, now, Lizzie was his auntie.

[Daisy] Mm, I don't know.

I tell you who, I tell you who. Raymond's mother. I know her name, I can't call her name. Oh, Lordy, whether ———. Raymond, he didn't no sisters. Did he? Did he, Jane? . . . No, Jane, 'cause you know. . . .

[Daisy] No, I didn't know his people.

No. He didn't have no sisters. I don't think he have no sisters. . . . He didn't have no brothers, I don't think.

[Daisy] I never know nobody but Raymond.

Nobody but Raymond, ole Raymond Payne.

Did you know Alex, Alex Payne?

[Daisy] I didn't never know him. He may have a brother but I never did see nobody but Raymond.

Now, he had an uncles. . . . William Martin was his uncle, but that too by his mammy. Let's see, because his mother, Rosie, was Rosie Martin before she met, yeah, before she married John Manyon Jordan. She was a Martin, Rosie Martin, wasn't she?

[Daisy] Rosie Martin and Lizzie Martin, wasn't it?

Lizzie was, uh, Rosie, wait, wait. I's getting it right, one of them girls, one of them women was Raymond's mother.

[Daisy] I thought Beulah was Raymond's mother.

I did, too. Yeah. Got to be. Rosie wasn't. Got to be Lizzie, got to be Lizzie Martin was his mother. . . .

[Daisy] He would have been dead. . . .

Long time, it's been. . . .

[Daisy] I don't know, now.

It's been, I don't know. All I can manage. I expect it's been around eighteen or nineteen years now, matter of fact. He's been dead a long time.

Was he very old when he died?

Sir?

[Daisy] No. He wasn't all that old, was he?

He wasn't very old. He wasn't very old. He wasn't very old.

[Daisy] No, they say he got killed there in Memphis. He used to drive, that's what happened to him.

Oh, Raymus ought to been, Raymus was around . . .

[Daisy] He used to drive a taxi cab and they say somebody . . .

Raymond ought to have been around up there in, Raymond was in his . . .

[Daisy] Hauled off and killed him, found him dead in his taxi cab, out there, I think in Binghampton, somewhere out there.

Binghampton is an African American neighborhood east of Overton Park and north of Summer Avenue in midtown Memphis.

Raymond would have been around in his thirties, something . . . I imagine.

[Daisy] Yeah, 'cause he used to, 'cause I was living in Arkansas and he could really play a box, too. And we used to come over.

He play, he playing a box when he, when he, he about like this, he about like that boy there, he playing box.

[Daisy] We used to, yeah, we used to come out there see Howard, see my daddy.

He about like him playing.

[Daisy] And he done there on Beale Street, playing his, playing box.

Sit up in his mother's lap and play the guitar. Play the piece and she hold him in his lap and he play a piece.

[Daisy] Used to carry the guitar around in his cab with him.

'Cause I didn't know nothing . . . about a guitar. I was a big ole fellow then, but I didn't know nothing about a guitar. But I'd seen him play one and ———. Guitar Payne.

[Daisy] His daddy used to blow harp.

Both Tom Pomposello (1990, 36) and Valerie Wilmer (1966, 23) quote McDowell recalling a trio consisting of his uncle Gene Shields on guitar, Cal Payne on harmonica, and Eli Green on guitar.

His dad blew a harp?

He blew a harp. . . . That's all I knowed, that's all I knowed him to do.

[Daisy] No, that's I knew ———, blew a harp.

Did Raymond play anything other than the guitar?

That's all I know him to play.

[Daisy] That's all he played.

But he played a slide guitar, didn't he?

Yes. . . . That's right, that's right. Ole Raymond played, he could play.

Fred McDowell told Pete Welding, "I learned a lot from one fellow, Raymond Payne in Rossville. He was really good, played guitar regular style, not bottleneck" (1971, 146).

Where was it that he was a taxi cab driver?

[Daisy] He was a taxi cab driver driving there in Memphis.

Memphis? Where was he raised? Was he raised up in Memphis, too?

He started out at Mount Pleasant.

[Daisy] Mount Pleasant, [Boose joins in] Mississippi.

Mount Pleasant is a community in Marshall County, Mississippi, southwest of Collierville on Highway 72.

[Daisy] Straight up that road out there.

Do you know how old he was when he come to Memphis?

I imagine Raymus . . .

[Daisy] Raymus was about in his thirties.

Thirties something, yeah.

[Daisy] 'Cause he was real young. He wasn't all that old. [Boose affirms Daisy's statements with frequent, soft-spoken yeahs and uh-huhs.] People just killed him, that what it was. They find him dead, his wife find him dead on his cab.

I played fiddle with Raymus. Last time I played with Raymus, played out yonder at Bud Martin's, at, uh [Burn Moment's?] right yonder where [Nurs?] and them, where Nellie B. stay right in that house down there.

[Daisy] You know, Jake Owens and all them used to play.

Jake Owens was a Rossville guitarist remembered by Fred McDowell (Cook 1973, 83).

Jack Kelly, Jack Kelly.

[Daisy] Well, he dead, too. . . . And Jake Owens dead.

Yeah, but he could play guitar, too. They'd come out there from Memphis, and I'd been over in Arkansas—I was staying over from up there on ———. I'd come over there and play with them.

You used to play with Jack Kelly's Jug Band?

I played with Jack Kelly and Raymus.

Jack Kelly was a well-known fixture of the Memphis blues scene for forty years. In the 1930s, records were released under his own name and that of his South Memphis Jug Band. (In 1933 Kelly and his band recorded for Vocalion in New York City and again in Memphis in 1939.) Willie Borum remembered accompanying Kelly's guitar playing with his own harp blowing in the 1930s, and Little Walter Jacobs recalled seeing Kelly, Little Son Joe (guitarist Ernest Lawlars, one of Memphis Minnie's husbands), and Walter Horton working together in Memphis. Borum stated, "He was a great big fellow. We'd go round playing at parties; they was giving house-parties. Jack was grey-haired. I know him a long time. He died around 1960. He was some fifty years old" (Olsson 1970, 38).

Furry Lewis, who sometimes played with Kelly, says Kelly was living in Orange Mound (in southeast Memphis) at the time of his death.

Bengt Olsson believes that Kelly recorded with Walter Horton for the Sun label in 1950 as "Jackie Boy and Little Walter" (1970, 38).

Did Raymus play with the jug band with?

Yeah . . . yeah, Raymus, . . . after he got in Memphis and got to driving a cab, Raymus went like, look like he going back on his guitar, you know. He quit fooling with it, trying to check it, kind of fooling with it. . . . He couldn't play it like he was when we stayed out there at Mount Pleasant. He, now, he play anything he want!

[Daisy] Yes, he could, too 'cause . . .

No, he wouldn't.

[Daisy] When I was living over in Arkansas, he started, we used to come over to Memphis.

But he better look up when I played with him. . . . 'Cause I played some pieces, he told me to lead some pieces on, I reckon this bare little ole fiddle, yeah, this bare little old fiddle. I reckon it t'was this . . .

[Daisy] But I know we used to come out from my mother-in-law's.

I know we used to play a couple of pieces, him and Jack Kelly. They played the same piece. And I told them, let me lead some pieces on them and they start to follow behind me some. On yonder at Bud [Momer?]. Bud Momer was giving a party; . . . Bud Momer call hisself giving a party. And they came out there, Jack Kelly and Raymus came out there and play.

Harmonica great Walter Horton recalled playing with the Memphis Jug Band in 1931, when he was thirteen years old. The band also included Gus Cannon, Jack Kelly, and Raymond Payne (Patterson 1971, 85).

Do you know whether Raymond's wife is still alive?

Knows his wife? His wife . . .

[Daisy] I know she's still in Memphis but I don't know where.

Oh yeah, Lucille, ain't it?

[Daisy] Yeah, her name Lucille. . . . Uh-huh, that's where she was, I know.

That's where she's been so far. She's in Memphis, she in Memphis, Daisy Mae.

[Daisy] She's in Memphis.

I don't think they gone out.

[Daisy] 'Cause that's where they were living when he got killed, there in Memphis. [Child crying.] And she still down there in Memphis somewhere, but where abouts I don't know.

Oh! [Boose rapidly bows fiddle.]

[Daisy] But she somewhere down there in Memphis.

[To child] I'll scare you there, boy.

[Older child] Bring that here boy.

When was the last time you saw Lucille?

Oh, I tell you [laughs], it's been a long time since I saw her, let me see when was the last time is. I saw that girl.

[Daisy] But we see her sister, though. . . . 'Might near every other Saturday.

Her sister every Saturday. . . . Seen her sister Saturday. Let me see, but it's been a long time since I've saw Lucille. Where was I at? . . . Sir?

Where does her sister live?

Her sister live up here.

[Daisy] Her sister name Jeannie.

She up here, at Rossville? Up here, don't she? . . . Her and the boys.

[Daisy] Up there somewhere, up there by Rossville.

Up here by Rossville, up here, her sister.

What's Jeannie's last name? You know? . . .

[Daisy] She's married, you know, she married dark Jody. He's a Hearn.

I imagine he is, but . . .

[Daisy] Yeah, 'cause he's kin with Kenta, Willard Hearn, and them.

Yeah, yeah. Well, he Joe Hearn. Yes, well, she . . .

[Daisy] She was an Albright before she married, but I think she's a Hearn now.

Yeah, uh-huh, Hearn, Jeannie Hearn.

Jeannie Hearn. Well, did anyone else play with you and Jack Kelly and Raymond when y'all used to get together?

Nobody but me and him, and just us three . . . just us three . . . They had two guitars, I had a fiddle. I just play with them when they come out from Memphis and come up in yonder. I stay at Piperton. They give picnics up there. . . . They had Raymus and Jack Kelly come up there to play and so they tell me to come on and play with them and I'd go ahead and play with, uh, play all night. That was the last time I played with Raymond, up there in Piperton, and so the next thing I heard he was dead. Jack Kelly, too, Jack Kelly, he dead. Jack Kelly, he'd play with a cigar in his mouth all the time [laughs]. . . . What's that?

According to Willie Borum, "Jack Kelly smoked a cigar all the time. It was never lit, it just always was there" (Olsson 1970, 38). Piperton is due east of Collierville and due west of Rossville in Fayette County, Tennessee.

How did Jack Kelly die?

I don't know. He, uh, I don't know. I imagine he, I imagine he just got sick, you know, or something.

Was he very old?

What, he was older. He was older, right?

[Daisy] But Raymond sure got killed, though, he driving the taxi when he got killed.

But that Jack Kelly, that Jack Kelly used to tickle me to death.

[Daisy] Boose, you ought to remember when Raymond got killed a driving a taxi?

Me? . . . Oh, I, yes, I remember. I, uh, you know, I heard when they say he got killed. The man was dead!

[Daisy, with breaking voice] Driving a taxi. They killed him in his taxi.

[Very quietly] Ah, well, somebody done that and they just killed the boy. [Louder] Well, William Martin, you know, William Martin, his uncle, used to play guitar. I thought he played pretty myself, I liked his playing. I thought it was pretty. . . . Sir?

William Martin still alive?

[Daisy, quietly] Oh, he might be. . . .

He living, ain't he, Jane?

[Daisy] Who? William Martin? . . . Yeah, he William Martin.

Yeah. He in Memphis.

[Daisy] No, he ain't! You know William Martin dead too!

Is he?

[Daisy] 'Cause you know they talking about, that girl did, his wife's time, get cold 'fore she was in the house with him at night. They said he dead.

Well, now, who was his wife at that time?

[Daisy] Well, he had Miss Frank Foster's daughter, Mary Foster.

Mary and Earl . . . And Mary Foster and . . .

[Daisy] And Beula Rae Foster.

Where did William Martin live before he moved to Memphis?

Well, he lived up here, too. He lived up here, too, about . . .

[Daisy] Rossville.

Rossville. . . . All around. . . . Sir?

Did he live there all his life?

Sir? . . . That's right, that's right. When I first got acquainted with him, that was, I imagine that he about been raised up around in there 'cause he, when I first got acquainted of him that's where he was, and he stayed there a lot of years after I got acquainted with him. That was his home. I imagine he was probably raised right up there. . . . Uncles? . . . Let's see. I don't believe I know no more.

[Daisy] It's been so long ago.

I don't believe I know no more than William and them and Amos. You know, Williams he, William and Amos and them was brothers then. . . . But that was Raymond's uncle, too. . . . Amos was, Amos Martin . . . He was Raymond's daddy, uncle, too.

Did he play any music?

No, sir, I never did know him to play nothing. He might have some uncles, but them's the onliest two that I can remember. . . . I don't know.

You never heard of Alex Payne or Little Willie Payne or any of those?

No, sir, I ain't. . . . I ain't heard of them.

[Daisy] It's been so long when I used to go up there to Rossville. I, uh, that's where I got acquainted with Raymond and them, up in there. I don't, it's been so long till might know them and just done forgot them because it's been a long time when I used to be in Rossville.

Yeah, it's been quite a while.

You ever met a man named Fred McDowell that plays the guitar?

[Daisy] Uh-huh.

Fred McDowell? . . .

[Dasiy] I know him, too.

Fred McDowell used to live with ———— when I first got a fiddle. That's the, them's the first fellows I played, tried to play like, tried to learn to play a fiddle with. Fred McDowell and Eli Green.

McDowell told Pete Welding, "The guitar player, he'd be behind the violin and I never could do that. I never could frail no guitar like that. That's why I never did play with them" (1971, 146).

Eli Green? Is he still alive?

No, he's dead, I think he's dead. . . . I think he's dead.

With McDowell's help, Chris Strachwitz located Eli Green near Holly Springs, Mississippi, in 1965. He was able to record two songs, "Brooks Run into the Oceans" and "Bull Dog Blues," by Green with backing from McDowell. These two songs are available on Arhoolie CD 304 *You Gotta Move* and are "all that remains for posterity of the remarkable artistry of Eli Green who in turn had apparently learned a good deal from Charlie Patton" (Strachwitz 1994, 5).

Sylvester Oliver states that Green was born in the first years of the twentieth century, making him a contemporary of both McDowell and Boose Taylor. McDowell remembered, "We did a lot of playing all around the Delta together—in Cleveland and Rosedale, towns like that" (Cook 1973, 84).

Junior Kimbrough, as a boy, learned guitar from McDowell and Green. The two musicians used to come on Sundays to get haircuts from Kimbrough's father. Kimbrough remembered Eli Green as "a bad guy" who "had a lil' man he kept in his pocket. He take that lil' man out and he dance around in his palm. If Eli git locked up in jail, that lil' man steal the keys for him." Kimbrough said that Green kept a magic bone that he had obtained by boiling a live cat. This bone allowed Green to walk through walls. Kimbrough also said that Green would "throw a deck of cards and they'd all stick in the ceiling. He'd name one and it would come down" (Lewis 1997, 53).

Oliver interviewed older residents of the area who remembered Green as a "bad and danger-ous" man who had "special hypnotic magic powers. One informant recounted the story of Green going into a café and hypnotizing all of the women, and apparently men also, making all of the women dance around with their dresses above their heads." Another of Oliver's informants told of how Green could change into an animal (like the Haitians' feared *loup garou*), eat light bulbs, and disappear at will (1996, 472).

Green was described as a gambler and a dandy dresser "in well-tailored black suits" and "white spats with his highly polished black shoes." He is rumored to have gotten drunk and lost his amulet and his power (473).

When Strachwitz found him in 1965, Green was living in a remote shack without electricity and a long ways from the road (1994). Oliver's report that Green died in 1963 is almost certainly a typo (since he also recounts Strachwitz's 1965 discovery of Green). Green is buried in the Greenwood Baptist Church Cemetery near Lamar in Benton County, Mississippi (Oliver 1996, 473). Elsewhere Oliver states that Green was from the McIntyre community near Chulahoma in Marshall County (413).

But Fred, now Fred, I think Fred . . .

Oh yeah, he's still alive, yeah. Lives down in Como, Mississippi. Was he playing the guitar at that time?

He sure was. I like to see him. [Laughs.]

[Daisy] He could play that guitar, too. Couldn't he?

[Drawn out slowly] Yeah, yeah, that guy could play it.

Fred McDowell was born January 12, 1904, in Rossville, Tennessee. McDowell first learned to play guitar while still a child in Rossville. He told Pete Welding that he had learned slide from his uncle there: "He didn't play with a bottleneck; you know this big bone you get out of a steak? Well, he had done let it dry and smoothed it off and it sounded just like that bottleneck" (1971, 146). McDowell's uncle was named Gene Shields (Wilmer 1966, 23). Howard Odum, who did field-work in the Mississippi hill country, wrote in 1911, "Instead of the knife, negroes often carry a piece of bone, polished and smooth, which they slip over a finger, and alternate between pick-ing the strings and rubbing them. This gives a combination of fiddle and guitar. The bone may also serve as a good-luck omen" (261). According to Gayle Dean Wardlow, King Solomon Hill (Mississippi / Louisiana artist Joe Holmes) used a cow bone slide on his 1932 Paramount record-ings (1998, 5).

   In the 1920s, McDowell sharecropped on a farm east of Hudsonville, Mississippi. It was there that he met Eli Green and the brothers Felix and Grady Kimbrough (Oliver 1996, 469). Accord-ing to other accounts (e.g., Welding 1971), McDowell moved to Memphis in the 1920s and then on to various locations in the Mississippi Delta before settling in the Mississippi hill country. In 1957, McDowell moved to Como, Mississippi, where he was discovered by Alan Lomax in 1959 (Lomax 1993).

   Subsequently, as "Mississippi" Fred McDowell, he made many exceptional recordings of the distinctive hill country blues sound. McDowell toured widely in the 1960s and was a major influence on many rock 'n' rollers, including Bonnie Raitt, who based much of her slide tech-nique on McDowell's.

   We contacted McDowell shortly after this interview with Boose Taylor and he was excited about a reunion with his old friend. Unfortunately, McDowell was ill, so we waited for him to recover. He did not recover but died July 3, 1972. According to Oliver, "Details regarding his death are uncertain. . . . some locals say it was from poison; others say it was from an undetected cancer" (1996, 468).

Did he help you learn to play the fiddle?

Well, I just went behind him, you know. . . . Play, trying to play what he sing and trying to play with them, this is the way I learnt, it t'was with him and Eli. They come to my house with their guitars and they sit there and play, and I tried to, and then I'd go off with them. I take the "carry your fiddle with you, man," that way they 'lowing. And I carried with me and, we walk to other folks's house and just play, go to other folks's house and just play, just play, and people want to hear them play, and he just, "Come on over to my house tomorrow night" or something, and, "play some. Let's have some fun." And they come over, they come, and the other night and they'd go and they'd be a house full that's here to hear them play. They could play a guitar, now, I tell you. Oh, Eli Green and Fred McDowell, they could play. They sure could play. Sure did. Ole Fred McDowell, you hear him about two miles hollering before you got there. And he could sing. . . . He could sing, sure enough, he could sing until you fell all the way out.

[Daisy] Used to be a lot of guitar pickers lived in and around Rossville then. Wasn't there.

According to Welding, McDowell said, "Pretty near everybody down around Rossville, them boys could play a guitar, some kind of thing" (1971, 146). He told Bruce Cook, "There wasn't hardly any seen who couldn't play guitar. There were some who pretty good, though—Van D. McKenna, and Raymond Payne, and Jake Owens" (1973, 83).

[Louder] Uh-huh . . . Yeah. Sir?

Do you remember any of the other guitar players around there?

[Daisy] Clem, but he dead, too.

Yeah.

[Daisy] Because he used to play guitar.

And . . . Clem . . . Clem [with Daisy] Martin. [Without Daisy] And Jim Shear, too. . . . But they dead. But them were guitar pickers at them times, you know. . . . Them were old guitar pickers.

Did they play blues or did they play old? . . .

[With Daisy] They played blues, they played blues. . . .

[Daisy] And they could pick them guitars, too.

And then [High?] Nelson at that time. He was a guitar picker there. High Nelson, he was good.

Is he still alive?

No, sir, he . . . he died, he's dead.

[Daisy] All them old guitar pickers, they gone ahead.

[Quietly] They sure have, them old guitar pickers, they all gone. Youngsters stay.

Were there any other types of musicians around there besides guitar pickers?

No, sir, I don't believe I can remember. I don't believe I can remember no more. You already know Junior Kimbrough, don't you? . . . Junior Kimber, Union Kimbo, Kimber.

No, I don't know him.

You don't know Junior Kim?

[Daisy] I know Sugar Jones, he a guitar picker.

Yeah, but Junior Kimbrough related to me. Junior Kimbrough.

[Daisy] Sugar Jones isn't, not Sugar, I mean Pete Jones.

Pete?

[Daisy] You know, Pete Jones who used to play guitar, a box, you know, he in Memphis.

Oh, oh yeah, oh yeah, yeah.

Is he still alive?

Jones? Yeah. Oh yeah.

[Daisy] I know where his sister live, but I don't know what street they on down there, but I know where they live.

I don't know where. Oh yeah. I forgot Pete Jones played that, played guitar.

Who was that you were talking about before Pete Jones?

Ah, Junior Kimble. . . . That's right.

Where does he live?

He's up in here about . . .

[Daisy] Holly Springs.

Holly Springs. . . . Uh-huh. Holly Springs, that right. But he used to come to, I imagine, he come down here where them boys play. He good guitar picker. . . . And he go for an ear. That's right, he got 'em, he go for an ear. I played with him a many a times.

David Kimbrough Jr., known both locally and worldwide as Junior Kimbrough, was born July 28, 1930, near Hudsonville in Marshall County, Mississippi. According to Oliver, Kimbrough is also locally known by "several corrupt version[s]" of his name, including "Junior Kimber" and "Junior Kimball" (1996, 479). Kimbrough learned guitar from his father, brothers, and from other local musicians such as Fred McDowell and Eli Green.

Kimbrough recorded a single for Philwood in 1966 (as Junior Kimbell), two cuts for a British anthology in 1975, and in 1982 two songs for David Evans's Highwater label. Recordings of Kimbrough have also been released on Swingmaster, Rustron, and Southland labels. It was not until Robert Palmer's documentary, *Deep Blues* (1992), that Kimbrough truly found a larger audience. In 1993, Fat Possum Records released Kimbrough's first CD, *All Night Long*. Other well-received recordings followed.

Rockabilly artist Charlie Feathers, who grew up near Kimbrough, refers to his music as "Cottonpatch Blues" (Oliver 1996, 481). David Nelson has described Kimbrough's music as the "trance-and-drone blues style" characteristic of the Mississippi hill country (1998, 50). Kimbrough's regular gigs in the Holly Springs area, which had attracted locals for years, began to attract others, from local college kids to famous rock musicians, during his last years. Oliver described Kimbrough's house parties as "a historic and colorful episode in the latter days of the Mississippi country blues tradition" (1996, 442). Indeed, the blues lost one of its last true practitioners when Junior Kimbrough died of a heart attack on January 17, 1998 (Nelson 1998, 50).

Do you know any other musicians that live in Memphis?

Well, let's see if I could remember any more in Memphis. [Slowly] Ummm, oh, I don't believe I can remember no more. I don't think. No, I can't remember no more living in Memphis there now. . . . No, you know that little ole . . .

[Daisy] Yeah, Billy Boy's here. He's here in Memphis.

Yes. Yeah I bet . . .

[Daisy] Know he's a guitar picker. . . . Billy Boy Shed.

Shade?

Oh, Shed? Yeah. Billy Boy here last night, you know. My cousin, you know, he say he play. [Laughs.]

[Daisy laughs] He say he ———, what's his name?

Yeah. [Still laughing.] His name Shit. What his name, girl?

[Child] O. J. Shit.

I think he say Shit.

You know how to spell that last name?

[Child] No, sir, I don't.

[Daisy] Okie Shit.

[Child] Obie.

[Daisy] Obie Shit. Looks like it ought to be s-h-i . . .

S-h-i-t?

[Daisy] That's the way I'd spell it.

[Child] Yeah, that's the way they spell it. Obie.

Now, he played, he played. . . . He tell it last night he about, he playing guitar. When me and my brother were playing, he took all that, he learned how behind us. . . . Well, I got another brother in Memphis, though, he play guitar pretty good. [Laughs.]

What's his name?

[Still laughing] Sam.

[Daisy] Yeah, I'd forgotten about him.

Yeah. [Still laughing] . . . Sam. [With Daisy] Taylor. [Boose only] . . . He's my brother. Right, I'd forgotten about him. Sam start to playing guitar.

Sam Taylor, Boose's younger brother, recalled that he was born March 22, 1911, in Red Banks, Mississippi. Sam started to play guitar when he was fourteen years old and remembered playing with brother Richard before Boose took up the fiddle. Richard and Sam would play nearby communities such as Olive Branch with other hill country musicians including Fred McDowell and Raymond Payne. Sam moved from Marshall County to Memphis in the mid-1960s.

Can he play as good as Richard could?

No, sir, not as good as Richard, but he can play. . . .

[Daisy] Well, you know he play.

And he play blues, too?

That's right.

[Daisy] Well, you know, trying to get my little brother to sell his ——— guitar to him.

Yeah, I'd forgot him, about him.

Do you know what street that he lives on?

I can't recall which street, I can't. I says he told me the other Saturday, too, when I met him. . . . I forgets. I forgets it fast he tell me. [Laughter.] He told me on Saturday. He's in Collierville Saturday before last, wasn't it? . . . Saturday before last? . . . I'm telling you all the time what did he ———, oh, but I can't think of it now.

[Daisy] He told you where he work at, too, didn't he?

Yeah. [Laughs.] You ought to know that I done forget it. [Laughs.] I wasn't paying much attention to him, you know, when he was telling me, I wasn't paying much attention to him.

Do you have any other brothers and sisters other than Sam and Richard?

Well, I had another one but I don't know where he at, my baby brother, I don't know where he at. He went out of the country and I ain't heard no more from him and he up the country.

[Daisy] Illinois, ——— says.

I ain't heard no more from him. I don't know where he's living or dead because he quit coming here, he ain't call, he ain't, he don't, he ain't nobody, he ain't writ to my mother, or nothing. I don't know. She's thinking might be dead, something done happen to him, he's—but I don't know, I hear he's gone up the country. . . . He was named Arthur Taylor.

Arthur. Now, your mother is still alive?

Uh-huh.

She live down in Mississippi?

That's right. She's name Lelia Taylor.

[Daisy] You know she don't live in no Mississippi. Your mother live in Memphis.

She lives in Memphis. That's right.

Is your father still alive?

No. He dead.

Have you ever known any banjo or mandolin pickers?

A banjo picker? . . . Did I ever know any? . . . Well, now, I know some old fellows a long time ago. . . . But I don't know no one now that's playing banjo. . . . One fellow was named Phillip Washington. Phillip Washington. He played banjo all the time. . . . Played the back of his banjo. And he could play, and the next fellow I know, he was named Henry Slate. . . . Henry Slate.

Where was he from?

Well, he was from up here in Rossville. . . . That's where, that was his home back up here in Rossville. And he . . . [To Daisy] What he say, sweetie? What you say?

The first one, was he from there, too?

Oh, talking about the first one? . . . Talking about Phillip? . . . Yeah, he was living, he, the last I heard, he in Memphis. I say, he dead. That where he die at, in Memphis. But he really had been, his home was out here. . . . Now, he was raised out yonder in Red Banks. . . . I believe that's, I believe them two are the only ones I know, that I remember. I know, that I remember. They's about the onliest two I know playing the banjo.

Did you ever know anyone who ever played mandolin?

Sir? Play who?

The mandolin.

Mando, mandoleen. No, sir, I never did know nobody [pauses] . . . [mumbles] that play the mandolin.

Did anyone ever help you learn to play the fiddle? You just picked it up by following . . .

Just picked it up by myself, just by myself. . . . What you say?

Where would y'all learn the songs?

[Daisy] Just make them up yourselves, wouldn't you?

Oh! We made up lots of songs. We make them songs and match them songs, match them words kind of the like, and made up them songs. . . . Lot of them songs we just made 'em. My brother, he can make up songs. He just, he even made up them songs. He got to singing, just got to singing, he just made up songs. I got a brother, older brother, he dead. . . . He was name was John Taylor. He sung for me and my other brother and Richard played, and he sang for us. . . . And, now, he would make up some songs, see.

Could you sing us some of those songs your brothers made up, you and your brothers? [Child beating out rhythm on chair with sticks as we talk.]

[Laughs.] I near about done about forgot it. I about near about forgot them, I tell you. Now, I try to touch them, we sung so many. Well, now, . . . he could sing some songs I couldn't play; I couldn't sing them. Now, he, I could play it, I play it where he sung, at that time when he singing, but me going to sing it, I couldn't sing it like him, I couldn't do it [laughs], and neither could, neither one of my other brothers; my other brother couldn't sing it. Now, he, that's all he could do, he just, that's all he did, practice singing. He couldn't play nothing and he just do singing. He didn't play no guitar or nothing. And he take it and play around with it, try to learn, never could learn how to play a guitar. But, now, singing a song, now, he could sing a song, man, he could really sing a song. And he used to sing a song about "close your wig and let your head go bald." Now, I just couldn't sing it, but he could sing it. . . . And . . . he'd tell you a song about he "went to the church and they called him to pray, he got on his knees and didn't know what to say" and all that. And, now, he could sing all them songs. . . . We'd play them just like he sing them, but we couldn't sing them like he sung them, but we could play them. . . . We could play—we made our fiddle and guitar say that what he say, you know. But we couldn't sing them like him.

You were talking earlier. You said that sometime you pick the fiddle instead of bowing it.

[Laughs.] . . . I pick those songs. I pick those songs. I know when I pick them [tunes fiddle, holds it like a guitar, starts picking it], that's a banjo piece. [In a falsetto voice, similar to that of Skip James, sings:]

> Going to New Orleans, get me a sack of greens,
> Get up on a possum, possum party if I can.
>
> Going to New Orleans, get me a sack of greens,
> Catch up on a possum party if I can.

Man, they got a dance there, man you ————. [Laughs.]

Man, that was great.

[Daisy] What that song was, can't get the sack out? . . .

That was it, that was it.

Did you ever see anybody pick a fiddle before you did it?

No, I made that up myself. . . . Sir?

Have you ever seen anybody do it since then?

[Daisy] I know I ain't.

No, no. I seen nobody do it [laughs]. Ain't seen nobody do it at t'all. I just took it up on myself. There's a song my Daddy used to sing that he used to play on his old guitar called ["Sheriff"?]. And I can't, I play it on a guitar, now, I play it on a guitar good, singing it, make those old strings say what I supposed to say on a guitar, but this littlest thing is hard. And then I'm off on this thing. I'm way off on this thing. I ain't, I don't fool with it, you see. It's been a long time since I . . .

Would you try to fiddle another song?

Been a long time since I pulled that thing out. I don't fool with it, I just forget about it. The children, sometimes the little grandchildren, they sometimes I say I'll go get the ———. And know I have done good, so good with it, have made money with it, I just believe I just keep it. I have made money with this thing, let me tell you. . . . [Laughs.]

[Daisy] He wants you to play. [Boose fiddles, rosins strings and bow, fiddles.] I want you to play that "Got to Bottom Up and Go."

[Laughs.] I ain't going to play that. [Plays and sings "Tease Me Over Blues."]

"Tease Me Over Blues" was recorded by Clarksdale's Tony Hollins for Okeh in 1941. Hollins, who first recorded the blues classic "Crosscut Saw" and an early and influential version of "Crawling Kingsnake," was a popular entertainer, often playing with a young Joe Willie Wilkins, in the northern Delta area. His influence on John Lee Hooker is especially significant.

Did you make that song up?

[Rosining strings] Did I make it? No, sir, that one come out on a record. I— my sister had it for a record a long time ago, so I learned it. . . . [Mumbles] I done forgot the fellows now that done sang that song. [Speaking at regular volume] I know, I can't remember who was singing it at that time. . . . Now, sure can't, 'cause I did know but I done forgot it now. Been such a long time! . . . That's been a long time that song, that song was put out, it been a many, many, many a year. . . . I learned it. . . . My sister had the record, so I learned it how he sung it, and I just went to playing it, and I just went to playing it, trying to play it like this. I did know little something, but I'll tell you, if you want to know the truth, I just near about forgot how to sing a reel, I just [laughs] . . . The truth [is] I don't practice them, see. . . . Out of program at that time, I don't practice them, now, I don't practice no reel now. I—that's the main thing, if I practice them like I used to now. I'm telling you, I'd hit them on, I'd hit them, I'd hit them over the head, partner. And playing with them. See, the motion's in the stick. . . . And if you can't that motion, you won't, you can't get it right, you won't get the note right. See, the motion's in this stick. So, I near about done forgot the motion of it. I near forgot, takes practice, you know. If you don't practice the thing, you done, y'all get back off . . . y'all get back way from it. And let me play you—let me, if I can—now a church song for you. . . .

Folklorist and fiddler Alan Jabbour writes that a reel, "a quick-paced instrumental tune in ¾ or ¼ originally associated with group dancing in lines (longways), dates from before the late 18th century" (Brunvand 1996, 254). Many older African American musicians used the term "reel" to include other types of songs, as Boose apparently does here.

I going to see if I can, and I don't know [rosining strings], I know I, the song, anyway, it don't, this thing ain't, I ain't played it in so long, it don't sound good to me. Let me see what I can play. [Draws bow across strings.] "Give Me That Old Time Religion" I believe. [Plays "Old Time Religion."]

[Daisy, during the song] He's playing a church song now called "Give Me That Old Time Religion."

Alright, now, you play that song for me. Let me hear you.

I'd like to, but I can't play. I brought [a guitar] to see if you could, if you'd play us that song you were talking about.

[Boose laughs, then Daisy laughs.] Alright, open it up, let's see what that is. Is it a guitar? . . .

[Daisy] I didn't know why he done went to.

[Still laughing.] Golly!

[Daisy] Got all kinds of things, what they making. [Boose laughing.] Y'all went and got them things.

They can bring them things, ow-wee.

[Daisy] Yeah, you can take one of these kids, they can really play them. [Boose tunes guitar.] You know that white man up yonder at [Tyler?], you know he can play as good as Boose.

Where does this man live?

[Daisy] Up there at [Tyler?]. His name is—what they call him? Mr. Sam, ain't it?

Yeah . . .

[Daisy] But now, he can really play, he pick a guitar, he play a fiddle, too.

Do you know his last name?

[Daisy] Maybe Boose know his last name. Boose, do you know his last name? . . .

No, all I know is Mr. Sam, now.

[Daisy] He's Miss [Beryl?], that's his sister. He ain't no [Beryl?].

Yeah, but he ain't no Sam, he ain't no Johnson, I don't . . .

[Daisy] But he can really pick that, play that fiddle, though, and that guitar, too. . . . His sister, her name, we call her Miss Beryl, she's married to, what his name, Goat, Mr. Goat Beryl?

I just call her Miss Barrow. [Laughs.] I don't know her name. . . .

[Daisy] What's the name of Miss Barrow's brother? I know his sister stay up there, but he stay right up there at Tyre. I think he play somewhere every Saturday in Memphis down in ———. [Boose and Daisy continue talking, but only snatches can be heard over Boose's tuning and playing licks.] My little ole boy, he trying to learn how to play. He do a few pieces on the, he got him a electric guitar in yonder but he got to get the speaker in there, he needs another of one of those old things there on it. . . . That there like them guitars them folks on that TV have in there. And them white people, they come on every Saturday. They be playing them boxes, too.

You ever heard of Furry Lewis? . . .

Furry Lewis? What, Furry Lewis? . . . No, sir. I don't know who he is.

That's whose guitar this is.

Is it? It's good and easy picking.

[Daisy] Sure sounds good.

[Boose plays licks, adjusts tuning.] I got to get them to the strings, strings so close. [Plays licks, clears throat, plays song:]

> Going to New Orleans, get me a sack of greens
> Get that pot a boiling if I can.
>
> Going back to Jones County, honey
> Going back and tell her howdy
> Going back and tell her howdy
> Howdy, Howdy, Howdy, how
> Howdy, Howdy, Howdy, how
>
> Going to New Orleans, get me a sack of greens
> Keep a pot a boiling if I can.
>
> Whoa mule, whoa mule
> Whoa mule, can't get
> Whoa mule, can't get salad
> Whoa mule, can't get salad
>
> Going back and tell her howdy
> Going back and tell her howdy
> Howdy, howdy, howdy, howdy
> Howdy, howdy, howdy, howdy.

[Song ends, tape ends, new tape starts. Boose messes around with guitar.]

Jones County is in southwestern Mississippi. The county seat is Laurel, hometown of African American opera diva Leontyne Price.

Old Eli Green used to play that. [Laughs.] Oh yeah, he used to play that. Old Eli Green used to play that, I telling you.

[Daisy] I believe ole Raymond used to play that too, didn't he? . . . [Boose keeps picking out different snatches of song.]

I trying to play it but I done forgot it. [Keeps trying then settles into instrumental piece.]

What was that?

That was the "Old Boogie Woogie." [Laughs] . . . I wished I could of played on this thing then, I tell you. This thing sure do play good. If I could play it, if

I knowed how to play it, I'd play it, but I can't play it. I never could play a guitar.

Did you ever try to play with a bottleneck? Slide?

Yes, sir. I have played, I have tried to play with a bottleneck.

Do you have one around here somewhere that you could try it?

I don't know. I seen one up there in the garden. I throwed it away, I throwed it away. I thought about the time I used to play a guitar with a bottleneck. [Laughs.] . . . I can't, I can't never could play it with a knife in-between my fingers, but I'd just put a bottleneck on my little finger. . . . On my little finger, like that.

Where did you learn how to do that from?

Well, my brother, he, uh, that's what he did. That's the way he played his guitar. That's the way when he in place of knife, he'd break a bottleneck and put it on that little finger. But he played it, too, with that bottleneck. . . . He really did. Oh, I can play it pretty good with a bottleneck. I can't find me another one. [Laughs.] I can't find one nowhere tonight. [Messes around with guitar.] I don't know. Man, I can't make it right now. I don't know. [Messes with guitar, retunes, plays a short piece.] Do it sound good to you? That make it sound good, don't it? . . . [Laughs.] It sure do pick good. Let me tell you, uh-huh. If I had a guitar like this, I'd go back to trying to pick guitar and try to learn. [Laughs.] Picks easy. [Continues playing same piece.] . . . Sure, that's the reason I couldn't never learn to play no guitar. See, my finger's off.

How did you do that?

My sister cut them off when I was a baby. . . . No, I crawled up, see, she had a old axe, to pick up a old axe and put a board in it, just like chidren do do, you know. When they growing up. . . . And she was beating on a board with a nail in it, they said. And I crawled up behind her, and she was beating the board, trying to bust it, bust the board, to get the nail out of it, with an old piece of axe, old rusty axe, and I stuck my fingers up there and she bust them off. . . . Now, if I had my good fingers, I could learn to play guitar. But that's the reason I can't, 'cause I ain't got no fingers. I can't [strikes guitar strings], that finger was cut off; that one caught cold [strums guitar]. Now y'all play me a good piece while y'all here. Now some of you can play, one of you.

I can't play nothing.

One of you, play me a good piece. . . . Ah, yes, sir, y'all can play the guitay. Yes, sir, y'all can play.

[Daisy] I mean to tell you, because . . .

Go ahead, they can play it. They don't want to play it. But y'all play me one. Let me hear it. . . . [Laughs.]

[Daisy] I mean, them white boys that come on that TV, don't they be ready with them boxes?

Yeahhhh. Y'all . . . may fool me, but I just believe y'all can play, some one of y'all can play. Both of y'all. . . . I bet y'all can play fiddle and guitar. . . . I bet y'all play fiddle and guitar. I'll bet y'all something, that's y'all come on that TV. . . . I bet! I bet! I bet that's some of y'all on TV. . . . [Still laughing; Daisy messing with guitar.] Next time come on the TV, next time come on TV, I'm going to look to see if it's some of y'all. [Laughter.] They don't play no more till Saturday.

[Daisy, strumming] I done forgot it now. I near about done learned that piece. I forgot where to put my fingers at. Up there, ain't it?

[Laughs.] It ain't in that, it ain't in that tune, what you trying to play. [Daisy strums.] It ain't in that tune you trying to play. I know what you was trying to play. You was trying to play this. [Boose plays a lick.]

[Daisy] Yeah. . . . And I didn't tune it.

[Laughs.] . . . You can't hit it best. That's a note. [Boose plays lick, retunes.]

[Daisy, speaking mostly inaudibly because of guitar] What you singing?

What? You talking about me?

[Daisy] They catching it on there.

Oh. [Daisy laughs.]

At the urging of Steve LaVere, musician Stephan Michelson set up his recording equipment at the Taylor family reunion in the summer of 1972. As of 1994, Michelson still had these tapes of Boose and Sam Taylor and sister Martha Howard but felt that their release on CD would not be a commercially feasible project (Michelson 1994).

Attempts to trace the whereabouts of Boose and Sam subsequent to the early 1970s have come up empty-handed. According to Kip Lornell, the last known link to the Taylor brothers, their nephew Fred Howard, died in the mid to late 1970s (1998).

Ukulady

6 My Daddy Put Me On Stage When I Was Five Years Old

Little Laura Dukes and Her Ukulele

Laura Dukes (1907–92) was born and died in Memphis, Tennessee. Known as "Little Laura" or "Little Bit," Dukes was indeed small, measuring four feet and seven inches and weighing only eighty-five pounds (McKee and Chisenhall 1981, 109). Dukes grew up in the black music community of Memphis. Her father, a musical associate of W. C. Handy, had put Dukes on stage by the time she was five years old.

Initially, Dukes was a dancer and singer with local shows working in and out of Memphis. While performing in one of these shows, Dukes met guitarist Robert McCollum, better known in later years as Robert Nighthawk, who showed her how to play rudimentary guitar. She adopted the appropriately small banjo ukulele, and later the standard ukulele, to accompany herself.

After splitting with McCollum, Dukes became a regular member, along with Will Shade and Will Batts, of the Memphis Jug Band. After 1956, Dukes performed mostly with Dixieland groups—which became increasingly interracial in composition—primarily for white parties and festivals. In 1972, Dukes lived alone in a small, comfortable house at 2758 Enterprise—east of downtown and near the Fairgrounds.

Field and commercial recordings of Dukes have been released on the Wolf (Austria), Albatross (Italy), and Flyright (England) labels and by the Tennessee Folklore Society. She appeared in the BBC's documentary on the blues, *The Devil's Music: A History of the Blues,* in 1976, and footage of her playing in Memphis was broadcast on NBC's *Saturday Night Live* in the late 1970s. Dukes was a primary informant for Bengt Olsson's (Swedish) book *Memphis Blues and Jug Bands* published by Studio Vista (England), and the subject of Robert

Springer's (French) interview published in *Blues Unlimited* (England) in 1977. A photograph by Ray Allen titled *Blues Singer Laura Dukes* (copyrighted in 1991 by the Center for Southern Folklore in Memphis) appeared on the cover of the Society of Applied Anthropology's newsletter *Practicing Anthropology* in the summer of 1991.

A relatively obscure figure to most blues aficionados, Dukes attracted the attention of European blues specialists and was a favorite with white Memphis audiences. Always accessible, Dukes was never interviewed for or written about —apart from the 1977 *Blues Unlimited* interview—in the blues periodicals. Likewise, her death in 1992 was not reported in any of these specialist magazines and journals.

. . . We are at the home of Little Laura Dukes, and the date today is May . . .

The fourth.

May 4, 1972. Thank you. [Giggles.] First, we would like to ask you a couple of questions. Could you tell us when you were born and where you were born?

I was born 1907, here in Memphis, Tennessee, in North Memphis, where they call, where they used to call it Crematory Place. This is my home, see, I've been here all of my life. My people's home, also, my son. [Coughs.]

Several sources, including Sheldon Harris (1979), give the date of June 10, 1907, as Duke's birthday.

When did you first start playing any instruments, getting interested in music?

In 1933.

Dukes told French researcher Robert Springer in 1976 that she had her first guitar lesson with Robert McCollum in 1933 (1977, 19).

Uh-huh. And was there any special reason why you started to take up . . .

Yes, see, my daddy was a musician. . . . And I wanted to learn how to play music so bad, and it was fellow that taught me how, a colored fellow taught me how to play a four-string instrument.

Do you remember what his name was?

Uh-huh, Robert McCollum.

Dukes told Springer, "After Robert McCollum and I got together, then he started teachin' me and then that's when I bought me a four-string instrument.... And when I got to East St. Louis, Illinois, then that's when I bought a banjo ukelele. I always did like a small instrument, you know, with four strings" (1977, 19; note: "ukulele" is the American spelling and "ukelele" is the British). The liner notes to Wolf Records 120.920 *Memphis Sessions 1956–1961* state that Dukes learned guitar from McCollum, whom she met in East St. Louis in 1933, and that she appeared with him as a duo in "local joints." According to Dukes, she accompanied McCollum to the St. Louis area (Springer 1977, 19).

And so that's when you learned to play the ukulele?

Well, no, I learned how to play four strings on the guitar first. . . . Uh-huh. And then after I learned how to play, well, he brought me a four-string instrument. I first played a ten-string tiple, then I left from that and went to a banjo ukulele, and after the banjo got out of fix, I just bought a little ukulele. [Laughs, sighs.]

Dukes told Springer that she began playing a "ten-string tipple" (1977, 19). According to John Schechter, the tiple is a stringed instrument of Spanish origin. Most Spanish and Latin American tiples are strummed instruments of four or five strings. Schechter mentions a Venezuelan tiple that "has five double or triple courses; it is strummed to accompany songs" (1984, 599–600). Sibyl Marcuse refers to the tiple as "in Cuba a small *bandurria* with 5 pairs of strings" (1975, 525).

The *machete da braga* was brought to the Sandwich Islands (Hawaii) from Madeira in the late nineteenth century. There it became the Hawaiian ukulele ("leaping flea"). Its presentation at the 1915 Panama-Pacific Exposition in San Francisco sparked a fad in the United States. In 1916, a Chicago company advertised Honolulu-made ukuleles as "the favorite of college men and women everywhere . . . the most popular instrument of the day . . . and the fad of the hour." Jay Scott Odel wrote that the ukulele's popularity peaked in the late 1940s and early 1950s "through the efforts of the popular American television entertainer Arthur Godfrey" (1984, 323).

The banjo ukulele is a small, four-stringed instrument with the banjo's shape and head but ukulele fingering. Neither the ukulele nor its miscegenational sibling, the banjo ukulele, have played a significant role in African American music. Henry Sampson includes a photograph of an anonymous child performer, circa 1897, with the caption "I'se a Little Alabama Coon." The photograph shows a boy holding a four-string banjo of the same size as a banjo ukulele. Since the ukulele had not yet been introduced on the mainland, this instrument probably did not have the ukulele fingerboard (1988, 122).

What kind of music did your father play?

Well, a long time ago, long time ago, he used to play with Handy, W. C. Handy. . . . Uh-huh. . . . Yeah, I think he was playing with Handy when Handy wrote the "Memphis Blues" and the "St. Louis Blues." I don't know. Well, after that then he commenced going with traveling with other bands, you know.

Handy published "Memphis Blues" in 1912 and "St. Louis Blues" in 1914. Dukes told Springer, "Sure, I met W. C. Handy long time ago. Before Beale Street went down and I was with the jug band then and I think . . . we played him a piece. See, that was after he'd lost his eyesight and I met him and his secretary. . . . We played one or two pieces for him. He liked it fine" (1977, 21).

What instrument did he play?

Drums. . . . Uh-huh. He was a drummer.

Dickerson refers to Laura Dukes as "the daughter of Alex Dukes, W. C. Handy's drummer back in the old days" (1996, 56).

Do you remember much about this Robert McCollum? Was he a blues singer?

Oh yeah, uh-huh, he was a very, he was a very nice, he was a real good guitar player. He could play, he could play mostly anything.

Robert McCollum, who recorded during the prewar years as Robert Lee McCoy and later as Robert Nighthawk, was born in Helena, Arkansas, in 1909 and died there in 1967. Nighthawk was an influential slide guitarist, vocalist, and song writer who recorded some of the best Delta blues ever. He claimed to be a cousin of Houston Stackhouse (see the Joe Willie Wilkins chapter), from whom he learned the basics of Tommy Johnson's style of playing and singing the blues. Nighthawk's sister Margaret was, at one time, guitarist Joe Willie Wilkins's wife. Wilkins remembered Laura Dukes as an old girlfriend of Nighthawk's. (For a description of an all-night guitar battle between friends and competitors Nighthawk and Stackhouse, see Hay 1992.)

. . . See? So, we traveled together for a while.

Dukes told Springer, "We hitch-hiked but we never would try to catch rides. We could ride the bus, like that, but we was just travellin' the highway, just makin' extra money" (1977, 20).

You traveled with him?

Uh-huh. . . . We traveled together for a while.

Dukes told Springer this story: "See, Robert and I, we started out traveling. We would hitch-hike along the roads and stop in stores. Every store we'd stop in to get a lunch or something, they'd want us to play 'em a piece. . . . We got a job in East St. Louis playin' every night at a man's place and he had a pool-room in the back and he had us to be in the front playin'. He had a Seeburg [jukebox] in there but he wanted us. And it was but just the two of us. Robert would play guitar and I would play the banjo-ukelele. He would sing some songs and I would sing mine. . . . We stayed there 'bout three months, then we started back towards Memphis" (1977, 19–20).

Playing blues or. . . ?

No, we played blues and every, practically every new song at that time that came out. I would learn it, we would practice on it.

"Mostly we played blues and other songs," Dukes told Springer. "We played other songs that came out, like 'The Old Spinnin' Wheel' and like that. . . . That's a song that come out way back yonder in the '30's and so I learned it and we used to go 'round and play that" (1977, 19–20). "Well, I *did* write a good many songs 'cause we would, of days, we'd sit down, you know, and study up songs. He showed me about everything" (19).

"Old Spinning Wheel" was a 1933 Billy Hill composition, first recorded by Sam Robbins, also in 1933.

. . . And we would go about playing different, you know, songs for people in different states.

Mostly around here in the South? Or all over?

Well, no, we went up in Illinois and places like that, you know.

Were you with a medicine show or a minstrel show or anything?

No, no, I have never been with a medicine show, but I used to be with minstrel shows on carnivals. Uh-huh.

Uh-huh. Can you remember any of the shows that you were on?

Yeah, you see, I never was with a one-night minstrel. I was always with carnivals. I was with Grace Sutton Carnival, then I was with Dad Hildred Carnival, and I used to be with carnivals. This woman was a manager, I manage, she was a blues singer, her name was Effie Moore, and I used to dance choruses on her show.

Dukes told Springer, "[Effie Moore] was a blues singer on the show. I never did know where Effie's home was. No. But she had been from Coast to Coast." Dukes stated that she began with Effie Moore in 1928: "I left Memphis with her and started to travellin'. We went about different places: Arkansas and Texas and Illinois, places like that. . . . She had a band, but, see, they were down in the orchestra pit. It was a regular band with horns. . . . Effie Moore's Nehi [Knee-high?] Steppers." Dukes also mentioned her work with "Dad [Hildredge?]" and "Great Sutton [Sudden?] Shows. Mr. Frank Sutton, was his name." It was with the Dad Hildredge Show that Dukes met the comedian/singer brothers Madder and Bubba Mack and where she first met Robert McCollum, who was playing guitar in the show's orchestra. Dukes played her last traveling carnival, "J. A. [Gant's?] Carnival," in 1947 before joining the jug band in Memphis (Springer 1977, 20).

Henry Sampson, in his chronological history of African Americans in show business, has documented a Frank Sutton who in 1893 performed in the Slavery Days Company, in 1894 performed as part of the Eclipse Colored Quintet, and in 1896 performed with the Golden Gate Quartet. In 1900, Sutton performed in the cast of the Williams and Walker Company's "new two-act musical comedy," "Sons of Ham," written by Jessie A. Shipp. This show included such African American show business luminaries as Bert Williams and Will Marion Cook (1988). It is not known whether this is the same Frank Sutton with whom Dukes later toured.

. . . I was a chorus girl.

What kind of dances were you doing then?

Oh, just regular chorus girl dances, you know. And that was way back yonder in the '20s and '30s.

According to Harris, Dukes worked as a dancer in Beale Street clubs in the early 1920s and as a singer/dancer in "passing carnivals out of Memphis working amusement parks/tent shows through Arkansas/Texas/Illinois, 1928 into 30s" (1979, 163).

Did these carnivals have a lot of other performers with them?

Yeah, they had rides, you know, had rides and they had what you call girl shows . . . like hula girls with grass skirts on [Dukes chuckles, laughter] and so on. . . . And that and so, where I got, I started to dancing before I started with music, playing music, see, because my daddy put me on the stage when I was five years old.

Would you travel with your father?

No, see, my mother wouldn't let me go. . . . It was right here in the city when I was with that, with her show. Her name was Laura Smith. She was a blues singer, but I wasn't but five years old, and she wanted to take me with her when they got ready to leave, but mother wouldn't let me go.

"When I was five years old, my daddy put me on a stage with a lady that had a show here in Memphis. Her name was Laura Smith," Dukes told Springer. "Well, [Laura Smith] had a show and she liked me so well she asked my mother to let me be on stage with her. So I did and the first song that I sang was 'Balling The Jack.' . . . I think it was a little over half a year. When she got ready to leave, mother wouldn't let me travel with her because I was too small." Dukes said that she made twenty-five dollars a week working for Laura Smith and that she gave it all to her mother (1977, 20).

A Laura Smith was recorded in the 1920s singing the blues. Little is known of her. Tom Lord writes that she was from Indianapolis; that she toured the South, Midwest, and East in the 1920s, sometimes with her "Ginger Pep Workers"; that by 1926 she was married to comedian Slim Jones and living in Baltimore; and that she died of high blood pressure in Los Angeles in 1932 (1976, 522–53). In the liner notes of Smith's *Complete Recorded Works*, Howard Rye noted that the *Chicago Defender* of November 22, 1930, reported that Smith had just completed a film (1996).

Dixon, Godrich, and Rye add that the *Chicago Defender* of April 27, 1929, reported Smith to be making a film for Paramount and Lasky Corporation titled *Lady Liz* (1997). The November 22, 1930, edition of the same paper stated that the film was completed. This film has not been traced.

Smith began her recording career in 1924 for Okeh. Her last known recordings were for Victor in June 1927. In all, thirty-five songs are known to have been recorded by Smith. It is not known whether this is the same Laura Smith that Dukes worked with as a child.

Would that be, would you play around Beale Street and places like that?

Mmm. No, the show wasn't but one block from Beale. That was at Fourth and Gayoso, uptown.

Was there any certain people that influenced your singing style?

Mmmm. What do you mean, when I was small or? . . . Influenced me? . . . Oh yeah. After I got grown, see, I started traveling then and when I stopped traveling, I started playing with different bands here in the city. I used to play with the jug band, Memphis Jug Band, and then after most of those boys died, well, I got with another band, and I am still with that band.

Mary Batts, widow of Memphis Jug Band member Will Batts, told Olsson: "I think it was 1938, Laura Dukes joined the band. She's a small woman—they call her 'Little Bit.' She did most of the singing, and played ukulele and danced" (1970, 43). In her interview with Robert Springer in 1976, Dukes gave both 1944 and 1947 as the year she first began playing with the jug bands (1977, 20–21). Helen Schrodt and Bailey Wilkinson, based on talks with Milton Roby, stated that Roby joined a "small group of other displaced musicians, the Memphis Jug Band, and together these men survived the lean years between 1933 and 1941. With Will Shade, the founder of the band, Will Batts, Wilfred Bell, Otto Gillman, and Laura Dukes, Roby played at parties when possible and on the streets when hungry until World War II brought an end to the hardships of the little group. The band held together until 1956 by playing at private parties and small clubs" (1964, 55–56).

Samuel Charters described the typical job: "These jobs were usually an hour's entertaining—most of the time in a sideroom, while a dance orchestra played for the social side of things in the main room. They were a kind of souvenir of the Old South, and as always there was a lot of drinking and a lot of clowning. . . . But as the years went by there were fewer people interested in what they were doing. . . . Will Batts kept his band going until 1956, when he died of a stroke. . . . Howard Yancey booked a lot of the jobs for the musicians—though Will Batts did his own bookings—and a woman named Mrs. Wagner used to book them for jobs outside of Memphis" (1977, 23).

Which band is that?

Well, one of our musicians taken sick—that was our trumpet player—and he is in a nursing home now. So got another trumpet player, and it was two, then later on, two more white fellows, you know, two white fellows, they joined our band, and one passed here last week. . . . They buried him this past Monday. Mmm, he name was Ed Morris. He was a clarinet player. [Sighs.]

Writing in 1970, Olsson stated of Dukes, "She still has a following in Memphis; she sings with Son Smith's band, and recently had an engagement on a riverboat, performing for tourists" (1970, 44). In 1976, Dukes told Springer that "our used-to-be trumpet player Son Smith, you know, he was blind and he was the manager of the band then, but here 'bout a month or two ago, he died. He was in his seventies." She was still working in a band managed by Charlie Banks, Smith's piano player and the former proprietor of Beale Street's Citizens Club (1977, 20).

River City Review Folk/Blues Editor Steve LaVere supplied the following in the promotional material for the 1973 River City Blues Festival: "Charlie Banks and the Beale Street Originals feature Little Laura Dukes on the banjo-ukulele. This group performs regularly aboard the Memphis and Delta Queen riverboats and include a good deal of Handy's material in their repertoire" (LaVere 1973).

What was the name of the band?

The Beale Street Originals. . . . Well, they played blues, played, you know, a little bit of everything, but they played what called Dixieland. . . . Dixieland music and other, you know, other old-timey songs. . . . Uh-huh.

Well, can you remember anyone specific that had influence on your vocal style?

 You mean the songs I sing now?

Dukes told Springer, "I never did like to imitate nobody" (1977, 21).

Huh? Well, I sing some blues, and then I sing other songs, "Darkness on the Delta" and, you know, like that—those songs came out a long time ago. But, see, when they came out, they was popular then, you know, and all like that. And "Honeysuckle Rose," and then I started to singing a number, looked like everybody like it, "Mr. Crump."

"Darkness on the Delta" was a popular song composed by Jerry Levinson with lyrics by Marty Symes and Allen J. Neiburg in 1933. Two recordings of the song were released that year, one by Del Lampe and one by Chick Bullock. "Honeysuckle Rose" is the classic composition of Fats Waller with words by Andy Razaf. They wrote it in 1929 and Wallers recorded it in 1934.

That was one of W. C. Handy's songs, isn't it?

Uh-huh. . . . Yeah. . . . But I got another different way of singing it, you know. . . . Uh-huh, so I would sing "Mr. Crump" and other numbers that the band, you know, knowed that I sang. See? "Why Don't You Come Home, Bill Bailey" and all of that.

Handy's "Memphis Blues" includes the famous lines: "Mister Crump don't 'low no easy riders here / We don't care what Mister Crump don't 'low / we gonna bar'l house anyhow" and "Mister Crump don't 'low it / ain't goin' have it here / Mister Crump can go and catch hisself some air" (Handy 1972, 70–72).

"Bill Bailey, Why Don't You Come Home" was written by Hughie Cannon in 1902 and recorded by numerous pop and jazz performers including Jimmy Durante and Mutt Carey.

When you were playing with jug bands here in Memphis could you tell us something about that, like some of the people you played with? Did you play with Gus Cannon or Will Shade or some of those?

Well, I played with Will Shade. And I played with, I didn't play much with Gus Cannon, you know. . . . He wasn't with them in the band very much. . . . So. I did play with Will Shade, Ukelele Kid, and . . .

According to Dukes, Ukelele Kid was Charlie Burse of the Memphis Jug Band (Springer 1977, 20). "I would go around with Ukelele. . . . Ukelele Kid and Will Shade," Dukes told Springer (1977, 20). Charlie Burse, a.k.a. "Uke" or "Ukelele Kid," was born in 1901 in Decatur, Alabama, and died in 1965 in Memphis. He moved to Memphis in 1928 and became an original member of the Memphis Jug Band. Whether on banjo, guitar, or mandolin, Burse was often found in Shade's company from 1928 until his death in the mid-1960s. Burse also recorded under his own name with jug band accompaniment (once as the Memphis Mudcats and another as Jolly Jug Band). Burse's younger brother Robert was also a musician associated with the Memphis jug band scene.

Dewey Corley?

Huh? . . . Yeah, played with Dewey Corley. We played with him sometimes. Sometimes he'd get a job, you know, and hire us and somebody else. So the jug band thinned out, so I started playing with a regular band. [Laura chuckles.] . . . Mmm, huh, we have, let me see, it was six of us, I believe it is five of us now, play in the band, and we do pretty good. Of course, we just, you know, when one person be done dropped out, what I mean something happened, you miss them. . . . You sure do. [Getting weepy] Because I know I did.

For more on Dewey Corley, see the Memphis Ma Rainey chapter.

I know what you mean, yeah. That's for sure. Could you tell us something about your days with the jug band?

... Well, sometimes we would play around on Beale Street and then we would get to play for house parties for people in, here in the city.... And we would go out of the city, too. We would play in Greenville, Mississippi, for Mr. Pryor, and then we'd play for Mr. Percy McDonald's parties. We played for him a lot. He used to be at the William Land Hotel all of the time.... Then he used to live at Bellevue and Peabody, but now he lives way out here on Warner Grove Road, but he's in a wheelchair now. See, he was a lawyer.... Mmm, and I know him very well, Mr. McDonald. So we played for a right smart of people here in the city, too.

Did you ever do any recordings? Make any records?

Well, no, we would go to a, we went to a lady's house out here on Highland, North Highland.... Way up there in North Highland. Mr. and Mrs. Newhouse. And we got to play for their parties, but they had a, what you call a, machine that would take a recording, you could make a recording of it.... And those are about the onliest recordings that I, you know, that we make. The others, the boys, they have put out records ... but I never have. Uh-huh.

Dukes told Springer in 1976, "I never did make no records, no" (1977, 21). According to Dixon, Goodrich, and Rye's *Blues and Gospel Records 1890–1943* (1997), Dukes played mandolin on the Memphis Jug Band 1934 Okeh recordings of "Mary Anna Cutoff" and "My Love Is Cold" and probably ukulele on "Little Green Slippers" (released on both Okeh and Vocalion) and "Fishin' in the Dark" (Vocalion). These four songs were recorded in two different sessions on November 7 and 8 in Chicago.

According to Olsson, the Memphis Jug Band—with Milton Roby and Will Batts on violin and guitar, Will Shade on bull fiddle, and Laura Dukes on banjo—went up north, "probably in Cleveland, Ohio," and recorded in 1954. They all sang. Among the songs they recorded were "Move to Kansas City" and the instrumental "Lady Be Good." None of these recordings were released (1970, 45). This session was released later on Flyright LP 113 *South Memphis Jug Band* in 1976. According to Mike Leadbitter and Neil Slaven, the performers were Will Batts on violin, guitar and vocals; Milton Roby on violin, guitar, and vocals; Will Shade on washtub bass; probably Mickey Mathis on clarinet; and Laura Dukes on banjo and vocal on "Kansas City Blues" (1987). Leadbitter and Slaven also list an unissued session recorded by Swedish radio in May 26, 1964, in Memphis. The session of five songs features Laura "Little Bit" Dukes on vocals and banjolele (banjo ukulele) and Will Shade on guitar. Charlie Musselwhite plays harmonica on one of two takes of "Nobody Loves Me." Nine songs by Dukes accompanied by Will Shade and Gus Cannon, recorded by Don Hill at a private party in Memphis on July 18–19, 1961, were released on Wolf 120.920 *Memphis Sessions 1956–1961*.

Four songs of Dukes playing and singing solo, recorded at her house on December 22, 1972, were issued on Albatros 8240 *Tennessee Blues, Vol 1*. Dukes recorded "Mr. Crump Don't 'Low" for the LP *Tennessee: The Folk Heritage, Volume I: The Delta* issued by the Tennessee Folklore Society in 1978.

When you first started singing, were there a lot of popular female blues singers there?

Uh-huh. Oh yes, it was, but I mean, they were with shows, you know, they were traveling with shows. That was even after I stopped traveling, you know.

Well, did you ever see them when they came through Memphis or when they were in Memphis?

Once in a while. I used to see them.

Did any of them ever impress you as being, you know, better than most?

No, no they did not.

Did any of them influence the way you perform?

No, they didn't. I tell you, at that time, majority of the girls was, I don't know, some of them would get kind of jealous, you know. . . . Jealous, because I know the show I was with when I was with Effie Moore, some of the girls on there, they looked like they were kind of jealous of me, you know. . . . But I never did pay that any attention. I'd have to do what the manager tell me. Uh-huh. And so, I would of come up a long ways, I have lived to be as old as I am, and so that's it. But I am still active. . . . I can't find many people my age as active as I am. . . . And some of them is not my age, and is not as active as I am. [Laughter.] . . . That's right. So I'm glad, I'm glad I am as active as I am, because I keeps going. See, I work, too. I have to work. . . . I work every Sunday morning and the first and third Tuesday. And I have been out there on that job going on twenty-seven years. . . . Yeah. Anytime you are fooling with thirty and forty children, you've got a job. Now I have, I mean those minutes sometimes, I mean I have to take care by myself. Uh-huh, see, I have been out, I been out there, I work in the church nursery. . . . And I have been out there a pretty good while. Some of the children that I used to take care of, they are married and got children, and they bring their children there for us to see after. [Chuckles.]

Do they all still remember you?

Uh-huh! Oh yeah! 'Cause some of them come by and say, "Hey, Laura, remember me?" I would say, "Yeah." "Well, I've got one for you to take care of out there." So I say, "So soon?" [Laughter.] He says, "Yeah." So they bring their children there, and, of course, some of them have moved out of town, you know. . . . But whenever they come back to visit, they about come by there at the church and come by and see me.

Would you mind playing a few of the songs you used to play with the jug band?

Well, the songs I used to play with the jug band, I don't know, I never practice, I never practice. [Coughs.] Now, this was one song that I play, that I used to play with Will Shade . . . and he really, he could play pretty good. . . . He really could play a guitar real, pretty good. . . . So, I just kept that, you know, just kept that in mind, then I would play some of my songs, you know, and he'd play with me. But we never did, you know, I never did, he put out records, too. . . . But I didn't. I don't know where I was when those guys were making records. [Laughter.] I don't know. Then I played this song that they used to play over the radio, "Stackolee. . . ." Now that's real old!

Yes, it is.

That song came out, I believe that song came out before I was born or after I was born one. . . . But I just got to the place where, when, uh, that I remember that song, and I started to singing it even before it got popular . . . on radio, because I could remember it, and I started to singing it. I started singing it in the white nightclubs that we used to play at, you know. . . . I played that song and sang it myself. See, when I heard it on radio, I said, "I bet you somebody done copied that from me." [Laughter.]

"The most important and longest-lived bad man in black lore," Stack O' Lee (Stagolee, Staggerlee, etc.) was celebrated in song as early as 1895 in Coahoma County, Mississippi. By 1911, Howard Odum had collected versions in Mississippi, Alabama, Tennessee, Louisiana, and Georgia (Levine 1977, 413). Early recordings of the ballad by blues musicians include those by Papa Harvey Hull and Long Cleve Reed, Furry Lewis, John Hurt, and Ma Rainey. Each version is somewhat different. In 1933, the Library of Congress recorded future recording star Ivory Joe Hunter performing "Stackolee" in Wiergate, Texas. In 1942, the Library recorded Will Starks performing "Stackerlee" near Clarksdale, Mississippi. New Orleans artist Archibald recorded a two-part "Stack-A-Lee" that rose to the number ten spot on the R&B charts for Imperial in 1950. Alabama soul singer Wilson Pickett's Atlantic recording of "Stag-O-Lee" rose to the number thirteen slot on the R&B charts in 1967 (Whitburn 1996). Other recordings of the song include those of John R. (1960), Good Time Charlie (1967), and Mary Wells (1968) (Paikos 1993). Dukes's version is most similar to Lloyd Price's remake from 1958. ABC-Paramount 9972, by the Louisiana singer/pianist, stayed at the number one slot on both the R&B and pop charts for four weeks and charted for a total of nineteen weeks (Whitburn 1996).

Where did you first hear "Stackolee"?

Oh! Long time ago. I heard "Stackolee," but you see, it came back into my mind. . . . Oh, it has been about, I say about ten years ago, and I believe I was living downtown, and I used to get my ukulele and sit out on the porch and play it for my neighbors, you know, out there, and sing. Then "Stackolee" come to my mind, and so I started practicing on it and got it down, you know. So I don't know, I don't know whether I can play any Son Brimmer song. Let me see. [Plays ukulele and sings.]

Son Brimmer was another name for Memphis musician Will Shade. For more on Shade and the jug bands, see the Gus Cannon and Furry Lewis chapters.

That was real good. What was that called?

I think the name of it "She's Gone But She Will Be Back Someday." [Laughter.] Uh-huh.

Kaiser Clifton sang this song accompanied by Will Shade on guitar (and spoken comments) and an unknown pianist, in Memphis on May 30, 1930, for Victor. Victor V38600, "She'll Be Back Someday," was released under Clifton's name. The recordings made at a private party in Memphis in the summer of 1961 (and released by Wolf Records) include Dukes performing (singing and playing the banjo ukulele) this song (titled "He's Gone") accompanied by Will Shade on the washtub bass.

Was that one of Son Brimmer's songs?

Yeah, that was one of his'n. . . . Now, let me see, [strums ukulele] now, this song here, I changed it, because the band was supposed to be singing . . . but I changed some parts of it, you know. . . . [Plays ukulele and sings.]

> Well, I ain't gonna marry, and I ain't gonna settle down,
>> Doggone my soul, hey Lordy, Lordy.
> Ain't gonna marry, and I ain't gonna settle down,
> I'm gonna stay right here until your whiskers drags the ground.
>
> Talk about your high yellows, give me my teasing brown,
>> Doggone my soul, yeah Lordy, Lordy.
> Talk about your high yellows, give me my teasing brown,
> 'Cause when you get in trouble your yellow papa can't be found.

[instrumental break]

When you see two women running hand in hand,
   Doggone my soul, yeah Lordy, Lordy.
When two women always running hand in hand,
   You can bet your last dollar that one's got the other's man.

Oh, my house is on afire, and the blaze is getting mighty big,
   Doggone my soul, yeah, Lordy, Lordy.
My house is on fire and the blaze's getting mighty big,
   I yelled the women in the alley, cried "Mama, won't you save my wig."

That was good. What was the name of that one?

Well, it been a while, ooh. I don't know, I done forgot. Let me see, "I Ain't Going Marry, And I Ain't Going Settle Down." That's it. [Laughter.]

Dukes recorded this song in December of 1972 for the Albatross label. The verses were the same but the order of the last two verses was reversed. Albatross listed the song title as "Doggone My Soul." She also recorded this song backed by Will Shade on guitar for Swedish Radio in 1964.

Do you know who wrote it?

Huh? . . . Oh no! That song came back out of way back yonder in the '20s.

Where did you learn that one from?

. . . I think that song came out on a record long time ago. I believe that was during the time when Bessie Smith was, you know . . . making records like that. That's an old number! . . . Uh-huh.

Memphis-born blues singer Viola McCoy, backed by Fletcher Henderson's band, recorded a version of this song for Brunswick in 1924. Bessie Smith's "Young Woman's Blues" included the line "I ain't going marry, ain't going settle down," a common phrase in American folk music. The couplet about two women running hand-in-hand also is a common blues expression.

Do you remember how to play "Mr. Crump"?

Well, I haven't practiced on that much. I have to get the right kind of, you know, chords on it and everything.

In 1970, Olsson wrote of Dukes, "A fine version of 'Mr. Crump Don't Like It' is part of her repertoire" (1970, 44). Duke learned this song, usually associated with Frank Stokes, who recorded it for Paramount in 1927, from another source. Dukes told Olsson, "I saw Stokes in the 'forties.

I was walking on a street with a friend, and we passed by an old man sitting on the porch. My friend told me that it was Frank Stokes. He was very famous in Memphis, but I had never seen him before" (1970, 17). A version of Dukes's "Mr. Crump" appeared on the Tennessee Folklore Society LP, *Tennessee: The Folk Heritage, Volume I: The Delta* in 1978.

Do you know any of the other W. C. Handy songs?

No, I used to play, let me see, I don't know. Pardon me a moment. Y'all excuse me. [Goes to tend to dog.] . . . Instead of one line, she goes round and round and round and round. [Laughter.] So, that poodle's a mess. [Laughter.]

You wouldn't know how to get along without him, would you?

No, my boyfriend brought that dog in here to me about two years ago. Uh-huh, well, I don't know what other songs. I, oh yeah, I just wrote this song. No, I better keep it a secret. . . . I just, I wrote this song over the last month. You know, sometimes when I don't have nothing to do, something comes in my mind, and I say, "That's a song, I believe I'll write it." Boy, well, let me see, I don't know, maybe I can play it for y'all. I don't care. I don't know whether I will do such a good job on it or not. [Plays ukulele and sings.]

> Oh, Jimmy, won't you come back? Oh, oh, Jimmy, you got something
>   I like,
> You know you are my heart and soul.
>
> Jimmy, what did I do, oh, oh, Jimmy, you know I love you,
> You know you are my heart and soul.
>
> Whenever we're together, we have a lot of fun,
> We don't worry 'bout the weather, even when day is done.
>
> Oh, oh, Jimmy, won't you come back, oh, oh, Jimmy, you've got something
>   I like,
> Jimmy, you are my heart and soul.

Dukes recorded a version of "Jimmy's Blues" for Albatross in December 1972 in which she added an instrumental break and repeated the last two verses. Albatross mistranscribed the line "day is done" as "day is dark."

Yeah. I like that.

Yeah, that's what my agent told me. He said, "That's a good song, Laura! Why don't you write some more?"

Yeah, that is good song. You got a name for that song?

Huh? "Jimmy . . . " Uh-huh.

"Jimmy." Well, that's really good. Can you remember "Stackolee"?

Huh? . . . Uh-huh.

Would you like to play it?

I didn't play it? [Strums ukulele] Oh, my. [Plays ukulele and sings.]

> I was standing by my window, when I heard my bulldog bark,
> He was barking at the men who were gambling in the dark.
>
> [poodle starts barking as if on cue]
>
> It was Stackolee and Billy, two men who were gambling,
> Stackolee threw seven, Billy swore that he threw eight.
>
> Stackolee told Billy, "Oh, you know I ain't going to let you go with that,
> You have won all of my money and my brand new Stetson hat."
>
> Stackolee went home and he got his forty-four,
> Said, "I'm going to the barroom just to pay that debt I owe."
>
> [instrumental break]
>
> Stackolee went to the barroom, looked across the barroom floor,
> He said, "Don't nobody move," and he pulled his forty-four.
>
> "Stackolee," cried Billy, "oh please don't take my life,
> I've got three little children and a very sickly wife."
>
> Stackolee shot Billy, oh, he shot that poor boy so bad,
> Shot the bullet right through Billy and it broke the bartender's glass.
>
> Oh Stackolee, Oh Stackolee, Oh Stackolee,
> Oh Stackolee, Oh Stackolee, Oh Stackolee-ee-ee.

[Yells at dog] Shut up! [Laughter.] Oh, that poodle! [Laughter.] I don't want you to sing. [Laughter, she strums ukulele.] Yeah, I practice on that, and a lot of more songs I've got to practice on 'cause I don't know, it so, my agent told me we are in that blues festival.

Dukes recorded an identical version (without dog) of "Stack O' Lee" for Albatross in December 1972. Albatross mistranscribed "bartender's glass" as "bar tinted glass."

One coming up?

Huh? . . . Uh-huh . . . And we was in the blues festival in, when was it, in '69, I believe.

Was that in the Cotton Carnival?

Uh-huh, during the Cotton Carnival.

The first Cotton Carnival, in March 1931, was Boss Crump's springtime fling to lift the spirits of Depression-era white Memphians. "The carnival idea in turn came from the old Memphis Mardi Gras celebrations of 1872 to 1881, when Ole King Cotton and his royal troupe entered Memphis triumphantly" (Shemanski 1984, 175). Louis Cantor described the event as "that most quintessentially Southern social event that living in the land of magnolias and honeysuckle ever produced. . . . It was an annual affair and clearly the highlight of the Memphis social season" (1992, 10). Black Memphians who participated were confined to menial, even "groveling" roles. In 1935, a black dentist, Dr. R. Q. Venson, created an African American alternative, the Cotton Makers' Jubilee. Its parade down Beale Street soon came to rival in popularity the original parade and had both black and white audiences. In 1983, the Memphis Cotton Carnival Association decided that all future Cotton Carnivals would commence on the third Saturday of May and end on the first Sunday in June. The Carnival begins with a River Pageant, has a major parade the following Saturday, and climaxes with a ten-day outdoor music festival (Shemanski 1984, 175).

Yeah, this picture here?

We was at the Downtown Motor Inn, and we were there one year, we were at Ellis Auditorium, and the next year we are at the coliseum.

Where are you going to be this year? Do you know?

Supposed to be out at Memphis State. . . . Uh-huh, that's what I heard. . . . I don't know.

Memphis State University is now the University of Memphis.

I noticed you had a little banjo, you . . .

I got two. . . . Yeah.

Do you play them?

Ut uh, they have to, they've got to be fixed. . . . And boy, you would be surprised the money you have to have to have them fixed. . . . That's right. I've got two, both of them is just alike, all but that one got a back on it, but the other one don't have no back on it, you know. So. [Long silence.] Well, that is about all I can tell you alls.

We saw Memphis Ma Rainey the other day.

Oh, you did? . . . Well, how is she doing?

She's doing pretty good.

Oh, I haven't seen here since I moved away from downtown.

She told us that she and you used to sing together a little bit.

Well, we did, and then I used, uh, no, I never did sing with Memphis Minnie.

For more on Memphis Minnie, see the Memphis Ma Rainey chapter.

Did you know Memphis Minnie?

Uh-huh, yeah, I knew her. . . . I don't know, is she still living?

Yeah, as far as I know she is.

Is she?

She had a stroke about ten years ago and quit singing.

I heard, I heard about it. Because she played guitar, Memphis Minnie did.

A good guitar player, too.

Yeah, she was. I knowed her from long, long time ago.

Did you ever sing with her?

No, because the fellow that taught me how to play music, I think he told me that she married his cousin. His name was Joe something.

Joe McCoy?

Yeah, I think so. . . . Yeah, but I've never, you know, I can't remember him, in a way, but I do know her.

Joe McCoy (1905–50) and his musician brother Charles grew up in Jackson, Mississippi. Joe later moved to Memphis, where his guitar and mandolin playing made him a featured performer on the Memphis jug band scene and where he began a longtime personal and musical partnership with Memphis Minnie. McCoy and Minnie moved to Chicago in the 1930s and made some remarkable records together as Memphis Minnie and Kansas Joe. McCoy recorded in a number of different contexts and under a lot of different pseudonyms, including in the risqué hokum bands of the 1930s. Sheldon Harris states that McCoy was "reportedly" a cousin of Robert Nighthawk (Harris 1979, 399).

Do you remember her other husband? Ernest Lawlars?

No, I don't. It has been so long since I have seen any of those people. That's the truth.

Ernest Lawlars (1900–61) was known as Little Son Joe. The Hughes, Arkansas, native played guitar and washboard and worked (and recorded) with Robert Wilkins before joining up with Memphis Minnie in 1939 in Chicago. By the late 1940s, Lawlars was again in the South working with Willie Love's Three Aces. In the 1950s, Lawlars and Minnie returned to Memphis as their health began to decline (Garon and Garon 1992).

What type stuff did you used to sing with Memphis Ma Rainey?

I don't know, we just sang, you know, just sang some blues and some like that, and I never was, I wasn't around Ma Rainey much, you know, during. . . . Of course, see, Ma Rainey was singing with those, with the, these bands here in Memphis. . . . Well, I wasn't unless, until I got with the jug band. . . . See, I never was singing with no band. Well, after I learnt how to play music, I just going by myself and be playing and singing by myself. See?

Can you still play "Bill Bailey"? You mentioned that earlier.

Well, I don't play, I don't play those numbers. See, the band plays those for me. . . . They play, let me see. It's one number that the band plays for me I think I have been playing on ukulele, one of—is that Fat Domino's or Big Joe Turner's "Flip, Flop, and Fly"? I believe.

I think that's Fats.

Huh? . . . Fats Domino. . . . I believe it is, let me see, I don't know. [Plays ukulele and sings "Flip, Flop, and Fly."] Oh, my!

"Flip, Flop, and Fly," composed by Charles E. Calhoun and Lou Willie Turner, was recorded in New York by Big Joe Turner on January 28, 1955. It was released as Atlantic 1053. Turner's follow-up to his 1954 chart-topping "Shake, Rattle, and Roll" rose to the number two slot after its release on March 19, 1955. "Flip, Flop, and Fly" stayed on the charts for a total of fifteen weeks (Whitburn 1996).

Where did you learn that song? From the radio?

Uh-huh. I sure did.

When you played the banjo, do you play it the same way you play this one [ukulele]?

Uh-huh, but the banjo is louder than this.

Louder? Sound better?

Yeah, it does, it sounds like one of those regular banjos, you know. But I can't, I have to have a pick to play that thing. . . . It's got steel strings. . . . But these are nylon, [strums ukulele] and I can't, I can't play it like I can this. I like this one better.

Do you use the same chords and all that?

Huh? . . . Uh-huh, you know, the same chords and everything, on this just like I do the banjo. But I haven't played that banjo in so long, it's pitiful. Course it was last year, or last summer, I tell you one of the fellows lives here, and the other one, he's from Sweden, . . . and so this fellow sent me a book from Sweden with myself and the jug band in it, and Shade, Will Shade's picture, Ukelele Kid.

Swedish researcher Bengt Olsson's *Memphis Blues and Jug Bands* was published in London by Studio Vista Limited in 1970. It appeared as part of the *Blues Paperbacks* series edited by Paul Oliver. This 112-page illustrated book is based on "research done by the author and Peter Mahlin in Memphis and its neighborhood in the summer of 1969" (Olsson 1970, 6).

Is that the one with Memphis Ma Rainey's picture, too?

Ut uh, no, just got all the, you know, I guess regular fellows that, you know, that was around then. And so, he came here to Memphis last year . . . and he borrowed a picture from me of Robert McCollum. See, Robert McCollum and his brother is on the same picture. . . . And he said he wanted to get a copy off it, and he was going to send it back to me. So, I haven't heard from him.

"Now I also had another picture with Robert McCollum and his brother Percy. Robert is sitting in a chair with his guitar and Percy was sittin' on the arm of the chair with his harmonica. The Swedish man . . . Olsson took it and said he'd bring it back like he did the other one, but he never did. I sure wish he'd send it back to me. That's the only picture of Robert McCollum I had," Dukes told Springer. Springer asks in a footnote to his *Blues Unlimited* interview with Dukes, "D'you hear, Mr. Olsson?" (1977, 21). This photograph has appeared in print including the cover of Mamlish LP S-3202 *Mississippi Bottom Blues*. Unfortunately, Dukes was not the only musician in 1972 who complained that Olsson borrowed pictures and had not returned them.

Royalties and copies of Olsson's field recordings made into commercial LP releases were also not forthcoming; Memphis musicians were unaware that records had even been released.

He never sent it back?

Not yet.

Do you remember his name?

His name is Ben-jit Olsen. Oh, I've got the address and everything. I got his name, address, everything, you know.

Where does he live?

Huh? . . . No. He's a, he is a Swede, uh-huh. . . . He is a Swede, and he stay in Sweden. But that, ohhh, I hate to write it, that's such a looong name, that whatever it is, I hate to write it. [Laughter.] I hate to write it. But I don't know, I was intending to write, you know, ask him what did he do with the picture, see, but, see, I've got my daddy, he was a drummer. I managed to get hold of his picture, and I managed to get, uh, have some of the musicians' pictures. 'Cause that is some of them's pictures over there.

Uh-huh. I saw that. Is that the band you play with now?

Uh-huh, and that band up there on the wall, that's the one, that's the band I play with now. . . . Uh-huh. Excusing that clarinet player and the trumpet player, they're not with us. . . . But we've got a bass player and another trumpet player. We still have our same drummer, same piano player, and the trombone player. That's right.

Do you still have that book that the man from Sweden sent you?

Uh-huh, yeah. . . . Yeah, I'll give it to you. [Walking away to get book] I'll let you see. I carries, I keeps it in my purse all the time. I don't know where it t'is she lay.

They have a thing in here about Harmonica Frank. Did you ever meet Harmonica Frank?

Nuh-uh. [Long silence.] Are they having school out there? . . . At Memphis State?

"Harmonica Frank" Floyd, born in Mississippi in 1908, was a white medicine show/carnival performer who traveled widely across the southern United States with his guitar, harmonica, and kazoo. His repertoire consisted of novelty, country, and blues-influenced songs. Before Floyd was located in Millington, Tennessee, in the early 1970s, British blues aficionados believed he was a black blues musician, perhaps because he had recorded for the Sun and Chess labels.

Well, Memphis State just finished, but where I'm from—we are all from South-western—and we are still in school. Southwestern is just, is by Overton Park.

Uh-huh. My son works up there. . . . Uh-huh, he works in the gym. . . . Uh-huh.

Southwestern at Memphis College is now Rhodes College.

Did the man that wrote the book take the picture?

I don't know where they got those pictures from, 'cause there isn't but one picture in there that I let those boys take a copy of, and that is that one over there on the table. Now, they had that picture, I let them have that picture to copy. . . . But I don't know where he went around and dug up some. There was two of them here from Sweden then. I don't know where they got all of they information from. . . . We used to play over there. We used to play at South-western. . . . A long time ago, uh-huh. We played over there. They were having a, I don't know, I think the young people was having a dance, and then the last time we went over there, I think the older people was having a dance.

This book is published by a different company than the previous.

See, it was published in London, you know. . . . I think it was published in London. But the boy that sent it to me, when it came to me, it was from, it came from Sweden. . . . Mrs. Van Hunt? . . . Now, not that I knowed of. Mrs. Van Hunt. What does she do?

Mrs. Van Zula Carter Hunt (1901–95), singer and guitarist, moved from her hometown of Somerville to Memphis when still young. She toured the South as a singer both with the larger minstrel shows (e.g., Rabbit Foot, Silas Green) as well as with her own show, Madame Hunt's Traveling Show. She worked with all the famous Memphis blues musicians, including the Memphis Jug Band. In 1930, she recorded the vocal "Selling That Jelly" with the Carolina Peanut Boys (Noah Lewis, John Estes, Ham Lewis, and others) for Victor. She reportedly made other recordings in the prewar era and recorded for Sun in the 1950s. Two songs were released on Adelphi LP 10105 *Memphis Blues Again, Vol. 2* in 1970. Steve LaVere, who learned of Hunt through Dewey Corley, said of her, "She knows everything about everybody" (LaVere n.d.). In an obituary, Ed Tremewan stated that Hunt appeared locally in festivals from the "early 1960's and well into the 1980's, when declining health slowed her activities down" (1995, 10).

She sings.

Oh, she does, uh-huh.

Used to sing with Bessie Smith.

Oh, sure enough. No, well, at that time that Bessie Smith and them was, I was, you know, I was real young. I never did go around like, I think about, I don't think I was big enough. My mother wouldn't let me. I might have been big enough to go around, because I couldn't go around like these children going around now. [Laughter.] Mama wouldn't let me. Always had to be at home. Especially at night, and couldn't get too far from home in the daytime. [Laughter.] 'Cause you see, when I was growing up, I went to, uh, our teachers were really strict. You know, I went to Catholic School.

Dukes told Springer that she had seen Bessie Smith on stage at Beale Street's Palace Theater but had not met her. She did meet the original Ma Rainey in Mississippi: "She and Effie Moore, they knew each other. See, I was always with Effie Moore, and Ma Rainey was there and we went to this roomin' house and Miss Effie she said she was gonna make me acquainted with her and she did" (1977, 20). Dukes told BBC interviewers (for the production *The Devil's Music*) in 1976 that she heard someone ask Ma Rainey, "Ma, do you have any money?" Rainey replied, "Honey enough to choke a ox!" (Oakley 1976, 102).

Mmm, did you first start singing in the church?

No. . . . Oh, well, they had children's choir there sometimes. . . . The nuns would, you know, just, on occasions, you know what I mean. And so, and the teacher said I had a very good voice, and so she put me in the choir. [Laughter.]

According to Larry Nager in his book *Memphis Beat: The Lives and Times of America's Musical Crossroads,* Little Laura Dukes died in 1992 (1998, 67).

Big Amos

7 Worth a Thousand Dollars a Note

Big Amos Patton on the Harmonica

In May 1972, Amos Patton was living at 557 Melton in South Memphis. His house was of recent construction and located in a middle-class black neighborhood. Patton had made his living and supported his large family not as a musician but primarily as a house painter.

In the 1940s, 1950s, and for a spell in the mid-1960s, Patton was an active contributor to the Delta blues. He tried again in the mid-1970s to reenter that scene when his old friend Joe Willie Wilkins was performing with his band before predominantly white and middle-class audiences. The competition, however, was fierce; Son Blakes, Nathaniel Armstrong, and Roland "Boy Blue" Hayes had all been working as Wilkins's harp players, and Henry "Little Wolf" Palmer and Woodrow Adams, among others, were trying to convince Wilkins of their fitness to be in his band.

It was apparent in 1972 that Patton, though out of practice, was still a superb musician. He had played a significant, if relatively unknown, role in fostering the important West Memphis blues scene of the 1950s. Unfortunately, Patton was, like many blues musicians, underrecorded. Furthermore, his 1960s recordings for Hi were an obvious attempt to market Patton to a soul music rather than a blues audience. These circumstances explain why white blues researchers have shown little interest in Patton and why we knew nothing about him, except that he played harmonica, when we arrived at his home for this interview.

[Radio playing.] Well, first we'd just like to get a little biographical information. Could you tell us when you were born and where you were born?

Yeah, now. [Laughs.] That's a woman's secret there, you know. [Laughter.] Well, I was born in, I was born December 25, 1921.

On Christmas Day, huh?

Right.

Sort of ruins your birthday, doesn't it?

Yeah, you know, get a Christmas present, you know [laughs]. . . . Course it's been a long time ago, since they, since I found out about Santa Claus; Christmas been kind of a . . . [Laughter.]

Where were you born?

Oh, it was in Panola County. Here in Mississippi, you know.

Is that in the Delta?

Well, kind of, kind of up, upside of that part of the Delta. Sardis. . . . Sardis, Mississippi, you know. The Delta's just a little below that, you know. . . . Yeah, Sardis in Panola. Yeah, uh-huh.

When did you start playing harmonica?

Let's see, I guess it was somewhere, '40, no, it was about '36, 'round there. . . . Humpf. Funny thing. Miller McFarlans, a cousin of mine. I used to go 'round and listen to him, you know, and he told me I used to, I steal his harp, you know, and then I'd tear them up, you know [laughs]. But, really, I guess that's how I learnt, you know. I really, you know, I'd listen to him and I used to steal his harps. And he'd miss them and then I'd been done tore them up, you know. [Laughs.] But it takes a pretty, takes a long time, you know, before I really learnt, you know. But I had plenty of weapons, you know, because I had a whole box of backs of harps that I had done already taken, you know. [Laughter.] Every time he'd buy a new one, I'd get the old one if I got my hands on it, you know.

Would you mind if I turn off the radio?

Oh. [Turns off radio, but TV in next room is still audible.] Now, let me.

Do you have any idea where your cousin learned to play?

No, I really don't. He, I guess ———— he wasn't very good, you know. He just, he could just play it, you know, a little bit.

You are better than he is now?

Oh yeah. [Laughs.] . . . Well, I mean it, well I mean, I guess maybe he was pretty good at that time, you know. . . . But, course, . . . he didn't do nothing with it, you know. He just, I mean, after I first learned, you know, what it wasn't, learned a couple of songs and, well, it wasn't six months, you know, I could play anything, you know, he could play after I got the hang of the things. And so that mostly settles that one, you know. With him. [Laughs.]

Was there anybody else in your family that played musical instruments?

Ah, well, ah course now Charlie Patton, you know, I'm sure you probably heard of him. . . . He's supposed to been my uncle. . . . I seen him one time. . . . But I didn't see him anymore. Course, he died in '37 or '27.

Charlie Patton (1887–1934) was one of the progenitors of Delta blues and one of its greatest performers. Much has been written about Patton, including John Fahey's *Charley Patton* (1970), Calt
and Wardlow's *King of the Delta Blues: The Life and Music of Charlie Patton* (1988), and *The Voice
of the Delta: Charley Patton and the Mississippi Blues Traditions, Influences, and Comparisons: An
International Symposium* (Sacre 1987).

What? Was he your, supposed to be your father's brother?

Right.

*What type of songs did you and your cousin play when you were first learning
to play?*

Oh, well, I don't know. Something, I mean, I think hounds or something. I mean, it really wasn't. . . . Yeah, it really wasn't anything. I can't even play it anymore now, you know. [Laughs.]

The "fox chase" with imitations of the sounds of hunting dogs barking, yapping, and baying was
a common harmonica theme among southern blacks.

But it was a church song that he played one time at church, you know. "Every-
body Got to Stand," you know. "It's nobody here, stand there for you, you got to stand there for yourself." I used could play that real good, which I learned how to play that one pretty good, you know, at the time, you know, when I hadn't played it now in how long. I probably could play it, though.

Did you ever do any traveling around or playing for money or anything?

Um, not, oh yeah, yeah, I made quite a few appearances, you know, before I started recording here. . . . I recorded for Hi, Hi Recording. 1350 South Lauderdale, which is Popular Tunes, you know, in Memphis. I mean, they own Hi Recordings, you know. And I got two or three records out, portion of an album. Me and Big Lucky, Don Himes.

Hi Records released six songs by Big Amos. "He Won't Bite Me Twice" and "Move with Me Baby" were issued on a 45 rpm (Hi 2108). "Going to Vietnam," "I'm Gone," "Dog Man," and "You're Too Young" were issued on the LP *River Town Blues* (SHL-32063). These six songs, recorded in the mid-1960s, were first built and rehearsed by Patton and Joe Willie Wilkins in the back bedroom of Wilkins's house in North Memphis. Patton taped these sessions, and it was that tape that Hi used as a model in the studio. On some of these cuts, the unknown guitarist even tries, with limited success, to copy Wilkins's elaborate guitar style.

Who is Don Himes?

Ah, well, I don't know Don Himes, really. He just a blues singer. And, other words, we had some tapes, mmm, tapes there at Hi, and they just got a couple of his tapes, you know, and a couple of mine and Lucky, you know, Big Lucky, you know. And just put them on an album, you know. . . . Oh, well, they pretty good. I wish, you know, I don't want, as I say, I don't know that much about Big Lucky, really know him. I never, I never seen him in person play, but he was recorded for Hi and so was I, and so was Don Himes, and so I didn't even meet either one until after the album was released. And I met them, we went out and make some pictures together, you know. And then I met them. But I never heard, never heard either one, you know, play or perform or anything like that, you see.

Don Himes was a Memphis soul singer, and Levester "Big Lucky" Carter (born 1920) is a blues guitarist and vocalist. Carter also recorded for the Westside, Bandstand USA, and the M.O.C. labels. For more on Carter, see the Tommy Gary chapter.

Well, how long did you stay in Mississippi? When did you move up here? Where did you go?

Huh, let's see, I stay to Mississippi until '42 and I left there and went to Norfolk, Virginia.

Were you in the navy? Is that why you went to Norfolk?

Well, no, I went there, you know, to work at the naval base. And then I was drafted into the army in '44. I had to come back to Mississippi, you know, my draft board was there. I went along and stayed about two and a half years and I came back to Mississippi where my family was and I—'46, I guess—I stayed there until '50 and I came to Memphis. . . . Yeah, in '50 or '51, somewhere in there, you know. . . . And so, I've been there ever since.

When you were back in Mississippi, though, did you play around the local places and things like that?

Yeah, I, well, uh-huh [laughs], when I came back out of the army, I bought me a guitar, a electric guitar and a—I would have bought one before then but I wasn't able. . . . And I bought me an electric guitar and drums and a mike and one harp and says, "Look out there!" Bud Lee and Willie Smith, which was, could play drums a little bit, you know. He was to play guitar a little bit, you know. And so. . . . Yeah, and so we . . . yeah, we got together. We went out, you know, and made a few gigs. Well, we made a bit of money, you know, really. And for about two years, you know, '40, '47, and '48, you know. And things got dull and everything and I just came on to Memphis. Then I substituted for Sonny Boy Williamson in '46 over to Helena, Arkansas, you know, playing harmonica with Joe Willie Wilkins, you know.

From the early 1940s, radio station KFFA in Helena, Arkansas, broadcast the extremely popular King Biscuit Time show each day at noon. This fifteen-minute broadcast originally featured Sonny Boy Williamson and guitar great Robert Jr. Lockwood. The cast grew rapidly and at various times included Joe Willie Wilkins and Houston Stackhouse on guitars, Robert "Dudlow" Taylor, Willie Love, and Joe Willie "Pinetop" Perkins on piano, and James Peck Curtis on drums. Sonny Boy often traveled, so Wilkins would get someone else to play harmonica. In 1973, Howlin' Wolf told Fred Hay and Steve LaVere, "Joe Willie Wilkins got me my first job on the radio. He came after me in Moorehead, Mississippi, in the 1940s when times were tough. He's a real nice guitar player."

. . . And James Peck Curtis. . . . Well, I would say, I would say they was the, they was the root of my getting started, you know. . . . I met Joe Willie out to Marks, Mississippi, when I first came out of the army. He was, Sonny Boy was gone at the time, you know. . . . And I met him, and I met him one night they was playing, and him and James Peck Curtis and Pinetop and Joe Willie was up there trying to blow the harp. He could blow the harp actually, a little bit, you know. And so, I was just standing out there which nothing but just me, you know, all my life. I could, I could play all the songs that Sonny Boy played, you know. I could hear them on the record and I could play them, you know, just, I mean, just as perfect as he could. But I didn't know anything about my time or keys. I didn't know what keys is. I didn't know nothing about that scoundrel, you know. I just blowing, playing the harp, you know. And so I asked him, I say, "Hey, man, how about letting me play you a piece, play you a number?" you know. And he said, "Can you blow?" I said, "Yeah." [Laughter.] And so, he said, well, "Come on up here," and I got on up there. I think I played this little ole song "Sugar Mama," you know. One of Sonny Boy's old numbers. And I didn't know too much what I was doing but I was playing, you know, I was playing my harp, you know. I know that. [Laughter.] And they liked it. I played a couple more pieces there with them, so, getting close, uh, pretty close to quitting time. And they comes up, "Come on and go to Helena, man. We need you." And I brought, I was gone on a Friday night, so I brought Joe and they came on back home with me. Batesville, where I was living there then. And we went back down there, that, went back down there that Saturday night. That was on Saturday night. We went back and I went on left them, I went on to Helena with them, you know. And I broadcast over there, about three months over there.

"Sugar Mama Blues" was recorded for the Bluebird label by John Lee "Sonny Boy" Williamson at his first recording session in May 1937. The Sonny Boy Williamson for whom Patton substituted on radio station KFFA was Rice (Alex or Willie) Miller. Sonny Boy's singing and harmonica were accompanied on "Sugar Mama Blues" by the guitars of Big Joe Williams and Robert Nighthawk. John Lee Williamson was born in Jackson, Tennessee, in 1914. He was stabbed to death on the streets of Chicago in 1948.

James Peck Curtis (1912–70), washboard player, drummer, and dancer, played drums for the King Biscuit Time show on radio station KFFA. Joe Willie "Pinetop" Perkins (born 1912) was a pianist with the King Biscuit Entertainers. Later he was a member of Muddy Waters's band. Perkins has recorded with Waters, Robert Nighthawk, Earl Hooker, Willie Williams, and others as well as under his own name.

Then Sonny Boy came back?

Yeah, Sonny Boy came back, and then I came back home. And then I went and got my, bought my own rig, you know. And, well, I could see there was a little money in the deal, you know. And I went out, uh, we played about two years, I guess. And so after I came to Memphis, I ran up on Joe Willie. We, cut some records, me and he and Joe Hill Louis. 1951. I don't know what, I don't know what happened.

Joe Willie Wilkins confirmed that he, Patton, and Joe Hill Louis had recorded together but could not remember the details. Louis (1921–57) often performed as a one-man band, singing and playing guitar, harmonica, and drums. Known as the "Be-Bop Boy," Louis performed over radio station WDIA. He also recorded a number of excellent sides for Sun, Modern, Checker, and other labels. Louis was influenced by the playing of both Sonny Boy and Joe Willie Wilkins.

Do you remember what label that was on?

No, I don't, tell you the truth. It came out, the record, I don't know, I don't know. Guy gave me fifteen dollars, I know that. [Laughter.] And I don't know what happened to the song, but I wrote the song myself that I play. "Love Is Strange," and I heard it seven different times, you know. And you know, 'cause it was my song I had never heard it, you know, before. . . . But after then, I don't know, I don't know how the song get out. "Love Is Strange." That was the title of it.

Did lots of other people sing it after that?

Yeah, yeah.

Can you remember who sang it?

I don't know, man. Let's see, let's see. Let's see who, I don't know right now. Who sang it, but it, I heard about three different people sing it. But they didn't use all the verses, but they used the biggest of them, you know. . . . And, well, in a way. I never did hear mine.

You never heard your record?

No. [Laughs.] . . . No, I never did, I never did hear it. But I heard one of the songs, which was an instrumental I grant, that I played. I knew, I knew my own play. It was on Joe Hill Louis, it was one of his, it was Joe Hill Louis. See, but I knew my . . .

Harp playing.

Yeah.

Was Joe Willie on that cut, too?

Yeah, so I mean, I didn't know. I didn't fool around no more until I was. . . . Frankly, I quit playing harmonica. I bought a house up here on Rochester. In '53, and I went, see, the house I was staying in when I got here, it was, they was going to remodel, and I was going to put a large family out—I got six kids, you know. And they, and I had to take my kids back home and, because you go to a guy's house and say you want to rent an apartment or a house or something. And you say, you got, he say, "How many kids you got?" And you say, "Six." Man, you might as well spit in your face, you know. 'Cause they don't want that stuff, man. And so I went and bought this house. In Walker Sub, stayed there sixteen years. And I quit playing music, 'cause I was playing regular over the weekend especially.

Where did you play, Beale Street or something, place like that?

Well, I mostly played in West Memphis in Arkansas, see, where we—Joe Willie and I—had a program over there. KWEM, West Memphis, you know, we broadcast on a Saturday. . . . No, uh, Sonny Boy, he was in Detroit at that time. But he used to come back in ever once in a while, you know. But, you know, he, well, anyway, anywhere Sonny Boy went, you know, he had, he could get a plug in on a radio station, you know. You know, he was a pretty famous guy, you know. . . . Sure enough, he blow some [harmonicas?], you know. [Laughs.]

Following the success of Helena's KFFA with blues broadcasting, KWEM in West Memphis ran a series of midday blues broadcasts beginning with Sonny Boy's show in 1948. Joe Willie Wilkins came to West Memphis to accompany Sonny Boy on KWEM and later broadcast with a number of other musicians, including Patton, Willie Love, Willie Nix, and Forest City Joe Pugh.

Did you ever play with Bo-Pete Fleming or Son Blakes or Sammy Lewis over in West Memphis?

Well, tell you really the truth, I mean, Bo-Pete play guitar; Sonny Blake, I taught Sonny near about everything he knew and also Sammy. . . . That's right. I taught Sammy. Oh, Sammy couldn't, he was young and he could play but he, his time was say off, you know. He didn't, you know, I had to go through that one time myself, you know. And so, I taught both of them boys. 'Cause Sonny was, oh, Sonny was a late starter, you know. Sonny wasn't, he, uh, 'cause Sammy was playing the harmonica long time, you know, but Sonny just probably started playing harmonica since '53 uh, to amount to anything at all, you know. But he pretty good, though. And I'm telling you. . . . Course now, one time Sammy, Sammy's, Sammy's real good. He become real good. As good as anybody that I have ever seen, including Little Walter. See. 'Cause I taught Little Walter how to play "Blues in the Night" in Helena, Arkansas, in '46.

Son Blakes didn't take up the harmonica until he was twenty-nine years old. He was a regular fixture on the Memphis/West Memphis music scene in the 1960s through the 1990s. He recorded in the mid-1970s. Sammy Lewis recorded one record with the Willie Johnson Combo in 1954 (Sun 218). Lewis sang "I Feel So Worried." The vocal on the flipside was by Willie Johnson. Bo-Pete Fleming was a West Memphis guitarist and Joe Willie Wilkins's protégé.

You taught him how to play harp?

No, he, see, one song, one song "Blues in the Night." See, Sonny Boy, he was broadcasting over there, and at the time I was over there, you know, I was substituting for Sonny Boy, you know. Well, Sonny Boy taken off. I was the first guy to ever tremor a harmonica to, that I can remember, and Walter got that tremor, you know, that trembling harp, he got it from me. But I didn't even think anything about it, really. Everybody was trying to play like Sonny Boy. You understand me. Because, you know, he was everybody's idol, you know. . . . And Sonny Boy was playing this song about, he used to play about "Blues in the Night," you know. "My mama done told me," and Walter couldn't play it, but, you know, it was just, was, you know, different style, you know, from the way Walter played. He played the harp, the harmonica, funny, different from anyone else, really, you know. And so, he said, "Man"— oh, I played, I played the thing on the radio one time, you know. He said, "You play thing near about like Sonny Boy, how you play it." So, I was sitting out there on Elm Street there, sitting out there on a porch, you know, in Helena, Arkansas, and I showed him, see, you had to play the thing in cross, see, you had to cross it, yeah.

Attracted by Sonny Boy's broadcast over KFFA, Little Walter Jacobs (1930–68) came to Helena from his native Louisiana in the 1940s. Joe Willie Wilkins remembered that the first time that he and Sonny Boy ever saw Jacobs, they were standing on a street corner in Helena. Jacobs rode by on the county truck (having been picked up for some minor crime such as vagrancy), and when he saw Sonny Boy, he asked him for a harmonica. Sonny Boy refused, but Wilkins convinced him to give Jacobs an old harp, reminding Sonny Boy that the boy was off to do roadwork for the county. The truck departed to the accompaniment of Jacobs's playing. Wilkins's widow, Carrie, remembered that Jacobs was just a "snotty-nosed kid" at the time.

Crossharp (or "second position") is developed from the "draw" rather than the "blow" notes ("straight" harp or "first position"), thus creating a different scale. According to Kim Field, "The note bending available in cross harp allowed players to achieve the minor thirds, flattened fifths, and minor sevenths that characterize the 'blue' scale" (1993, 158).

You had to cross it.

You got to cross it, yeah. And so he picked it up nicely. When I left there, I didn't see Walter anymore, so I reckon, till after he put out "Juke," you know. He had done gone to Chicago with Muddy Water, you know, and, uh, the boy was good, out of sight. But now, Sammy, well, Sammy was the kind of—he had too much confidence in himself or something. And didn't, and didn't have any confidence, see. Now, he wanted to, he wanted to be the greatest harmonica player there was in the world. Which he was great, but he wasn't as good as he thought he was, see. He wasn't good enough to get out there and try to make a living with his harp, see. He stand around and listen to other people play and then he'd tell the people, "I could cut your throat," you know. And when he would, he'd get up on the stage and cut his throat. 'Cause he played with Bo-Pete about three years and then he wouldn't blow the harp. Blowed all the time he played with Bo-Pete, see. But he was just good, but he wasn't a, you know what I mean. Anybody can follow, you know. He told Walter himself, you know, Walter say, he was playing one time, Walter came down there and he, oh, I don't know, it was sometime before Walter died, maybe in '67, something in the '60s. He came down, Walter down there, and he was playing and he said, uh, Walter said, "You know, you really play that harp. I haven't never heard nobody play near like me as you." He said, "I'm going to, I'm going to make you crawl." But he didn't, one thing he didn't think about, he don't think about that Walter build all the stuff that he play, see. See, but he didn't, Sammy ain't built nothing. See, naturally a person, you can hear something you can always trail behind it, but he could play anything Walter play just like he play it, but he never play anything for hisself, see. And so, that's why I figured, I say, "Well, Sammy old boy, I don't think you need to tell the old man that," you know. The guy's good, but, you know, Walter's one of the greatest harmonica players that went through this country, you know. What I mean, what I think really, today, I mean, I mean for noting a harmonica, I give it to Sonny Boy Williamson, you see. I think he's the greatest, but his style and all that is all way behind him, you understand. What we come up with, you got your new styles, but what I mean, making a monkey out of Sonny Boy, noting a harp, you know, but I's telling you, that guy, he could make a note on that harmonica. He could take one harp and he could, I'm going to tell you right now, he could [sings] bi ba ma mom bam. [Laughs.]

Was there any harp player that was a great influence on your style after you learned how to play?

Yeah. I like, of course, you know, there was two Sonny Boys. I'm sure you know about that, you know. . . . But, now, the old original Sonny Boy was, he was really my idol, but when, after when he died, got killed, or something, you know, and then Sonny Boy, he was broadcasting, well, you know, I just, oh, took up behind him. And this guy what died, he could play, he was kind of like the two Walters. Walter Jacobs and Walter Hawkins [i.e., Horton], see. Both them guys can play harp, play good. Well, now, Walter Jacobs, is, he was middle ——— man, and Hawkins, he was bogus harp player, see. He played bogus, see. He just like the two Sonny Boys. One of them, both of them was good, but the old original Sonny Boy, he was middle ———, and but Willie Miller, you know, he was bogus, you know, but he, he, he could, he could play it, though! I guarantee it. [Laughs.] And both of them Little, Walters, I can take James Cotton. James Cotton, he was, well, James Cotton was pretty good now. He and I was coming along at the same time along with Sammy. Sammy was younger than we were, you know. . . . And James Cotton helped me play the last gig I played in '40, in '53 before I quit. And I even quit playing harmonica, I didn't touch a harp, I'm sure, until Slim Harpo came out with "Scratch My Back."

James Cotton was born in Tunica, Mississippi, in 1935. While still quite young, Cotton left the farm for Helena, Arkansas, where he followed Sonny Boy Williamson. Later, he followed Sonny Boy to West Memphis, where he worked with Howlin' Wolf, Willie Nix, Joe Willie Wilkins, and others. He recorded for Sun Records in the early 1950s, joined Muddy Waters's band in the mid-1950s, and left Waters's band in 1966 to go out on his own. He's still going strong as one of the blues's greatest harp blowers and recording artists.

Big Walter Horton (1917–81) was one of the most influential and original of blues harmonica players. He was raised in Memphis and as a child played with the Memphis Jug Band. Horton made brilliant recordings under his own name and was the consummate sideman on the recordings of others (including Muddy Waters, Johnny Shines, and Otis Rush).

Slim Harpo?

Yeah, Slim Harpo, when the record came out "Scratch My Back," and was just, I justs the way, that's the way I learnt how to play a harmonica. The key in the, you know, just a, the whole thing was just, that's the way I learned how to play harmonica, when you hit, just hit, his rhythm of "Scratch My Back," was how I learned how. I mean, you know, and I said, well, "I'm going to make me a record and I can play that, I bet you." I was going to say Slim, to hear you, he's dead, too, you know. But I bets you one thing. If he's, if he was still, if he was up there and let me play it, "Scratch My Back," before he play it, he would not play it. [Laughter.]

James Moore (1924–70) was a Louisiana bluesman who recorded under the name of Slim Harpo for the Excello label. He recorded his hit "Baby Scratch My Back" in 1966, which was also the year in which Patton recorded for Hi Records.

Have you ever heard any records or seen a guy named Sonny Terry?

Little Sonny Terry. I heard his records, you know. I don't know him, I've never seen him. . . . Well, I hadn't really had, I hadn't been paying him any attention, but I just happened to, uh, little lady had his, one of his albums. . . . And then I got to listening at it, you know, and, well, he plays pretty, he plays pretty good, you know, you know. Well, he just got, he's got his one particular way he play and he ain't, 'cause everybody's in that bag, you know. . . . Everybody's got their own bag and they ain't going to get out of it. I don't care, even James Brown, if he was to get out from what he is now, he's lost. [Laughter.]

Patton is not thinking of Sonny Terry here but of the Detroit musician Aaron Willis, whose stage name was Little Sonny and who had, at the time, recently released an album. Willis, an Alabama native, was Sonny Boy's protégé and namesake from the latter's Detroit years. Willis made a few singles beginning in 1958 and recorded his first LP for Enterprise, the Stax subsidiary label, in 1969.

But he makes some pretty good plain notes on a harp, you know. He ain't, he ain't, he don't, make no, he don't make no, he don't make no notes on a harmonica, not that can't anybody that play harmonica near about make, you see. He ain't got nothing, there ain't nothing he got is strange, you know, that you know make a harmonica player listen too much, you know. . . . Now, all of the, you know, anybody can go "wah, wah, wah, em, wah, wah, wah, wah," you know. Just playing that stuff. But he ain't got no big breaks in there, see. I mean, course I, uh, oh, sure, I like his. He's got a couple of songs, got some pretty good beats, you know, that I like. I like his songs, some of them, I mean, but especially about that one, "that woman is named trouble," you know. [Laughs.] . . . But, I mean, I was speaking strictly about his harmonica, you know. 'Cause I'm a harmonica player, see. And if you a guitar player or a horn blower and, I mean, I can come up with most ole anything, but if he come up with something makes some funny keys there, makes you wonder about it. Then you going to get there. But Sonny's not making anything on harmonica that no harmonica player can't make, see. Now, I just likes what Slim Harpo came out with, "Scratch My Back." Ain't five peoples can play it, see. It's just simple, but he's making some funny, funny runs on there, but Little Sonny, he's just making, he's just playing straight harmonica, you know. Now, it's not nothing, but it's good, you know.

Do you play the harmonica any now?

Oh, a little bit. If I, you know, take a notion, I play. Wind's kind of short, you know.

Can I talk you into a song or two?

Oh, man [laughs], I don't even got a harmonica, though, you see.

You don't have one?

I probably ain't got no 'count around here. I might have an old piece somewhere around here.

We should have brought—I'd sure like to hear you play. Yeah, we'd like to hear a little sample.

Oh, uh.

To get an idea.

[Laughs.] Well, you all had better cut that thing off. You wasting some tape now. [Laughter.] Let's see, man, I don't know. Y'all ain't got no harmonica? [Goes to shelf, opens box, and gets harmonica. Plays harmonica and laughs.]

Wow.

Ah [panting]. . . . Well, man, that's worth a thousand dollars a note, man. [Laughs.]

Wow, that was good.

Umh, shu. . . . [Plays riff.] Mm, huh. [Plays song accompanied by foot patting plainly audible on tape.] Shu.

Wow. That was really good. [Patton laughs.] What was that?

Man, I don't know, don't ask me, man. [Laughter.] Oh, I, uh, I just wrote something. I don't know.

Just something that came to your head?

Just something. [Laughs and pants.] . . . Um, mmm, jus' a ———. When I was a young man, you know, like y'all, you know, I, boy, I could sweat all night, man, sweat popping out, I was running ice, was playing, man. I used to get up out of my seat and [laughs] it be full of water. [Laughter.]

Like ole James Cotton does now?

Yeah, yeah. . . . Yeah, ole James Cotton, oh, we had some pretty good times together, James Cotton and I. He was playing with Willie Nix. Willie Nix got in trouble over there in Arkansas, in Joiner, I think. See, Joe Willie had a little ole band and—which I was Joe's harp blower—and Willie Nix had a band ——— got in trouble. James Cotton, he just taken over Willie's band, you know. Then he had, you know, pretty popular, you know. . . . When Muddy came down, after Little Walter, you know, had done pull out, you know, for hisself. Muddy came down. Well, frankly, Muddy came after Sammy, but Sammy was, he was playing at Black Fish Lake somewhere. And, of course, Sammy was, uh, he's a better harp blower than Cotton, you know. At the time. I don't know. I think Cotton pretty good now, but I don't—Sammy quit, kind of halfway quit or something. I don't know, but I hadn't heard either one of them play in a long time, but at that time, uh, uh, Sammy was a better harmonica player than Cotton was. But Cotton, he just got a lot of nerve like Joe Hill Louis, man, he plays harmonica anywhere and Sonny Boy, too, you know, and I just didn't have that nerve, you know.

I, well, anyway, any guy make a success, man, in music when he eat, he can break his own plate, you know, and then eat somewhere else. You know about getting no success, man. See, I got a wife and six kids, you know. . . . And, you know, they got to have some bread, you know. . . . And you can't make no bread ——— messing around with this music, laying around these juke halls, you know, and, well, you get a good break sometimes, you know. Even making records, if you get a smashing hit, man. Well, every recording company in the world, man, is at you. Until you make that hit, don't nobody, you can't even talk to a man hardly, you know. So.

Willie Nix (1922–91), a native of Memphis, was a superb singer and drummer who recorded in Memphis and Chicago in the early 1950s.

Joe Willie Wilkins remembered that when Muddy Waters came south to find Sammy Lewis, that Wilkins recommended that he take Cotton instead. Wilkins also encouraged Waters to take his protégé and Cotton's frequent associate, guitarist Pat Hare.

They don't want you till you already done made your hit.

Yeah. . . . That's right. They all want you then, see. So, I see, that's the whole damn thing in a nutshell, you see. But I got a couple of records over there. Have y'all heard any of my records?

No. We'd like to.

[Laughs.] I got a couple over there; you may, you can hear them if you want. . . . But you got to have enough time if you want to hear them.

Oh, we'd love to hear them.

[Plays records while tape recorder is turned off, laughs. Plays harp.] Ah, whew! [Laughs.]

Ah, wow. That's some fine playing.

I even forgot the song, man. [Laughter.]

What was the name of the song?

———— that's it. I forgot it. [Laughter.] It was supposed to have been "Eyesight to the Blind," you know.

"Eyesight to the Blind" was Sonny Boy's composition. He recorded it at his first recording session, for the Trumpet label, in Jackson, Mississippi, in 1951.

[Patton plays and sings "Truckin' Little Woman"—snaps fingers in time as he sings.]

Willie Nix recorded this song in 1952. It was released on the Checker label.

In the spring of 1999, Amos Patton was still living in his house at 557 Melton in South Memphis. According to his son, Patton was quite ill and incapable of talking on the telephone.

Biscuit Kings

8 Why Don't You Cut Me Up Some Bream There

Beer Party at Joe Willie Wilkins's
House with Houston Stackhouse
and Willis "Hillbilly" Kenibrew

Earlier in the year, during wintertime, we had visited the house at 1656 Carpenter Street to interview Houston Stackhouse. When we set up that interview, we did not know that it was Joe Willie Wilkins's house that we were to visit. Wilkins witnessed our interview with Stackhouse and agreed to be interviewed himself at a later date. In May 1972, we returned to this house on a residential street surrounded by factories and warehouses. The air in the vicinity had a sweet burning odor from the nearby meat packer.

On this day, as at the time of our first meeting, Wilkins was sick; his legs and feet were swollen. The doctor told Wilkins's wife and Hay that this condition was caused by Wilkins's heavy drinking. According to David "Honeyboy" Edwards, whom Fred Hay interviewed in 1992, Wilkins had apparently suffered from this sickness since at least the 1950s. Carrie Wilkins and Hay finally convinced Wilkins to quit drinking and have the colostomy operation that the doctor recommended. For several years Wilkins did not drink, but by the mid-1970s he was once again drinking, only by this time he had gained substantial weight and given up smoking.

Wilkins's house, where his widow continued to reside until her death in 1998, was a small frame house that his parents, Frank and Parlee, had built when they moved to Memphis from the Mississippi Delta. Wilkins himself had been living there, off and on, since the late 1940s. Stackhouse and Willis

197

"Hillbilly" Kenibrew were currently living there with the Wilkinses. Through the years, many different musicians either visited or lived in that house with Wilkins. Those who stayed for longer periods of time included Pat Hare, Roland "Boy Blue" Hayes, and Wilkins's one-time brother-in-law, Robert Nighthawk. Kenibrew moved to Marianna, Arkansas, in 1973; Stackhouse stayed at Wilkins's until the late 1970s, when he returned to Crystal Springs, Mississippi, and Helena, Arkansas.

Wilkins mastered the guitar at an early age and became so proficient at playing other musicians' songs—learned in person and off records—that he was known in the northern Delta as the "Walking Seeburg," for a brand of jukebox. Give him a nickel and he would play your request. By the time he was in his mid-twenties, he was the most influential guitarist active in the Delta. Marc Ryan observed, "His ultimate contribution to the development of a modern blues guitar style is immense; his precociously early refinement and dissemination of his music place him alongside T-Bone Walker and Lonnie Johnson as a progenitor of the genre" (1992, 43).

Nearly every significant postwar Delta guitarist has recognized Wilkins's influence. For example, Jimmy Rogers said, "Joe Willie Wilkins was my favorite. He had a tone. He carried a good bottom. . . . I got a lotta licks from [Wilkins]" (Brisbin 1997, 17). Willie Johnson said, "He could play the blues the way he developed it. . . . he could play bass on his guitar and lead all at the same time. He'd stretch them fingers, man. Joe Willie, he was a terrific guitar player" (Brisbin 1995, 45). Music journalist Robert Palmer, in his well-received 1981 book *Deep Blues,* remarked that Willie Johnson's playing, via broadcasts from West Memphis radio station KWEM, were a significant but generally unrecognized influence on the development of white rockabilly and rock and roll guitar (1981a). Palmer was undoubtedly correct in his claim that West Memphis blues guitar was in many ways the progenitor of rock guitar, but he was wrong to limit this influence to Johnson's playing. In fact, it was that whole generation of guitarists who studied and played with Wilkins in the West Memphis area that should, more accurately, be credited with that impact. These musicians include not only Wilkins and his cousin Willie Johnson but also Pat Hare, Hubert Sumlin, L. D. McGee, and others. The impact that Wilkins had on guitar playing in early rock and roll and in those great postwar Chicago blues bands (especially those of Muddy Waters and Howlin' Wolf) can hardly be overstated.

While Wilkins was a mentor for many of blues' best musicians, he also taught them, and others, about life—the mundane and the spiritual. To many, Wilkins was nothing less than a master teacher and adviser. Little Milton Campbell told Steve LaVere and Hay of Wilkins' personal and musical influence: "Joe Willie taught me a heck of a lot; I never could do as much with a guitar as he could. To me, he is very artistic; sounds like two guitars at once— he plays rhythm and lead at the same time. He influenced me tremendously. Me personally, I think he's the greatest of blues guitarists. I think the world of him."

Wilkins's friend Houston Stackhouse (1910–80) was also a well-known and influential guitarist. He once played a number of string instruments and harmonica, but he is best known for the slide guitar style he had learned from Delta blues pioneer Tommy Johnson and which he later taught his cousin Robert Nighthawk. Earl Hooker and Sammy Lawhorn are among the many guitarists who have been influenced by Stackhouse's playing. In the liner notes of *Houston Stackhouse 1910–1980,* David Evans wrote, "There was no more central figure in the Delta blues scene over such a long period as it passed from a pre-war acoustic style to a post-war electric style than Houston Stackhouse" (Evans n.d.).

Wilkins played guitar on recordings of many of his fellow blues musicians, including Sonny Boy Williamson (Rice Miller), Willie Nix, Willie Love, Little Walter Jacobs, Big Walter Horton, Mose Vinson, Roosevelt Sykes, Joe Hill Louis, Elmore James, Arthur "Big Boy" Crudup, Floyd Jones, Jimmy DeBerry, and Memphis Al Williams. In 1973, Mimosa Records released the first record of Wilkins's singing on a 45 rpm. These two cuts, combined with eight live recordings and an impromptu tribute to Wilkins by Johnny Shines, were released on Adamo LP 9507, *Joe Willie Wilkins and His King Biscuit Boys,* in 1977. Field, concert, and studio recordings by Houston Stackhouse have been released on Arhoolie, Testament, Flyright, Blue Moon, Genes, and Wolf Records. Stackhouse accompanies Wilkins on some of the cuts on the Adamo LP.

The day of our visit, Wilkins, Stackhouse, and Kenibrew were recovering from their heavy drinking the night before. Things started slowly—with Wilkins being, not uncharacteristically, reticent and uninterested (though he could be, and often was, the exact opposite)—but became festive after sufficient beer had been consumed.

Houston, where did you go when you went up to New York with Hacksaw Harney?

[Stackhouse] First in Boston and then . . . We played, uh, one place there. I reckon they call it a club. It was a big place, you know. I was in Boston on the thirteenth, fourteenth, and the fifteenth. We played New York City a couple of times. ———I can't think of that fellow.

Did you do any recording records?

[Stackhouse] In Silver Springs. Silver Springs, Maryland.

What label was that for? Remember?

[Stackhouse] Adelphi.

The recordings that Harney and Stackhouse made for Adelphi Records in February 1972 were released posthumously, in the 1990s: Genes CD 9909 *Sweet Man,* by Richard "Hacksaw" Harney, and Genes CD 9904 *Cryin' Won't Help You,* by Houston Stackhouse.

Mr. Kenibrew, we talked to Houston pretty much the last time we come, but we didn't find out where you learned to play the bass or anything like that.

[Kenibrew] Well, uh, we learned it in Arkansas. And, uh, that's been about twenty-two years ago, now. Started to playing bass. Near as I can guess it.

Is that where you were born?

[Kenibrew] I was born in Mississippi. Crystal Springs, Mississippi.

Crystal Springs, [to Stackhouse] that's where you were born, too. Right?

[Stackhouse] That's right.

Did you two know each other when you were little?

[Kenibrew] I didn't know him when I's little. I was grown.

Did you go over to Arkansas with Houston?

[Kenibrew] I didn't go over there with him. He was over there before I was.

How did you learn to play?

[Kenibrew] Well, about him [Stackhouse] teaching me some and whatever I could see. Joe Willie Wilkins. So I just come on up with it the best I could, then . . .

Did you play on the radio show with Houston, Joe Willie, and Sonny Boy?

[Kenibrew] I never could play for that.

When did you come over to Memphis?

[Kenibrew] Oh, I came over to Memphis the year before last.

[Stackhouse] In '70, wasn't it?

[Kenibrew] In '70. What's it, '72?

[Stackhouse] Sixty-nine. Because . . .

[Wilkins] Umph.

[Stackhouse] I come up here in '70, I started staying up here in '70, right after we went to Washington.

[Wilkins] You go to see Washington.

[Stackhouse] You're ready, you're all ready? In '69 when we started staying up here.

Was that the, did you go to that big festival [to which] they had brought a lot of blues players in Washington?

[Kenibrew] We sure did. . . . I never had so much fun until I got there. I got to the place where I enjoyed myself just regular now.

In 1970, Wilkins, Stackhouse, and Kenibrew performed at the Festival of American Folklife in Washington, D.C.

See a lot of people you knew there?

[Kenibrew] I ain't see none that I knew about ————. [Laughter.]

[Stackhouse] Lot of people there, I can tell you that. Seventy-seven, seven hundred and fifty thousand people 'round there.

[Kenibrew] There's some up there say they was eight hundred thousand.

Whew, that's a lot! . . . Are you about ready to start, Mr. Wilkins?

[Wilkins] What you want me to do now? [Stackhouse and Kenibrew laugh.]

We just want to ask you a few questions and things [Stackhouse laughs]. . . . And get you to play a little bit [Stackhouse laughs].

[Wilkins] Mmmmm. [Laughter, Wilkins feigns laughter.] Uhh. I'm mighty
————. [Stackhouse laughs, Wilkins feigns laughter.]

[Stackhouse] Ah, weekends, we ———— and so, you know, we can ————.
[Stackhouse is inaudible here but was apparently referring to his having played
at the University of Arkansas the previous weekend.] . . . That's right. Here one
of the old bill. This fellow, you know, that Mose and them that played with
them, just have a bill sketched in, you know, that's who all was on there. . . .
Yeah, had a nice time on it. . . . I enjoyed it. . . . They was having a big goat barbecue and a fresh glass of ———— on Saturday night. I told them I'd keep playing Saturday evenings. . . . Yeah, it was a nice time, oh, a nice time.

Mose "Boogie" Vinson (born 1917 in Holly Springs, Mississippi) is a fine pianist still performing
in Memphis today. Wilkins recorded with Vinson for Sun Records in 1953. These sides were released on Bear CD 15524 AH *Joe Hill Louis: The Be-Bop Boy with Walter Horton and Mose Vinson*.

Mr. Wilkins, would you mind answering a few questions?

[Wilkins] Uh-huh, no suh. If I may. [Stackhouse laughs.]

Can you tell us where and when you were born?

[Wilkins] In, at Bobo, Mississippi.

Wilkins described Bobo as "a big place. One store and a gin" (O'Neal 1973, 13). Bobo is in
Coahoma County, east of Clarksdale. Winifred Kellersberger Vass lists Bobo as one of the possible Bantu place-names in the southern United States. *Bobo* is Bantu for "they" or "them." Vass
described Bobo, Mississippi, as "an early plantation settlement with a population of 110 in the
1930s. This disjunctive pronoun was probably the only needed reference to the white masters
and owners" (1979, 52). W. C. Handy, in his autobiography, recounts tales of President Theodore
Roosevelt's visit to Bobo to hunt bear (1970, 88–89). Wilkins remembered it as a wild country
in his childhood, one inhabited by bears and panthers (Hay 1979).

And where was that in Mississippi?

[Wilkins] Delta part.

And do you remember what year that was?

[Wilkins] Nineteen twenty-three.

Wilkins told others (including Jim O'Neal and Steve LaVere) that he was born January 7, 1923
(O'Neal 1973; LaVere 1977). Fred Davis reported in *Blues Unlimited* in 1968 that Wilkins was

born January 7, 1922 (1971b, 144). Wilkins's birth certificate states his birth date as January 7, 1921.

How did you first start learning to play the guitar?

[Wilkins] Well, I picked up the first one I came to. [Stackhouse laughs, and Wilkins's voice is muffled.] . . . I didn't put it down after I picked it up.

Did your father play guitar?

[Wilkins] Yes.

He didn't like your, did he like your playing or did he? . . .

[Wilkins] No, he just didn't want me to mess with that guitar. [Stackhouse laughs.]

He didn't want you to learn guitar. Why?

[Wilkins] He was just crazy about that guitar. Wasn't no use me messing with it at t'all.

Did he play the blues?

[Wilkins] That's all he played.

And what was his name?

[Wilkins] Frank Wilkins.

Frank Wilkins (1894–1966) was well known in the northern Delta. His son remembered him playing with Richard "Hacksaw" Harney, Walter "Pat" Rhodes, Fiddlin' Sam Harris, Willie Brown, and other Delta musicians.

Did he ever record?

[Wilkins] I really don't know.

Did you ever play any other instruments besides, than the guitar?

[Wilkins] No, the guitar was all I could walk away with. [Laughter.] The others were too tough for me. [Laughter.] Too tough for me.

On other occasions, Wilkins told Hay that he had started on harmonica and learned some accordion and fiddle before settling in with the guitar. Wilkins said his mother had made him give up the harmonica because it caused him nosebleeds. He still occasionally played harmonica as an adult (see the Big Amos Patton chapter).

Davis wrote that Wilkins got his first guitar, at age sixteen, when he walked the nine miles from Bobo to Alligator to M. C. Kline's Hardware and paid six dollars for a Stella guitar (1971b, 144).

When did you go to Arkansas to start working with Sonny Boy?

[Wilkins] In '41.

You stayed in Mississippi all that time?

[Wilkins] All that time. All over Mississippi. [Stackhouse laughs.] . . . Bottom to top. . . . Playing around.

Was there any other influential guitarists influenced your style of guitar playing besides your father?

[Wilkins] Well, I just liked it all. I likes all music. . . . All of it sounds good to me. . . . I'm just crazy about music.

But did any individual player teach you any techniques or anything or you learn anything from listening to him play?

[Wilkins] Oh, I was, could, I picked up, I pick up a whole lot from different people, myself. I never had nobody teach me. I just picked it up myself.

Did you ever do any playing on the medicine show or any of the things like that, the traveling groups that would go around?

[Wilkins] No, I'd be by myself and find somebody to work. We two would play a week or two or a day or two and I'd be gone somewhere else. [Laughter.]

Did you ever have any partner that you stuck with for, you know, a long period of time?

[Wilkins] Oh, Stack is the one I can remember now. We been together a long time. All of the rest of them are dead but me, and so about the onliest one who stuck with it so long time. All the rest of them dead but me.

Did you learn to sing just to sing while you play guitar?

[Wilkins] Same way I learned to play guitar. . . . Nuu, I just open my mouth and start to hollering. [Laughter.]

Did you used to hear blues singers or guitarists around your hometown and all when you were growing up?

[Wilkins] Oh, well, there weren't too many around my hometown, but after I started running around, I run up on a gang of them.

Who did you used to see?

[Wilkins] Oh-ohh, man, I can't, I can't even remember who all I didn't see.... That's been a long time ago.

Did you ever come in contact with Charlie Patton?

[Wilkins] Well, uh, I got close enough to him, I could, I hear from him all right, but I never did play none with him.

Charlie Patton (1887–1934) is the legendary Delta blues guitarist who influenced a whole generation of blues musicians. Wilkins told Jim O'Neal, "Oh, he was all the world to me. I thought there wasn't nobody else but him. This fellow was playin' his guitar and hollerin' loud. So I wonder how can one man do that?" (1973, 14).

Did you play with Tommy Johnson like Houston played?

[Wilkins] No, I never played with Tommy, but I knew him.

Tommy Johnson (1896–1956) was one of the first generation of Delta blues artists to record, and it was Johnson from whom Stackhouse had learned to play and whose vocal style, with its falsetto "yodels," Stackhouse copied. David Evans published a biography, *Tommy Johnson* (1971), and *Big Road Blues: Tradition and Creativity in Folk Blues* (1982), an analysis of the larger group of musicians and songs of Johnson's milieu.

Did you know Sonny Boy before you went over to Arkansas or did you happen to just meet him there?

[Wilkins] Yeah, I knowed him for some time.

Sonny Boy Williamson (a.k.a. Rice, Willie, or Aleck Miller), who had passed away in 1965, was the influential harmonica player, singer, and poet who started the King Biscuit Time show on Helena Arkansas radio station KFFA (Hay 1987).

He ask you to come over?

[Wilkins] Uh-huh.

You met him in Mississippi?

[Wilkins sings] Mississippi, Mississippi.

Had you played with him before?

[Wilkins] Yeah, I'd played with him before. I didn't broadcast with him before, we just . . . First time I broadcast with him was when I came to Helena.

How long did you play with Sonny Boy?

[Wilkins] Lord, '41 until he died, off and on.

In 1941, Wilkins joined Sonny Boy broadcasting on Helena radio station KFFA's King Biscuit Time show. In the 1940s, Helena was a center of blues activity, and most of the active blues musicians of the day played there at one time or another. Sonny Boy and Wilkins were at the heart of this scene. Other accounts have Wilkins joining the King Biscuit Time show anywhere from 1940 to 1943.

Did you do other playing around [in the] Arkansas area besides the radio show?

[Wilkins] Well, we broadcast Jonesboro back to Helena; we broadcast Clarksdale awhile.

[Stackhouse] Monroe, Louisiana.

[Wilkins] Uh-huh, yeah. . . .

[Stackhouse] And you went to Monroe, Louisiana, wasn't you?

[Wilkins] Clarksdale. Yeah, we was down there three months, Little Rock, and then we'd go somewhere else, some of the different places. . . . Yeah. . . . We worked for Guy Croix. We worked for Guy Croix in a, uh, I can't think of the name of the station. Jackson. Broadcast out of Jackson for about three or four months.

[Stackhouse] You was in Monroe, Louisiana, where you . . .

[Wilkins] Yeah.

I understand. You either played with or you had some influence on, influenced B. B. King. Could you tell us something about your relationship with him?

[Wilkins] Oh, we worked together. He came, B. B. King came to West Memphis before I did. . . . He got to there about three or four weeks before I got to West Memphis. I left Helena and came to West Memphis and broadcast from a West Memphis station, and B. came on over here to Memphis.

Can you remember when this was?

[Wilkins] Oh, it was '50, I say '50, about '49 or '50.

Wilkins joined Sonny Boy on radio station KWEM in West Memphis, Arkansas. He later broadcast with other musicians over KWEM, including Willie Love and Willie Nix. King had temporarily accompanied Sonny Boy before Wilkins's arrival. King later became a DJ and performer on Memphis station WDIA. On other occasions, Wilkins recalled how he had worked with the young King and had encouraged him to play in the less technically demanding single-string style for which he has become world famous. Wilkins loved King's singing and always regarded King essentially as a blues vocalist.

Wilkins played an important role in the development of the very popular postwar, single-string style of guitar playing popularized by B. B. King, Albert King, Little Milton, and others. Marc Ryan has perceptively observed that "Wilkins' style became the template for a whole generation of aspiring guitarists throughout the Delta, including two who would help to forge the next link in the evolution of the style, B. B. King and Little Milton" (1992, 43).

Yeah. Did you play with him?

[Wilkins] Em-huh. We played together.

What did you think of his playing?

[Wilkins] I like it. I just like it. That boy sing the blues so good that it just makes me, I don't know [Stackhouse giggles], like I'm fixing to shout or something. [Laughter.]

[Stackhouse] ———— also Robert Junior Lockwood. [Laughs.]

Robert Lockwood (born in 1915 in Marvel, Arkansas), a brilliant and influential guitarist, played with Sonny Boy and Wilkins in the South and later became the premier sideman in the blues recording center of Chicago. He moved to Cleveland, Ohio, in 1961 and is still actively performing. Lockwood is often celebrated today for having been Robert Johnson's step-son.

[Wilkins, to Stackhouse] Keep it easy, kin'.

Have you seen him since?

[Wilkins] Seen B.? . . . Yeah, I saw B. several times. I seen, I seen him often when he come here, but the biggest time I'd be out of town. . . . He'd be here, so I ain't seen him now in about five, four or five years. But he's been here since then, but I just have not, you know, been in town. . . . Yeah.

[Stackhouse] He supposed to be ————.

[Wilkins, to Stackhouse] That's where y'all were Saturday night?

[Stackhouse] Uh-huh.

Well, would you mind trying to play a little for us?

[Wilkins] Shoooooot no. [Stackhouse laughs.] Don't know how bad I feel. Throat sore. [Stackhouse laughs.] Imagine old Stack play some now. I may play some in a while.

Like some more beer?

[Stackhouse] No.

[Wilkins] No, I can, I reckon, I hope that will help me out some.

You drink some more of that, looks like it might help you a little.

[Wilkins] ——— y'all reach in, reach in, y'all reach in and get you [cans popping].

[Stackhouse] I think I'll try one more. That will make me feel a little better. . . . I got on one of those bad hangovers over at ———. . . . Having my fun; getting into those bottles and stuff. . . . Sometimes trying to taste a little too much and I [laughs], and it's a drag when you feeling bad, you know, when uh, you puke.

[Wilkins] When you turn on your box [amplifier] there, just . . .

[Stackhouse] Be fine in a minute ———. Have to get me ——— [speaking as he walks into next room] . . .

Did you come here to Memphis with Houston?

[Wilkins] No, no. I came to West Memphis . . . with Sonny Boy, yeah, he sent for me.

[Stackhouse] See how the cords do together on this thing, 'cause one started, one of these knobs off my rig and I have to shimmy [Stackhouse working on guitar and amp].

When did you come here, to live in Memphis?

[Wilkins] Uh, '48. [Stackhouse trying out guitar in background. He and Kenibrew discuss tuning, mostly inaudibly.]

[Kenibrew, to Stackhouse] We're together.

[Stackhouse] Oh yeah.

[Kenibrew] Yeah. [Stackhouse plays some licks.]

[Wilkins] Where did you learn that, cousin?

[Stackhouse] Huh?

[Wilkins] Why don't you cut me up some bream there?

Bream is a common freshwater fish with a mild, sweet flavor.

[Stackhouse] Oh, Lord! I just want to be on a little small boogie or something.

[Wilkins] I don't see nothing that would be no better. [Laughter. Stackhouse plays lead, Wilkins chords along, and Kenibrew plays bass on instrumental boogie. Midway through, when Kenibrew starts speeding up, Stackhouse yells, "Wait a minute!" Wilkins strums last chorus and brings song to its conclusion.]

That was real good. What was the name of that?

[Kenibrew] Uh? . . . The "Boogie-Woogie" or the "Stackhouse and the Joe Willie and Hillbill." [Laughter.]

[Stackhouse] The "Stackhouse, Joe Willie, and Hillbilly Boogie-Woogie." [Laughter.]

That's an original song?

[Wilkins] Ah, no.

[Stackhouse laughs] Ties a rope on you, wouldn't it?

[Wilkins] I thought it, how many more times. [Wilkins coughs badly and tries to clear his throat.]

That's what you're called, "Hillbilly"?

[Kenibrew] That's what they call me.

Why do they, how did you get that name? [Stackhouse laughs.]

[Kenibrew indicating Stackhouse] He gave it to me. [Laughter.]

[Wilkins] Good to the last taste. [Laughter.]

Did you finish it? Need another one?

[Wilkins] Yes, she dead. She dead and gone. [Plays "Mean Little Woman"; Stackhouse sings and Wilkins plays lead.] Behave yourself! Behave yourself! [Laughter.] Yeahhhhhh.

That was good. What was the name of that one?

[Wilkins] Yeah, yeah, yeah.

[Stackhouse] That was "Mean Little Woman."

Did you write that one?

[Wilkins] Uh-huh.

[Stackhouse] Well, uh, I's just put it on record, I ain't, you know, I put it on record.

That's on record?

[Wilkins] I say yeah, yeah, yeah. [Stackhouse laughs, beer cans popping.] I don't know, sounds pretty good.

[Stackhouse] Uh-huh.

[Wilkins] Can you, can't you whup that back on me once? . . . Whup it on me there once and we can see how it going to be. [We play back the song. Laughter.] Mmm uh mm.

Can you play any other instruments besides the bass guitar?

[Kenibrew's response is inaudible as Stackhouse tunes guitar.]

[Wilkins] What you got [coughs] going on there, cousin?

[Stackhouse] I just don't [Wilkins coughs], I just as well give them a little slide or something.

[Wilkins] This Christmas cold is getting me.

[Stackhouse] A little slide might could the microphone might pick it up clearly. Then we can reel back here. [Stackhouse plays some licks while microphones are adjusted.] You boys want to play "Sweet Life Man" or "Getting Tired"?

[Wilkins] Yeah, better "Get Tired" on me once.

[Stackhouse] "Getting Tired." [Stackhouse sings and plays slide, Kenibrew plays, Wilkins plays quietly in the background. Stackhouse hollers just before he takes guitar solo: "Well, alright, let's work ———!"] Whup that back and see if it picked it up any better. [Song is played back. Laughter.] I'm like Joe Willie. [Laughter.]

LaVere attributes authorship of "I'm Getting Tired" to Stackhouse on Stackhouse's Genes CD. The music publisher is listed as Blind Basement Music, BMI (1994). Stackhouse's cousin Robert Nighthawk recorded the same song for Pete Welding's Testament label in Chicago in 1964 (Testament LP 2215 *Masters of Modern Blues, Vol. 4: Robert Nighthawk—Houston Stackhouse*).

[Wilkins] My my, um, um-um, um.

Mr. Wilkins, did you ever play slide yourself?

[Wilkins] That I never did, sometime, but I never let him [Stackhouse] know it. [Laughter.] Yeah, lawd.

Would you try a little bit of it out?

[Wilkins] Yeah, I ought to be able to do whiles he's around. [Laughter.] Yeah, well, uh, that's sort of too daring behind that, I put mine, I hid it the first time I see'd him. [Laughter.] He would pull it out and he went to wailing down on it. I said, "Let me put this thing back in my pocket." [Laughter.] He's bad, man. Everyone scared to slide around him, man. I told him, "I ain't going, I ain't." [Laughter.] Man, I hurried up and let him alone. [Laughter, Wilkins coughs.]

Wilkins was a superb slide guitarist, as illustrated on his Mimosa recording of "Mr. Downchild" and his versions of "Me and the Devil" and "I Feel like Going Home" on the Adamo LP.

[Stackhouse] A fellow said he's got to ——— over of something.

[Wilkins] . . . Yes, sir.

I know you do some pretty fine singing. We'd sure like to hear you do some of your singing.

[Wilkins] I know, but I, uh, the other night here—y'all better catch me some other time when I more at myself than now, because I ain't, I ain't ne'r good now. [Stackhouse laughs.] I've been so sorry.

[Stackhouse] Weekend done killed you. [Laughs.]

We'd like to hear you anyways, even though—I think he's out of beer. You better give him another one now.

[Wilkins] Nooo, ut-uh, beer ain't going to stand ———. Plenty more from where that come? [Laughter.]

Here, I tell you what.

[Wilkins] That's okay.

Here we go [offers money to Wilkins].

[Wilkins] Ain't nobody to go get the beer?

You want another beer right here?

[Wilkins] No, I got some more of this here right now. Think I got a little bitty swallow. No. You better hand me that one there, 'cause this one's near about out. . . . [Laughter.] Well, I see. Somebody's going to have to get the beer.

[Stackhouse] Got the beer.

[Wilkins] Keep that then. I keep that, that's what I've been looking for. [Stackhouse playing in background.]

That's just to make it worth you singing, if you'd sing some.

[Wilkins] Oh, well, I tell you better do then. You'd better let me put it in my pocket first, because when I get through singing you going to take it back. [Laughter.]

If we give it to you first, y'all only have to do one or two songs for it.

[Wilkins] Now, I ain't going to make, to sing no two of them. [Laughter.] I'm going to try one. Maybe. Now, wait a minute. [Emphatically] Y'all don't know, y'all don't know, y'all don't know how sick I am.

[Stackhouse] See that boy got on a party last night and didn't get in until two o'clock. . . . Big card party. . . . See, I was already dead. I didn't go out. They kept partying. [Laughter.]

Here you go, you go ahead and put it in your pocket first and you sing what you can.

[Stackhouse] Well, start him a little number. I've done bust my throat trying a little bit.

[Wilkins] Mm uh.

[Stackhouse] Now you sing them a number. . . .

[Wilkins] I'm going to ease back here in C. [Stackhouse laughs, Wilkins plays "I Believe I'll Dust My Broom." Eventually Stackhouse sings it and Wilkins forces him to play lead without slide.]

Robert Johnson recorded "I Believe I'll Dust My Broom" in 1936. Elmore James made the song his signature piece. He first recorded "Broom" in 1951 for Trumpet Records in Jackson, Mississippi. According to Wilkins, James got upset with Sonny Boy for duplicating his famous guitar lick on the harmonica and refused to record any other songs.

That was real good. Where did you learn that song?

[Stackhouse] Well, I learned it around, you know, traveling around. . . . That was one of Elmore James's tunes. . . . I used to work with him.

Joe Willie "Elmore" James (1918–63) was a close friend of Wilkins. They often played together. They recorded together, and Wilkins was an important influence on James's nonslide guitar playing. According to Wilkins, James began to go by the name Elmore rather than Joe Willie to distinguish himself from Wilkins.

Did you like his playing?

[Stackhouse] I liked it. Yeah. We used to work together a whole lot, me and him. . . . We used to, all in Mississippi. Well, he used to come out of Mississippi over in Arkansas and work with us up around Parkins and Wynnes and different places. . . . He and I used to work a whole lot together down in Drew. I used to go there with him and play a ———, Boyd Gilmore and them, they was staying in Mississippi at that time. They was farming down there at the time, and so I worked with them down there. Then we worked down there for a long time and then, I reckon better than a year.

[Wilkins] Where would that be? . . .

[Stackhouse] That was in the, uh, early fifties, late, around the early fifties. . . . Maybe around '51 or '52 or somewhere along there. It was just a little bit before Boyd Gilmore done his recording. Do you remember what year he done his recording in? . . . Well, you know, he done some recording along, when he left here, then he went on to St. Louis or somewhere or somewhere down in Florida, one thing. That was in either '51 or '52, I believe. I don't know for sure, now. Because I played at Tunica then a whole lot after he done his recording and left. I had quit playing at Drew with him. He'd be down there to [Kerman?], I'd be playing at Tunica for, had a little, what I call a hard place down there. He ——— for me on the weekend, every Saturday night and Sunday. At Tunica, Mississippi. That's where I lost track of Boyd Gilmore at until '61, when he came out of St. Louis, Florida, and different places. He went on to Pine Bluff and started living over there. Playing, and working at the old folks home, you know, nursing home. . . . But he play music all, every weekend, you know. So I went over there and found him and tried working together and worked over there about three years over there together. . . . Now he's out in California, now. . . . Elmore died.

Boyd Gilmore (born 1913 in Belzoni, Mississippi, died 1976 in Fresno, California) was a popular slide guitarist and rumored to be Elmore James's cousin. Gilmore recorded with Ike Turner for Modern Records in 1952.

[Wilkins] . . . Oh, Popeye gone. . . . I said old Popeye gone.

[Stackhouse] Mmm. Done got back on? Okay.

[Wilkins clears throat, whispers sigh,] Little Max say, "I'se just a little bit ashamed right along now."

[Stackhouse, laughing] Ain't no need to be ashamed. . . . Well, I should be ashamed Saturday evening [in Fayetteville, Arkansas] over there ——— those people out [laughs]. Out on the mountain with that wind blowing so I couldn't keep my hat on. It blowed right off my head ———. [Laughter.] Had to go pick it up for me. [Laughter.] Made me put it on my knee. When the sun was shining it was pretty, but the wind was just howling over there.

Yeah. Was there a lot of people there?

[Stackhouse] A lot of people.

[Wilkins] Say they had a big time. [Wilkins plays softly on guitar, then plays "Glory of the Man," complete with spoken asides and general laughter.] Lay it on me, Brother Stack.

[Stackhouse] Well, alright [phone rings] . . .

[Wilkins] Joe Willie? Ahh, hello. That's right. No ma'am, sure ain't. Well, because they hadn't told her, but I [tape recorder turned off] . . . little thing. I don't know.

Did you make it up as you went?

[Wilkins] Since you been sitting here telling me to do the singing. [Laughter.]

Let me play that back for you, let you hear how good that sounds.

[Wilkins] Okay. ———. [We play back song.] Yes, sirre! Boy, tell a mule and then some. [Laughter.] Yes, um, before we brought Stack home Sunday, we brought him on down to Hughes, where we was working. Hughes, where we was working Sunday night. They brought him over and I think they forgot to go home. [Laughter.]

For a description of Wilkins, Stackhouse, and Kenibrew performing at Robinson's Café in Hughes, Arkansas, see Jim O'Neal's "Live Blues" (1972).

[Stackhouse] We all got together and went to clowning, boy—talk about having fun. [Laughter.]

You forget to go home, too?

[Wilkins] No, I like to, they brought me, though. [Laughter.]

[Carrie] Had to bring you home. [Laughter.]

Louise "Carrie" Ethridge Wilkins, or "Ma," as she was known in the community, was Wilkins's wife. Wilkins asked Ethridge's mother for the Arkansas belle when she was only fourteen years old. Carrie worked as a cook in 1972 and had previously been a professional dancer and vocalist on the traveling minstrel show circuit. She died on Labor Day, September 7, 1998 (Hay 1999).

[Wilkins] Boy, them peoples enjoyed theirselves Sunday night. [Laughter.] Yeah, down there. . . . And we's fighting back hard, you know. I was already mad at him. Me and Stack; was already about mad with him. He was late getting in there. I was looking for him.

[Stackhouse] That's just such a long way, and it was about 9:30 before we got kicked off. That's a long way from Little Rock. . . . We arrived . . .

[Wilkins] It over there somewhere. I don't know. I never been there.

[Stackhouse] We arrived . . .

[Wilkins] Fayetteville, I ain't never been to Fayetteville.

[Stackhouse] We arrived at twenty minutes of ten and we got to Memphis at 6:30, and then they had to carry back to Hughes, and that's forty miles.

[Wilkins] Had to bring Steve [LaVere] home and then had to go back. See? Past by where he was supposed to come, where we was working at, to come to town, Memphis, to bring Steve home and then had to come back.

[Stackhouse] On the other side, you know, when there was Bukka White and everyone.

[Wilkins] They bring all them with them. . . .

[Stackhouse] And Big Charlene [Peeples] and, you know, different ones. . . . To bring them all on to Memphis with Steve, now. I had to go back, had to go to Lehi, cut off and go down 79 to Hughes, and, uh, that's forty miles from Memphis ———. They was glad to see me, though, when I got in there. [Laughter.] They wasn't too mad, they was smiling when they saw me walk in there. [Laughter.] That amplifier was cutting up with them, you know. I reckon that was what had them so mad. It wasn't acting right. Put it in the shop and got it out and it went to clowning with them, you know. Something wasn't right there.

[Wilkins] It's like sticking it in and it keep slipping out. [Laughter.] If this ain't a biscuit to cancel anybody. [Laughter.] Well, I can get the ——— playing anybody you ever seen in your life.

[Stackhouse] Now, he can't, he ain't going to get to carry it [the amp] this evening, now, 'cause he went to take care of them.

[Wilkins] Yes, he got them cold again. So, well, he want in, me and you, here, I stand looking here.

[Stackhouse] He'll probably check it out tomorrow.

[Wilkins] Tomorrow! Tomorrow just another day. [Laughter.] So I, well, okay. Yeah, Stack came in there, made me so doggone mad, I said, "You going to go get me a bottle of gin or I don't know what I'm going to do to you." [Laughter.] He hurried on up there and got that for me. [Stackhouse laughs.] Somebody ask me, he say, Hillbill, I think, uh, boy say he don't drink gin much.

"No, it ain't none of mine, it belong to Stack." I done killed it then. [Laughter.] He said, "What you do that for?" I said, "He told me to keep it for him." [Laughter.] I put it where I knowed it would be safe. [Laughter.]

Trumpet Records owner Lillian McMurry (always referred to fondly as "Miss Lillian" by Wilkins) told Hay in 1993, "Pass a fifth of liquor between Sonny Boy, Elmore, and Joe Willie, and by the time they'd each raised that bottle once, it would be empty." Hay heard many stories (warnings) from Wilkins's fellow musicians that Wilkins could (and often did) lift a full pint to his lips, looking as if he were taking a little swig, and drain the bottle.

[Stackhouse] We had some fun. I laid the whiskey on him. I commence pouring them half pints to him and he went to standing up rocking that bass there then, you know. [Laughter.]

[Kenibrew] Yeah, feel like laying down out there now. [Laughter.]

[Stackhouse] Well, this . . .

[Wilkins] I'm glad to be seeing that somebody . . .

[Kenibrew] I think I was still drinking out there. I've been down in the dumps.

[Wilkins] You wasn't down much last night, was you? [Laughter.]

[Kenibrew] Down just as low as a snake belly last night. [Laughter.]

[Wilkins] You know nobody knowed it.

[Kenibrew] I just wouldn't be [laughter] . . .

[Stackhouse] You drunk as me, telling me about you done fooled around and got drunk again when they come. [Laughter.]

[Wilkins] Boy, boy, boy. I know there wasn't no need of me going up there and I already knocked out, I ain't going up there and let them kill me there. All that Scotch and beer and whiskey and everything. [Laughter.] Yeah, ole Stack deduct that, boy, he deduct that. He said, "I'll be on in a few minutes." [Laughter.]

[Stackhouse] Joe Willie speaking of the Mule there.

"Mule" was a popular nickname for Wilkins. Piano great Roosevelt Sykes told Hay, in 1973, that St. Louis guitarist Henry Townsend, who was also known by the nickname "Mule," was "Mr. Mule" and that Wilkins was "Mr. Mr. Mule."

[Wilkins] All the drinks he got up there, he bought it. He started the party rolling again. I said, "Well, now, I know I be too weak to be getting up." I said, "You just bring it here, 'cause I ain't going to be able to reach at the bottle and drink, too." [Laughter.] He says [laughs] ———, so I just lay on down there and wait. [Laughter.] And yesterday evening they went to doubling back on us. [Laughing hard] He done got weak, and I'm beginning to feel better now. I looked at him and change my mind. I say, "I feel sorry for you but ain't nothing I can do; I'm going to hurry up and try to get back down there with you." [Laughter.]

[Stackhouse] Two o'clock when they come in the other night. But they wore me out, jumping up answering phone. "Who is this? ——— give them a message. What you want with the space ———?"

[Wilkins] [High pitched] Mm huh.

[Stackhouse] I just give them a message. I was sick like a coon.

[Wilkins] Lordy, Lordy, Lordy. It was something else there. [Blows nose.]

[Stackhouse] That sure brought me to life. I did have, I feeling rough.

[Wilkins] Some good for this cold I got on me, too, you know that.

[Stackhouse] I was feeling pretty rough last night when I went to bed, but now I'm feeling right smart better.

[Wilkins] Ah, cold better leave now. . . .

[Stackhouse] But if I had a went up there and doubled up on it last night, I'd might not be any good today. [Laughter, Stackhouse plays guitar softly in background.]

Mr. Wilkins, I notice you don't use a pick. Do you, have you ever used a pick before?

[Wilkins] I used to. . . . Mm huh.

Why did you, is there any special reason you decided to . . .

[Wilkins] I just stop using it. Got a little, picked up the back a little bit [in reference to the thumbnail on his right hand]. I went to getting old and real slow. I just stop using the picks 'cause I make a mistake with one finger, I get with the whole hand now quick, see, but it going to want to pick it that a way. It going to break the strings or something, so I just let them alone. [Laughter.]

Well, your thumbnail does pretty good.

[Wilkins] Yeahhh, but it's [his thumbnail] getting awful mighty skinny there [laughter]. . . . See where the shavings getting to be at? That brother had me going up side that ———. [With great hilarity] Now, you, golly, let me look at that scoundrel, you all. Shit. I ain't in a bit better shape. Uhh, shit. [Wild laughter.]

[Stackhouse] That's, that's the sign of real ———.

[Wilkins, laughing] Man, what you done talking about, sure enough.

[Stackhouse] You had done broke it off on the end.

[Wilkins] I know that scoundrel whipped y'all, but I didn't know y'all let him go and tear all that off. [Laughter] . . . What did Hacksaw tell you to say? What did Hacksaw tell you?

Richard "Hacksaw" Harney (1902–73) was an outstanding guitarist and pianist whom Wilkins had known since childhood. Harney made his living primarily from tuning pianos and he traveled up and down the Mississippi River Valley plying his trade. He and his brother (as "Pet and Can") accompanied accordionist Walter Rhodes and vocalist Pearl Dickson on recordings for Columbia in 1927. Harney and Stackhouse toured the Northeast in 1972 as "Hack 'n' Stack."

[Stackhouse, laughing] You talking about the guitar?

[Wilkins] Yeah. . . . Yeah, what did he tell you about the guitar? Still not give you no piece of that pie.

[Stackhouse, laughing] Uh-huh, I didn't need a piece of that pie.

[Wilkins] Oh, Lord.

[Stackhouse] That was down here at the festival over there to D.C., uh-huh. . . .

[Wilkins] That's a fellow you used to see. I remember when . . .

[Stackhouse] He eat that pie. He too lazy to get up there and walk, but every time I moved he wanted me to get up and bring him a piece. [Laughter.]

[Wilkins, laughing] Get yourself a little. [Laughter.]

[Stackhouse] I got him an armful. I said ———— put them on the table where he lay his guitar at. I went out, I left him in there. I don't know whether he finished them all or not. [Laughter.]

[Wilkins, laughing] Wow, Lordy. [Stackhouse plays "What's That Taste like Gravy?"]

Tampa Red (Hudson Whittaker) and Georgia Tom (Thomas Dorsey) recorded this song in Chicago for Vocalion in 1929. Jackson, Mississippi, artist Johnny Temple recorded a version called "What Is That Smells like Gravy?" in New York for Decca in 1938. When Stackhouse performed this song, he added the line, in response to the question asked in the song's title, "Go ask Tampa Red and his best ole lady, too."

That was real good.

[Stackhouse] Thank you so much. [Laughs] . . . That was "What's That Flying So High," the astronauts, you know. [Laughter.]

Did you make that up yourself?

[Stackhouse] Eh, I got it off, thinking about recording it pretty soon.

[Wilkins] That's a ———— over there, though. . . . What, is that, what's that say do? . . . You know I like the way you say 'cause you sure going to get ———— guitar. Pass it here to me. [Laughter.]

You want to play us another song since that one was interrupted? [Stackhouse picking away in the background.]

[Wilkins] Ut-o, ut-o, ut-o [laughter] . . . Ut-o . . . Ut-o. Ut-o . . .

[Stackhouse] Sing them the little number there.

Sounded so good, look like you'd want to do it.

[Wilkins] No, no. No, what number?

[Stackhouse] The number you sung in Washington.

[Wilkins] I don't know what it is.

Yeah, sure you do.

[Wilkins] No, drunk as I was. [Laughter.]

[Stackhouse] Can't get your hands on no money, my women keep tipping out on you.

[Wilkins] Oh, that one.

[Stackhouse] Yeah. Sing that one for me.

[Wilkins] I hear you. I'd done a whole lot better if that Big Boy Crudup wasn't there.

Arthur "Big Boy" Crudup (1905–74) was a popular Mississippi singer/guitarist. He recorded prolifically from 1941 to the 1970s. Many of the songs he penned became classics. He and Wilkins had worked together often in the past. In 1952, Wilkins and Sonny Boy accompanied Crudup on his recordings for the Trumpet label.

[Stackhouse, laughing] That scoundrel got with you, didn't he!

Were you playing with him?

[Wilkins] Who?

Big Boy Crudup?

[Wilkins] Mm huh.

[Stackhouse] Big Boy Crudup was getting so much of that fire water, he call it. Everywhere you look around Big Boy Crudup would be a fifth of that fire water. [Laughter.]

[Wilkins] I told him I didn't want anything to drink. I told him I didn't want anything to drink, time I seen him. [Laughter.] I didn't want anything to drink now. And he went to talking about me and all, calling me all kinds of bad names and going on. I say, "I don't care what you get to drink, I'm going to drink some of it anyhow, now." [Laughter.]

[Stackhouse] Every time I looked around up there y'all had a fifth of fire water, a quart or something.

[Wilkins] That [Ralph?] kept on toting there. James did. Mess around and he done got us two fifths there whupped up together. And he done got near about drunk and forgot about it now. And now I'm getting drunk, too. And now we had to go and leave ———. And that motherhopper, he didn't want to go to bed that night 'cause he thought I'd beat him back and get it, and

I didn't want to go to bed because I thought he'd beat me back to get it. [Laughter.] Whenever he'd come up, I'd say, "Here, here I is." [Laughter.] Yeah, yeah, yeah. [Wilkins plays "It's Too Bad"; Stackhouse and Kenibrew accompany. Wilkins includes an additional verse to the version he recorded for the Mimosa label.]

In 1973, Steve LaVere and Fred Hay recorded Joe Willie Wilkins and the King Biscuit Boys for LaVere's Mimosa label. The band included Stackhouse, guitar; Roland "Boy Blue" Hayes, harmonica; Melvin Lee, bass; and Homer Jackson, drums. The songs "It's Too Bad" and "Mr. Downchild" were released on Mimosa. "Mr. Downchild" (first recorded by Sonny Boy and Wilkins for the Trumpet label in 1951) and a longer version of "It's Too Bad" (with Boy Blue's full chorus) were released on Adamo 9507 *Joe Willie Wilkins and His King Biscuit Boys*. Wilkins claimed authorship of "It's Too Bad"; however, his old playing partner, pianist Eddie Boyd, first recorded it in the mid-1960s, and his version was released as a single on Mojo 2167.

Oh yeah! [Stackhouse laughs.]

[Wilkins] Yeah.

Did you write that song?

[Wilkins] Since you been sitting here. [Laughter.]

You going to name it?

[Wilkins] Well, if you want to. . . . You do it. [Stackhouse laughs.] . . . Yeah, Lordy. . . . Yeah, just let me, let me lick it one time there. [Stackhouse laughs.] ——— a lemon, let me lick it once. [We play back the song.] Yes, yes, yes. Boy, boy, boy. Yes, sir. Just need this day and one more like it. [Sneezes.]

Bless you.

[Wilkins] Huh? [Laughter.]

[Stackhouse] Oh, my.

[Wilkins, softly] Well, y'all just . . . [emphatically] I know, I know, I looked at those old people saying, I woke up this day, I said, "Now, what is that in that paper sack? Is that anything in there that will help any?" [Laughter.] They all went to pulling it out, I said, "Mm, uh, mm."

[Stackhouse] Knowed you was going wake up then, didn't you?

[Wilkins] I got so ashamed. I started to turn around and wouldn't look at it. [Laughter.] Ah, Lordy. That sure give me a lift for this day. Mmmm, y'all have no idea how good that did me. Yeah, sure. . . . Really, I'd of been, I'd of been laying over there now trying to go to sleep and weep. [Laughter.]

[Stackhouse] Oh, man, oh, man. I'm telling you, sure made me feel lot better. 'Cause I've been feeling bad all day.

[Wilkins] Yeah, I really appreciate it. The old song say "Anytime y'all need us, y'all knows wheres us at. . . ." [Aside to someone: "I'll follow y'all, I don't care."]

[Stackhouse] Got some gigs going somewhere, sometime, where you can definitely, you know [laughs]. . . .

How did you like playing at that new place, Hot Mama's, or something like that?

Hot Mama's on Lamar Avenue in Memphis was a popular club that often featured blues. Wilkins played at Hot Mama's frequently in the early 1970s.

[Stackhouse] I like that.

[Wilkins] I ain't been there.

[Kenibrew] Let's go.

[Wilkins, to Stackhouse] You hear that, Jack? [To everyone] I ain't been there yet.

[Stackhouse] Steve say they going to try . . .

[Wilkins] If y'all plan to go with me, y'all don't even, I ain't thinking about Steve.

[Stackhouse] He say they say they going try steer us in there.

[Wilkins] I ain't thinking about Steve bigger than a [gestures].

[Stackhouse] Ain't you . . . [Carrie shrieks with laughter.]

[Wilkins] Steve's my buddy, he's a good person. Oh yeah. . . . He argue at me too much.

Does he? Why?

[Wilkins] Well, he don't want me drinking. Getting, he know I'm going to drink. 'Cause I've been a little sick, you know. . . . I say it don't make, don't make a difference anyhow. He going buy it for me anyhow. [Laughter.] . . . He know if I'm on the guitar, I'm going to drink some, though. [Laughter.]

[Stackhouse] Well, you going to drink it anyway.

[Wilkins] He know he don't know, have to tell me something. [Laughter.] [Softly] Um umph.

[Stackhouse] Well, nice place. I enjoyed it down there. Hot Mama's, you call it? . . . Yeah, I enjoyed that down there.

[Wilkins] Yeah, you had to tell it. You done forgot it about the ———. He come back here so wet behind the ears, he didn't know where he's at. "Nows, is that my Cousin Stack there?" [Laughter.]

[Stackhouse sighs] I enjoyed myself.

[Wilkins] He said he had the time of his life down there, though.

[Stackhouse] I enjoyed myself.

[Wilkins] Yeah, y'all can't do us no more harm now, so okay. [Laughter.]

Steve told me you sing early Muddy Waters songs real fine.

In 1973, Muddy Waters told Fred Hay and Steve LaVere, "I really like Joe, you know, as a person, as a friend and as a musician; I like him all around. I think, at this time, he's one of the greatest I know of. The man is great, the man is stone great. For blues, like I say, he's the best." In 1975, Waters told Hay that, in 1948, after he had released "I Feel like Going Back Home" on Aristocrat, he was traveling to a gig down South and heard someone over the car radio singing and playing his new hit better than he could; it was Wilkins. On this occasion, when he was performing at Memphis State University, as he had on other occasions in Hay's presence, Waters tried to convince Wilkins to join his band. Wilkins had known Waters since he was a kid, when Waters would play with him and Wilkins's father, Frank.

[Wilkins] Steve? Steve? . . . Didn't I tell you that! Didn't I just get through telling you about Steve! Oh, man, I know! [Laughter.]

I notice you got a lot of Muddy Waters records over here.

[Wilkins] Well, I hold them over there sometimes. I just look at them. [Laughs.]

Y'all sing one last song for us, though. Won't you?

[Wilkins] Next time I see you. [Laughter.] . . . Who made that number? . . . Who made that number? Oh, let me see. That was Junior Parker, wasn't it ———? "Next time I see you things won't be the same."

Though Arkansas is sometimes reported as Herman "Little Junior" Parker's (1932–71) birthplace, Wilkins claimed that he and an uncle witnessed Parker's birth while peeking in the window of the house in Coahoma County, Mississippi, where Parker was born. Parker was one of the many younger musicians who followed Sonny Boy and Wilkins in the 1940s and 1950s. In 1956, he recorded "Next Time You See Me" for the Duke label in Houston.

[Stackhouse] Oh, I don't know who that is.

[Wilkins] Who made that number? . . . "Next Time I See You, Things Won't Be the Same."

[Kenibrew] Little Junior Parker.

[Wilkins] I believe it was.

[Stackhouse] It wasn't Louis [Lowell] Fulsom, was it?

Lowell Fulson or Fulsom (1921–99) was an Oklahoma-born performer and T-Bone Walker disciple who made many popular records.

[Wilkins] No, I think it was Herman Parker.

[Stackhouse] It might have been.

[Wilkins, singing] Next time I see you, things won't be the same. [Speaking] Yeah, that's him. Mmm uh. I know now, yeah, I know now. . . . Huh?

You like that song?

[Wilkins, sputtering] I, uh, uh, dah, I told you, I crazy about all music. I'm prejudiced to music. [Laughter.]

Why don't you sing us that song?

[Wilkins] I don't know that one. . . . I don't know that one about the next time I see you things won't be the same.

You couldn't sing one more song?

[Wilkins] No, I couldn't do that just this minute because this beer getting me tight. [Laughter.]

I thought that was the best way to sing, though.

[Wilkins] No, you can't holler in tights. When I go to hollering and fire my voice over to Arkansas [rest inaudible because of loud laughter]. . . . Yeah, I thought just a while ago I was to belch and my mind said, "You'd better go to the bathroom." It's a good thing I did go. [Laughter.]

Looks like as good as you can sing, though, you'd want to sing some.

[Wilkins] Yeah, I know. [Laughter.] Y'all done made me feel too good. I need, God doggit, I said, "I'm going to feel this good everyday." [Laughter.] I tried to lay on it later on this evening to feel a little better, but Goddangit, but y'all got me feeling good already it.

[Stackhouse] 'Fore night ain't it.

[Wilkins] 'Fore night, I know it, I got to clown some tonight somewhere. [Laughter.] Or am I too weak? . . . Yeah, but I going to make a pass at that bottle that be blow it in a minute. [Laughter.] I ain't going nowhere, though. I ain't going nowhere now. I'm going to stay at home this night.

[Stackhouse] It ain't going to let you stay home now. [Laughter.] Not with them Little Wallaces and things there. "Cousin Joe, come over here."

Little Wallace, Wilkins's cousin, was a younger man who lived two houses up on Carpenter Street.

[Wilkins] I seem . . . [Seriously] No, see, my little cousin over there. They going to stay out of school, too. They're here then. They don't drink nothing much, but I tell them I don't really need none, anyhow, I don't like to drink nothing. [Laughter.] Actually, you know, whatever it is they drink, I say, "Let me have a taste of it." When I get through going around all them different tastes and things. . . . [Laughing] Worried Stack. That's a worried Stackhouse. . . . That's a worried Stack here.

[Stackhouse] Cases of beer, great man. Whew! Alright, boy was wrong, ain't he?

[Wilkins] Two cases, three cases, two cases of beer last night.

[Stackhouse] I didn't let them get a hold of me last night.

[Wilkins] Two cases of beer and three fifths Scotch and how much Bourbon. And I, uh, I mean, I ain't got no business being in no place like that. [Laughter.] I know myself. No, I know myself. [Laughter.] See all them bodies, see all them kin folks up there. And the one set the glass over here, and I, I forget where, I done always lose my glass. That's what I hate about myself. [Laughter] . . . First thing I know I done drunk up somebody else's glass, "And now where am my." [Laughter.] Oh, man, don't get me, I don't be playing when I'm drinking.

Y'all play one last number, though, won't you?

[Wilkins sighs. Stackhouse laughs. Wilkins mumbles] Oh, what I'm going to play? . . . No, I meant, I'm doing this for y'all because I can. . . . You know, the idea of family, you do something because, you know. I don't know, maybe y'all can help me someday. . . . And don't forget I will appreciate it. [Laughter.] . . . Yeah, I will. Got to appreciate it. So, yeah, I mean, it don't matter. This old rusty guitar here, been clowning on me so much. [Stackhouse laughs.] Stackhouse make me so mad there with him. [Laughter. Wilkins sighs.] What can I do now? Now.

[Stackhouse] I'm going to get me one of those old, old ——— Gibsons or something just to sit around and play like this ———. Give you so much a better a sound.

[Wilkins] Goddang. Eh, eh. [Laughter.] No, no. No, no, no. Jimmy Reed says, "Man, look, first you got to choose these things, then next you got to play it." [Laughter.] First you choose these things. See.

Wilkins played a Gibson L5 hollow-body electric guitar that his mother had purchased for him in the 1950s. Stackhouse, at this time, played an inexpensive, solid-body Sears Silvertone guitar. He later replaced it with an Epiphone.

Jimmy Reed (1925–76) was immensely popular for a blues artist. The guitarist/harmonicist wrote many blues classics of the 1950s and 1960s.

If you don't choose it, you can't play it. [Wilkins plays and sings "Wake Up, Baby." Laughter.]

Sonny Boy recorded "Wake Up, Baby" in 1958 for the Chicago-based Checker label. This song is actually Child Ballad 274. Francis James Child published versions of this ballad in his monumental *The English and Scottish Popular Ballads* (1882–98). Variants of this favorite English ballad have been widely collected in the United States as well. Cecil Sharp published five versions of this song (sometimes known as "Our Goodman"), which he had collected in the southern mountains, in his *English Folk Songs From the Appalachians* (1932).

Boy, that was good.

[Wilkins] Yeah, that will get it.

Well, thank you. [Laughter.]

[Wilkins] Well. [Wilkins laughs, then sighs.] My, my. I so scared. I so ashamed I wasn't going to make it. [Laughter.]

[Stackhouse] Yeah, Lord.

[Wilkins] Yeah, yeah. Lordy, lordy.

You want to hear that one back?

[Wilkins] Yeah, I sure do. Please. [Laughter.] Lay it cold to me.

[Stackhouse, laughing] Lay it cold to you. [We play back the song.] That Lipscomb, Robert E. Lipscomb, live in California.

Mance Lipscomb? Yeah, I think he staying out there now. . . . You ever see Blind Lemon Jefferson?

Mance Lipscomb (1895–1976) was a songster and guitarist from Navosta, Texas. He first recorded in 1960 for the folk revival market. Blind Lemon Jefferson (1897–1929) was the great Texas guitarist, singer, and poet who had a tremendous influence on black and white guitarists throughout the South. He was an especial favorite of Wilkins.

[Wilkins] Uh-huh.

Did he come, did you see him when come through Mississippi?

[Wilkins] Uh-huh, uh-huh. I was staying in Clarksdale when he got off the train. They told him to hurry up and get back on it.

[Stackhouse] They did?

[Wilkins] Shit.

Why did they tell him that?

[Wilkins] Because he was playing that guitar and them blues.

They didn't like that in Clarksdale?

[Wilkins] They didn't there. [Nervous laughter.] Oh, them peoples going on playing them blues. Big legged women . . .

[Stackhouse] They paid to see him in Crystal Springs. When he played there, they was glad to see him. Everybody was there.

Did you like the way he played?

[Stackhouse] Yeah, I like it.

[Wilkins] Did I like who? Who wouldn't like the way Lemon played?

Hay remembers fondly a night in the mid-1970s, when Wilkins sat alone in his house, after everyone had retired, playing Stackhouse's National Steel guitar. He played for several hours the songs he could recall from his youth. Many of them were Blind Lemon Jefferson composi- tions. It was startling to hear this postwar Delta guitar innovator play those brilliant, sometimes Thelonious Monk–like, guitar runs from an earlier time and a very different place.

[Stackhouse] He was tremendous. . . . He came from Texas loping like a mule. [Laughter.]

Did you ever meet or hear Blind Willie McTell? Down in Georgia.

Blind Willie McTell (1901–59) was a Georgia twelve-string guitarist and singer.

[Wilkins] Uh-huh, uh-huh.

Where did you see him?

[Wilkins] Man, you know, in fifty some years of doing something, you got a whole lot of toe tapping you come up with. [Laughter.]

[Stackhouse] Meet a whole lot of folks, huh.

But old Willie, he's one of the best singers there.

[Wilkins] Who's that? . . . Well, I mean, you know, it's just, I mean, to me, as I told you, I mean, like some music . . . all of it is good. I mean, likes music, just music, music by music, I likes it. I mean, I likes doing this thing. I likes hear- ing it. And if you don't like mine, I don't give a damn. [Stackhouse laughs loudly.] I got to eat just like he does.

[Stackhouse, laughing] Say you got to eat just like he does.

[Wilkins] Just like he does. . . . Uh-huh.

Did you ever see Leadbelly? You got some of his records here?

[Wilkins] Yeah, mm huh, mm huh.

As Hay learned later, the tone of Wilkins's reply here meant that he was tired of this line of questioning and would answer in whatever way he thought might bring it to an end most quickly. Sometimes, when he was tired of discussing a particular topic, Wilkins would say, paraphrasing Sonny Boy's song, "Don't start me to lying."

Did you see him in Mississippi?

[Wilkins] Yup. Yup. Mm huh.

You must have liked his playing?

[Wilkins] Mm huh.

[Stackhouse] Blind Blake, that bad scoundrel, he come through Mississippi, wasn't it?

Arthur "Blind Blake" Phelps was a phenomenal Florida/Georgia guitarist who played complicated fingerings at high speed in a ragtime-influenced style. His style was especially influential among East Coast musicians.

You saw Blind Blake?

[Stackhouse] I saw him a long time ago, you know.

Did you like his guitar playing, that ragtime?

[Stackhouse] Yeah, I liked his stuff.

Did you do any playing with him?

[Wilkins, sings tune in background.] That's his number. What is some of the numbers he used to play?

[Stackhouse] I didn't do no playing with him but I come in on him some. . . . Play one sort of like this. I don't know if I can keep up with it or not but I can . . .

[Wilkins] Oh yeah. I have done forgot now. [Stackhouse plays his standard "Blind Blake" piece.]

Did the Mississippi musicians like Blind Blake?

[Stackhouse] They liked him.

Yeah. Did Tommy Johnson see him?

[Stackhouse] Yeah. . . . Tommy Johnson used to play with him some. . . . Tommy Johnson was grown. I wasn't grown then. I wasn't getting out this, you know. Tommy Johnson just play with Blake some. Ishman Bracey and all them cats, you know. . . . Tommy Johnson was out on the road then, you know.

Ishman Bracey (1901–70) was a Jackson, Mississippi, guitarist/pianist who recorded 1928–30.

Did you ever meet any of the other guys from over there in Georgia, South Carolina, Florida?

[Stackhouse] I never did, I never did meet too many people out of Georgia and Alabama.

Did you ever see Blind Willie McTell?

[Stackhouse] He used to come to Crystal Springs and play.

Did he come with Willie Johnson?

[Stackhouse] No, he was playing by hisself but he was on a medicine show or with some doctor or other and he come play at the big school there in 1927. . . . He sure played that guitar that night.

What, did he have the big twelve-string?

[Stackhouse] Right. . . . Yeah, he was wailing that thing that night. . . . Blind Lemon Jefferson. [Laughs.] There were some people there, too. Where he played.

Did you ever see Big Bill Broonzy? When you were over in Arkansas?

William Lee Conley Broonzy (1893–1958) was a popular blues recording artist with both African American and folk revivalist audiences.

[Stackhouse] I never did meet him.

He probably left by the time you got there.

[Stackhouse] Right, I came over in Arkansas in '46.

[Wilkins walks up, clicking fingers in time with stride] Back in the boat. In the dark. [Can pops, Wilkins takes a gulp.] Ahh. Anybody got any brew? . . . [Inaudible muttering.] No. You sure, we can wait. [Purposefully mumbles, pops can, laughs. Everyone laughs. Stackhouse sighs.] Now, see what we got. [Laughter.] Yeah, Ole Milwaukee, he drank the first one.

You want one, too?

[Stackhouse] I reckon I might freshen up a little, maybe.

[Wilkins] Yes, sir. Now, he too, he too young to drink. [Laughter.]

[Stackhouse] Hillbill likes that flat soda water.

[Wilkins] Yeah, he's going to drink beer he said he'd be a whole lot bigger. He like that strong alcohol, and so I can't stand to be around that stuff. . . . That whiskey stuff get me way too drunk. Yeah, boy.

[Stackhouse] That ole Gibson been many a mile, ain't they? [Laughs.]

[Wilkins] I've been with it, I, uh, ain't messed with me, if I don't be with me. I don't ———.

[Stackhouse] Were you playing it in Detroit when you and Sonny Boy were together? Or in Helena?

[Wilkins] In Helena.

When did you go up to Detroit?

[Wilkins] Ah, shit, I don't know. Fifty-six or -four, I don't know.

Did you live up there?

[Wilkins] For a while.

Did you play with Roosevelt Sykes and all those . . .

Roosevelt Sykes (1906–84) was an influential pianist who recorded prolifically from 1929 until his death. Wilkins recorded a session with Sykes for the House of Sound label in Memphis in

1957. One single was released with "She's Jail Bait" and "Sputnik Baby." On "Sputnik," Wilkins imitates the sound of a satellite traveling through space with his guitar. These songs have been reissued on Document CD 6050 *Roosevelt Sykes: Complete Recorded Works in Chronological Order, Vol. 10, 12 July 1951 to 1957.*

[Wilkins] Mm huh. . . . No, I didn't play with all of them up there. I didn't see all of them.

[Stackhouse] In Chicago?

[Wilkins] Yep.

Robert Nighthawk was there then, wasn't he?

Robert "Nighthawk" McCollum (1909–67), Stackhouse's cousin, student, and later, teacher, was an outstanding slide guitarist (Hay 1992). Wilkins lived with McCollum's sister Margaret for a number of years. They had at least one child together. For more on Nighthawk, see the Little Laura Dukes chapter.

[Wilkins] No, not when I was there. . . . Somebody was up there that I was thinking of.

[Stackhouse] No, Robert mostly hung around Chicago until he went to Canada.

[Wilkins] Uh-huh.

[Stackhouse] I don't think he done too much in Michigan.

[Wilkins] See, we was bypassing one another.

[Stackhouse] Yeah, one going over this place and one going somewhere else.

[Wilkins] Yeah, yeah. . . . Yeah, you know Sonny Boy, as bull-headed as he was.

[Stackhouse] Yeah.

[Wilkins] He going to go wrong with anybody else, anyhow.

[Stackhouse, laughing.] Hammie.

Hammie Nixon (1908–84) was a Brownsville, Tennessee, harmonica player who often accompanied Sleepy John Estes. For more on Nixon, see the Tommy Gary chapter.

[Wilkins] You hear me say "anyway"?

[Stackhouse] Yeah, Hammie.

[Wilkins] I was the biggest fool there was in the world. I just say "let's go." [Laughter.]

You went up there with Sonny Boy?

[Wilkins] Mm huh. . . . Ohh, in those days, I been, didn't have no business dealing with them. [Laughter] Lord, I mean . . .

[Stackhouse] You mean the time he carried you in that big club there about a half-mile long.

[Wilkins] Got me so ashamed. Yep. [Laughter.] I was so ashamed. [Laughter.] Oh wee, looked like it was so far trying to get down to that stage, and now nobody but me and him, guitar. And where they was a dancing there was bigger than this house and I say, "Shit, I wished I knowed the way out of here." [Laughter.]

Fred Davis reports that Joe worked the King Solomon Bar in Detroit in 1954 (1971b, 145).

[Stackhouse] You going there trying to get kicked off by yourselves ———.

[Wilkins] See, he didn't give a damn 'cause he knows, he knows, I mean, but that's one. I needs some drums, guitar, some bass, horn, harp. Excusing harp, ain't nothing but him sitting up there with that dry harp and that guitar. I said, "Man, goddamn." [Laughter.] "You ought to be ashamed of yourself do me this way." [Laughter.]

[Stackhouse] Then he told you he going to play around with you ———, your guitar . . .

[Wilkins] Mm huh. That's what I told him I'm going to do. I say, "Look, I'm going to play my harp." He say, well now, he ———, "You motherfucker, you. [Laughter.] I'm going to play goddamn guitar if that's the way it is." [Laughter.] Boy, uh, old man was ———.

[Stackhouse] You had to come on in there when he got to blowing good, huh?

[Wilkins] Yeah, I had to work anyway, but I was just, you know, ashamed, to be ashamed going in there.

[Stackhouse] So many people, huh?

[Wilkins] Yeah, man, just me and him and that harp there, I say, "Shit." [Laughter.]

[Stackhouse] Peck say that's the way got him doing, uh, down there in Indianola, Mississippi, you know. That's Big Johnnie Jones's nightclub. Just harp and drums. "Guitar player be here directly," but Robert and ———— done left him. [Laughter.] But Peck said he made three hundred and some dollars there that . . .

James Peck Curtis (1912–70), drummer, washboard player, and dancer, was the regular drummer for the King Biscuit Time show in Helena. He often played with Wilkins and Stackhouse.

[Wilkins] That son-of-a-gun would work by hisself. . . . Now, he took my guitar case one night. I said, "Where you going with it without asking? You doing wrong again now, 'cause." He said, "I'll tell you what you do." Say, "I'm going to this job and you go to this one and you take and, uh, and y'all make some and I make this one, I go by myself. Give me your guitar case." I didn't give him my guitar case. He said, "Just let me have you guitar case." I said, "Okay, if that's the way it is, you can have it." . . . Shit. Sonny Boy say, "Joe Willie will be here directly." Yeah, I see his guitar. Joe will be here directly." Joe ain't got there yet. [Laughter.] Said, "I was ahead of Joe." Joe still ain't got there. He worked down there by hisself. He come back where we were.

[Stackhouse] Case with a scound in it.

Wilkins, Stackhouse, and their friends referred to genitalia as "scound" (short for scoundrel). Having sex was "scounding."

[Wilkins] But that old man sure could blow a harp. . . . Love to blow that harp.

Did you go with him to Europe?

Sonny Boy toured with the American Blues Festival Tours of Europe in 1963 and 1964.

[Wilkins] No, I couldn't go. [Stackhouse laughs.] He came in, but I couldn't go. At this time, my mother was sick, you know. . . . And I was sick, so.

He wanted to go back over there and live, didn't he?

In the liner notes of *"The Original" Sonny Boy Williamson,* Paul Oliver stated that Sonny Boy was "very anxious to return to England to live" (1965b).

[Wilkins] Hum? I don't know. Because we never did talk too much after he come back. I got the chance to see him once. After he came back. . . . He came over here.

[Stackhouse] Ah, he wasn't going to go . . .

[Wilkins] At me, so.

You were living over here then?

[Wilkins] Yeah, uh-huh. Living here all the time. At least my people were, but you know I'd be out and gone somewhere ———— was playing. . . . He came back, he'd call me. He'd be sitting in the car every once in awhile, you know, he'd call me, so I . . .

[Stackhouse] He wasn't going to go 'cause the man come after him. He was down to Helena there. Said he'd come back home to die.

[Wilkins] Nah, he said he wasn't going back no more. He didn't want to go back no more. In other words, he didn't want to go that time. In other words, he done had to go and I was supposed to go with him. . . . Things happen like they did, I couldn't go. So he just had to go on.

He liked it over there, didn't he?

[Wilkins] Yeah, uh-huh, yes.

[Stackhouse] There's a picture of us. That guy from California took of me, him, and Peck there. Trying to get him to go back but he wouldn't go. . . . So next time the fellow come back again, Sonny Boy had passed.

The "guy from California" was Chris Strachwitz, who visited Sonny Boy in Helena in May 1965, several weeks before Sonny Boy's death.

What year was that picture taken? Do you know?

[Stackhouse] Sixty-five. Sonny Boy died in '65.

Yeah. The same picture on the front of that album there.

Blues Classics LP no. 9, *"The Original" Sonny Boy Williamson,* is a reissue of the best of Sonny Boy and Wilkins's trumpet recordings from the early 1950s.

[Stackhouse] Yeah, uh.

Because they didn't, they cut you out.

[Stackhouse] Cut me and Peck out. . . . He got me to go up to the station and play the program with him that day. I tried to tape that down.

Are you on that record?

[Stackhouse] I don't know if I'm on that record or not. Maybe, I don't know. But it seems that just Joe Willie and them, that record there.

[Wilkins] What? [Inaudible, everyone talking and moving about.]

[Stackhouse] That's just y'all?

[Wilkins] Yeah, uh-huh.

[Stackhouse] Steve [LaVere] give me this up in the, he wouldn't give me the whole book, he just give me the back off of it, up there in Boston. He kept the book. I wanted the whole book up there, but he wouldn't. [Laughter.] Sometimes Steve is something else, I tell you, but he did a lot of record business up there in Boston.

Ole Paul Oliver the one that took that picture there, though, wasn't he?

Chris Strachwitz took the photograph.

[Stackhouse] Uh-huh, down there at Helena. . . . He's the one from California, wasn't he?

He's from England.

[Stackhouse] That's what I'm talking about. . . . He was trying to get Sonny Boy to go back with him, but Sonny Boy wouldn't go. . . . When he come back at Sonny Boy trying to get him again, Sonny Boy had passed. Cried like a baby. . . . [Sighs.] This was me when we was at Ann Arbor, up there at . . .

In 1970 and again in 1973, Wilkins, Stackhouse, and Sonny Blake played the Ann Arbor Blues and Jazz Festival in Ann Arbor, Michigan. Wilkins, Stackhouse, and Blake's 1973 Ann Arbor performance was released on Schoolkids Records CD 2104-2 "*Well All Right!*": *Ann Arbor Blues and Jazz Festival, Vol. 4.*

I read that in that Living Blues, *that* Living Blues *magazine about you and, uh. You going, you went up there, too, didn't you? It said you two sounded real good.*

[Stackhouse] It said that? [Laughs.]

It said y'all sounded better than you did on record.

[Wilkins] Ha ha.

[Stackhouse] I was feeling pretty good because they weren't bringing me nothing but them fifths of Grandad. [Laughter.] I was tapping them pretty good. Enjoyed it. Every time we go on ———, you know.

Dr. Ross came down, blew some harp.

"Doctor" Charles Isaiah Ross (1925–93) played guitar, harmonica, and drums and often worked as a one-man band. The influence of Sonny Boy and Wilkins is evident in Ross's recordings.

[Stackhouse] That's right.

[Wilkins] That Doctor is something else.

How was Sonny Boy Blake?

Sonny Blake, a fine harmonica player in the style of Sonny Boy Williamson, still performs regularly in Memphis. Blake, another protégé of Wilkins, played regularly with Wilkins's band in the early 1970s. He recorded singles for the CMC and Rooster labels. For more on Blake, see the Big Amos Patton chapter.

[Stackhouse] He's good, he do okay.

Yeah, he live over in West Memphis.

[Wilkins] West Memphis.

[Stackhouse] Yes.

Did he ever play over there with Sonny Boy Williamson?

[Wilkins] Who? . . . Yeah, he would be around but he wasn't playing nothing.

Joe Willie Wilkins and Houston Stackhouse played frequently in the 1970s in places like Hughes, Arkansas, for their traditional African American fans, but also for white clubs and college audiences. They played together or as solo acts, and Stackhouse played for a time in Wilkins's band, the King Biscuit Boys. Stackhouse toured Europe, and Wilkins turned down invitations to do the same. Stackhouse and Wilkins and band were featured artists with the touring Memphis Blues Caravan. Recordings from some of their live appearances appear on Memphis Archive CDs 7008/7009 *Memphis Blues Caravan, Vol. 1 and 2.*

Willis Kenibrew died in Marianna, Arkansas, in the early 1970s. Joe Willie Wilkins died in Memphis, March 28, 1979. Soon after Wilkins's death, Stackhouse proposed marriage to Wilkins's widow, Carrie. She turned him down. Stackhouse died in Helena on September 23, 1980.

The North Memphis neighborhood where Wilkins lived for several decades experienced a serious decline in the 1980s. Crack houses began to dot the street and the crime rate soared. Carrie Wilkins continued to live in the house at 1656 Carpenter Street even though it was deteriorating as quickly as her health and the neighborhood. Her house was robbed on several occasions. Carrie Wilkins, "Ma," died on Labor Day 1998.

In 1993, the African country of Gambia (the area of the ancestral continent that some scholars have identified as the source of American blues) honored Joe Willie Wilkins by issuing a stamp with his portrait. Only a few blues artists were so honored by the Gambian government. Someone back home, at the source, discerned a greatness in this kindred genius that escaped the notice of many contemporary Euro-American blues fans.

Recommended Listening

Note: All recordings listed below are currently available on compact disc.

Bukka White

The Complete Bukka White. Columbia 52782.

Includes all of White's prewar commercial recordings.

Sky Songs. Arhoolie 323.

All of the musical selections from White's phenomenal Arhoolie LPs.

1963 Isn't 1962. Genes 9903.

Excellent material recorded in 1963 but not released until the 1990s.

Memphis Ma Rainey

No recordings are currently available. However, many recordings of the original Ma Rainey are available. For example:

Ma Rainey. Milestone 47201.

Reissue of Milestone double LP of the *Mother of the Blues*.

Tommy Gary

Mississippi Delta Blues Jam in Memphis, Vol. 2. Arhoolie 386.

Gary accompanies Sleepy John Estes on this reissue of Blue Thumb's *Memphis Swamp Jam* LP.

Furry Lewis

In His Prime 1927–1928. Yazoo 1050.

Lewis's outstanding prewar recordings.

Shake 'Em On Down. Fantasy 24703.

Reissue of two Prestige/Bluesville LPs from 1961. Lewis's first commercially recorded "rediscovery" recordings.

Fourth & Beale. Lucky Seven 9202.

Nice set of 1969 recordings.

Boose Taylor

No recordings of Taylor have ever been released. However, excellent recordings of his friends Fred McDowell and Junior Kimbrough do exist:

McDowell: *You Gotta Move.* Arhoolie 304.

1964–65 recordings with two songs by Eli Green.

Kimbrough: *Do the Rump!* High Water 6503.

Selection of 1982 and 1988 recordings.

Little Laura Dukes

No recordings are currently available. Recordings are available of her mentor Laura Smith, teacher Robert Nighthawk, and her associates in the Memphis Jug Band.

Smith: *Complete Recorded Works, Vol. 1: 1924–1927.* Document 5429.

Nighthawk: *Robert Lee McCoy, The Bluebird Recordings, 1937–1938.* RCA 67416.

The Memphis Jug Band. Yazoo 1067.

Great material recorded 1927–34.

Big Amos Patton

River Town Blues. Hi (UK) 118.

Reissue of the Hi LP and the British Hi double LP, which includes songs by Patton, Big Lucky Carter, and others.

Joe Willie Wilkins and Houston Stackhouse

"Well All Right!": Ann Arbor Blues and Jazz Festival, Vol 4. Schoolkids Records 2104–2.

Includes Wilkins, Stackhouse, and others live from 1973.

Memphis Blues Caravan, Vols. 1 and 2. Memphis Archives 7008/7009.

Includes live selections by Wilkins and Stackhouse (also Bukka White and Furry Lewis).

King Biscuit Time. Arhoolie 310.

Classic Trumpet recordings from the early 1950s of Sonny Boy Williamson accompanied by Wilkins's astounding guitar playing.

Goin' in Your Direction. Trumpet AA–801.

More Trumpet sides of Wilkins accompanying Sonny Boy and Arthur "Big Boy" Crudup.

Big Road Blues. Wolf 120.915.

Field and live performance recordings of Houston Stackhouse made from 1967–76.

Cryin' Won't Help You. Genes 9904.

Stackhouse's 1972 studio recordings.

Robert Nighthawk/Houston Stackhouse. Testament 5010.

Includes late 1960s field recordings of Stackhouse accompanied by Nighthawk and drummer James "Peck" Curtis.

Bibliography

Albertson, Chris. 1972. *Bessie Smith*. New York: Stein and Day.

Andrews, Dwight D. 1989. "From Black to Blues." In *The Blues Aesthetic: Black Culture and Modernism,* edited by Richard Powell. Washington, D.C.: Washington Arts Project.

Bane, Michael. 1982. *White Boy Singin' the Blues: The Black Roots of White Rock.* New York: Da Capo.

Barlow, William. 1989. *Looking Up at Down: The Emergence of Blues Culture.* Philadelphia: Temple University Press.

———. 1990. "Fattening Frogs for Snakes: Blues and the Music Industry." *Popular Music and Society* 14, no. 2 (summer): 7–35.

Bindas, Kenneth J., ed. 1992. *America's Musical Pulse: Popular Music in Twentieth-Century Society.* Westport, Conn.: Greenwood.

Booth, Stanley. 1991. *Rhythm Oil: A Journey through the Music of the American South.* New York: Pantheon.

Bowman, Rob. 1977. "Beale Street Blues." *Southern Exposure* 5, no. 1: 75–79.

———. 1997. *Soulsville U.S.A.: The Story of Stax Records.* London: Books with Attitude.

Brisbin, John Anthony. 1995. "Howlin' Wolf's Early Guitarists: Willie Johnson." *Living Blues,* no. 124 (November/December): 40–49.

———. 1997. "Jimmy Rogers: I'm Havin' Fun Right Today." *Living Blues,* no. 135 (September/October): 12–27.

Brunvand, Jan Harold, ed. 1996. *American Folklore: An Encyclopedia.* New York: Garland.

Burton, Thomas G., ed. 1981. *Tom Ashley, Sam McGee, Bukka White: Tennessee Traditional Singers.* Knoxville: University of Tennessee Press.

Calt, Stephen. n.d. *Furry Lewis in His Prime 1927–1928.* Yazoo LP 1050 liner notes.

Calt, Stephen, and Gayle Wardlow. 1988. *King of the Delta Blues: The Life and Music of Charlie Patton.* Newton, N.J.: Rock Chapel Press.

Campbell, John C. 1921. *The Southern Highlander and His Homeland.* New York: Russell Sage Foundation.

Cannon, Gus. 1963. "Narration." *Walk Right In.* Memphis, Tenn.: Stax Records LP 702.

Cantor, Louis. 1992. *Wheelin' on Beale: How WDIA-Memphis Became the Nation's First All-Black Radio Station and Created the Sound that Changed America.* New York: Pharos Books.

Charters, Samuel B. 1975. *The Country Blues.* 1959; reprint, New York: DaCapo Press.

———. 1977. *Sweet as the Showers of Rain (The Bluesmen, Vol. 2).* New York: Oak Publications.

———. 1993. "Workin' On the Building: Roots and Influences." In *Nothing but the Blues: The Music and the Musicians,* edited by Lawrence Cohn. New York: Abbeville Press.

Child, Francis James. 1965. *The English and Scottish Ballads.* 1882–98; reprint, New York: Dover Publications.

Clayton, Rose. 1981. "Furry Lewis, 1893–1981." *Rolling Stone,* no. 355 (29 October): 49.

Cohen, Norm. 1981. *Long Steel Rail: The Railroad in American Folksong.* Urbana: University of Illinois Press.

Cohn, Lawrence, ed. 1993. *Nothing but the Blues: The Music and the Musicians.* New York: Abbeville Press.

Cone, James H. 1972. *The Spirituals and the Blues: An Interpretation.* New York: Seabury Press.

Cook, Bruce. 1973. *Listen to the Blues.* New York: Charles Scribner's Sons.

Cook, K. W. 1963. "Fame 'Walks Right In' Out of Cold." *Memphis Commercial Appeal,* 16 February.

Courlander, Harold. 1970. *Negro Folk Music U.S.A.* 1963; reprint, New York: Columbia University Press.

Davidson, George D. 1994. *Carvin' the Blues.* Tokyo: Libroport.

Davis, Angela Y. 1998. *Blues Legacies and Black Feminism: Gertrude "Ma" Rainey, Bessie Smith, and Billie Holiday.* New York: Pantheon.

Davis, Fred. 1971a. [Gus Cannon.] In *Nothing but the Blues: An Illustrated Documentary,* edited by Mike Leadbitter. London: Hanover Books.

———. 1971b. "Joe Willis [sic] Wilkins." In *Nothing but the Blues: An Illustrated Documentary,* edited by Mike Leadbitter. London: Hanover Books.

Dickerson, James. 1996. *Goin' Back to Memphis: A Century of Blues, Rock 'n' Roll, and Glorious Soul.* New York: Schirmer Books.

Dixon, Robert M. W., and John Godrich. 1970. *Recording the Blues.* New York: Stein and Day.

Dixon, Robert M. W., John Godrich, and Howard W. Rye. 1997. *Blues and Gospel Records, 1890–1943.* 4th ed. Oxford, England: Clarendon Press.

Dixon, Willie, with Don Snowden. 1989. *I Am the Blues: The Willie Dixon Story.* New York: Da Capo.

Edwards, David. 1992. "Honeyboy." Interview by author with John Brisbin and Michael Franks. Manchester, N.H.

Escott, Colin, and Martin Hawkins. 1975. *The Complete Sun Label Session Files*. East Sussex, England: Swift Record Distributors.

Escott, Colin with Martin Hawkins. 1991. *Good Rockin' Tonight: Sun Records and the Birth of Rock 'n' Roll*. New York: St. Martin's.

Evans, David. 1971a. "Booker White." In *Nothing but the Blues: An Illustrated Documentary*, edited by Mike Leadbitter. London: Hanover Books.

———. 1971b. *Tommy Johnson*. London: Studio Vista.

———. 1982a. *Big Road Blues: Tradition and Creativity in Folk Blues*. Berkeley: University of California Press.

———. 1982b. "Walter 'Furry' Lewis, 1893–1981." *Living Blues*, no. 52 (spring): 55.

———. 1993. "Goin' Up the Country: Blues in Texas and the Deep South." In *Nothing but the Blues: The Music and the Musicians*, edited by Lawrence Cohn. New York: Abbeville Press.

———. n.d. *Houston Stackhouse (1910–1980)*. Wolf LP 120779 liner notes.

Fabre, Genevieve. 1990. "The Stomping of the Blues in Urban America or the Emergence of a Blues Culture: 1900–1930." *Storia Nordamericana* 7, no. 2: 103–15.

Fahey, John. 1970. *Charley Patton*. London: Studio Vista.

Field, Kim. 1993. *Harmonicas, Harps, and Heavy Breathers: The Evolution of the People's Instrument*. New York: Fireside.

Finn, Julio. 1986. *The Bluesman: The Musical Heritage of Black Men and Women in the Americas*. New York: Quartet Books.

Fox, Mrs. Jessie W. 1959. "Beale Street and the Blues." *West Tennessee Historical Society Papers*, no. 8: 128–47.

Friedman, Albert B., ed. 1971. *The Viking Book of Folk Ballads of the English-Speaking World*. 1956; reprint, New York: Viking.

Garon, Paul. 1971. *The Devil's Son-in-Law: The Story of Peetie Wheatstraw and his Songs*. London: Studio Vista.

Garon, Paul, and Beth Garon. 1992. *Woman with Guitar: Memphis Minnie's Blues*. New York: Da Capo.

Gordon, Robert. 1995. *It Came from Memphis*. Boston: Faber and Faber.

Greene, Maude. 1941. "The Background of the Beale Street Blues." *Tennessee Folklore Society Bulletin* 7, no. 1: 1–10.

Groom, Bob. 1971. *The Blues Revival*. London: Studio Vista.

———. 1986/1987. "Big Lucky: Memphis Bluesman." *Juke Blues*, no. 7 (winter): 12–13.

Handy, W. C. 1970. *Father of the Blues: An Autobiography*, edited by Arna Bontemps. 1941; reprint, New York: Collier.

———. 1972. *Blues: An Anthology*. 1926; reprint, New York: Collier.

Harris, Sheldon. 1979. *Blues Who's Who: A Biographical Dictionary of Blues Singers.* New Rochelle, N.Y.: Arlington House.

Harrison, Max. 1986. "Jazz." In *The New Grove Gospel, Blues, and Jazz,* edited by Paul Oliver. New York: W. W. Norton.

Hay, Fred J. 1975. "Tommy Gary." *Living Blues,* no. 24 (November/December): 5–6.

———. 1979. "Joe Willie Wilkins, 1923–1979." *Living Blues,* no. 42: 8.

———. 1981. "The Delta Blues and Black Society: An Examination of Change (1900–1960) in Style and Community." M.A. diss., University of Virginia.

———. 1987. "The Sacred/Profane Dialectic in Delta Blues as Exemplified in Excerpts from the Life and Lyrics of Sonny Boy Williamson." *Phylon* 48, no. 4: 317–26.

———. 1992. "Blues What Am: Blues Consciousness and Social Protest." In *America's Musical Pulse: Popular Music in Twentieth-Century Society,* edited by Kenneth J. Bindas. Westport, Conn.: Greenwood.

———. 1998. Review of *Blues Legacies and Black Feminism: Gertrude "Ma" Rainey, Bessie Smith, and Billie Holiday,* by Angela Y. Davis. *Appalachian Journal* 25, no. 4: 442–45.

———. 1999. "Carrie Wilkins." *Living Blues,* no. 144 (March/April): 74.

Herskovits, Melville J. 1966. *The New World Negro: Selected Papers in Afroamerican Studies.* Bloomington: Indiana University Press.

———. 1967. *Cultural Dynamics.* New York: Alfred A. Knopf.

Humphrey, Mark. 1996. "Prodigal Sons: Son House and Robert Wilkins." In *Saints and Sinners: Religion, Blues, and (D)evil in African-American Music and Literature: Proceedings of the Conference held at the Université de Liège (October 1991),* edited by Robert Saire. Liège, Belgium: Société Liègeoise de Musicologie.

Hurley, F. Jack, and David Evans. 1981. "Bukka White." In *Tom Ashley, Sam McGee, Bukka White: Tennessee Traditional Singers,* edited by Thomas G. Burton. Knoxville: University of Tennessee Press.

Hyde, Gene. 1998. Letter to author.

"I'm a Yard Man." 1963. *Time* (5 April): 50–51.

"In Memoriam: Walter 'Furry' Lewis." 1981. *Guitar Player* 15, no. 12 (December): 14.

Jabbour, Alan. 1996. "Fiddle Music." In *American Folklore: An Encyclopedia,* edited by Jan Harold Brunrand. New York: Garland.

James, Michael. 1997. "Yank Rachel." *Living Blues,* no. 135 (September/October): 54–55.

Jones, Wilbur. 1979. Interview by author. Athens, Georgia.

Kay, Jackie. 1997. *Bessie Smith.* Bath, England: Absolute.

Keil, Charles. 1966. *Urban Blues.* Chicago: University of Chicago Press.

Kirby, Edward. 1983. "Prince Gabe." *From Africa to Beale Street.* Memphis, Tenn.: Lubin Press.

Kluckhohn, Clyde. 1949. *Mirror for Man: The Relation of Anthropology to Modern Life.* New York: Whittlesey House.

Kubik, Gerhard. 1999. *Africa and the Blues.* Jackson: University Press of Mississippi.

LaVere, Steve. 1973. "The River City Blues Festival." *River City Review* 3, no. 8: 1.

———. 1977. *Joe Willie Wilkins and His King Biscuit Boys.* Adamo LP 9507 liner notes.

———. 1978. "Earl Bell." *Living Blues,* no. 36 (January/February): 31.

———. 1993. Conversation with author.

———. 1994. *Houston Stackhouse: Cryin' Won't Help You.* Genes CD 9904 liner notes.

———. n.d. *The Memphis Blues Again: An Anthology of the Blues Today in Memphis,* 2 vols. Adelphi Records 1009s/1010s liner notes.

Leadbitter, Mike, ed. 1971. *Nothing but the Blues: An Illustrated Documentary.* London: Hanover Books.

Leadbitter, Mike, Leslie Fancourt, and Paul Pelletier. 1994. *Blues Records, 1943 – 1970: "The Bible of the Blues,"* vol. 2. London: Record Information Services.

Leadbitter, Mike, and Neil Slaven. 1968. *Blues Records: January, 1943 to December, 1966.* New York: Oak.

———. 1987. *Blues Records 1943–1970: A Selective Discography,* vol 1. London: Record Information Services.

Lee, George W. 1972. "Poetic Memories of Beale Street." *West Tennessee Historical Society Papers* 26: 64–73.

Levet, Jean-Paul. 1992. *Talkin' That Talk: Le Langue du Blues et du Jazz.* Paris: Hatier.

Levine, Lawrence W. 1977. *Black Culture and Black Consciousness: Afro-American Folk Thought From Slavery to Freedom.* Oxford, England: Oxford University Press.

Lewis, John. 1997. "Drink, Drank, Drunk: Junior Kimbrough's Intoxicatin' Blues." *Option,* no. 74 (1 May): 48–53.

Lieb, Sandra. 1981. *Mother of the Blues: A Study of Ma Rainey.* Amherst: University of Massachusetts Press.

Lomax, Alan. 1993. *The Land Where the Blues Began.* New York: Pantheon.

Lord, Tom. 1976. *Clarence Williams.* Essex, England: Storyville Publications.

Lornell, Kip. 1975. "Living Blues Interview: Hammie Nixon and Sleepy John Estes." *Living Blues,* no. 19 (January/February): 13–19.

———. 1995. *"Happy in the Service of the Lord": African-American Sacred Vocal Harmony Quartets in Memphis,* 2nd ed. Knoxville: University of Tennessee Press.

———. 1998. Telephone conversation with author.

Lovett, Bobby L. 1998. "Beale Street." In *The Tennessee Encyclopedia of History and Culture,* edited by Carroll Van West. Nashville: Tennessee Historical Society and Rutledge Hill Press.

McKee, Margaret, and Fred Chisenhall. 1981. *Beale Black and Blue: Life and Music on Black America's Main Street.* Baton Rouge: Louisiana State University Press.

McMurry, Lillian. 1993. Telephone interview by author.

Major, Clarence. 1994. *Juba to Jive: A Dictionary of African-American Slang.* New York: Penguin.

Manning, Terry. 1999. *W. Furry Lewis: Blues Magician.* Lucky Seven Records CD 9206 AAD liner notes (dist. by Rounder Records).

Marcuse, Sibyl. 1975. *Musical Instruments: A Comprehensive Dictionary.* New York: W. W. Norton and Co.

Means, John. 1963. "Plink, Plink and a Hee Hee Hee." Unidentified newspaper clipping. 23 March. In John Quincy Wolf Papers, Lyon College, Batesville, Arkansas.

———. n.d. *Memphis Swamp Jam.* Blue Thumb LP 6000 liner notes.

Michelson, Stephan. 1994. Personal communication.

Mitchell, George. 1971. *Blow My Blues Away.* Baton Rouge: Louisiana State University Press.

Morton, David C. with Charles K. Wolfe. 1991. *DeFord Bailey: A Black Star in Early Country Music.* Knoxville: University of Tennessee Press.

Nager, Larry. 1998. *Memphis Beat: The Lives and Times of America's Crossroads.* New York: St. Martin's.

Napier, Simon. 1971. "The Story of Bukka White." In *Nothing but the Blues: An Illustrated Documentary,* edited by Mike Leadbitter. London: Hanover Books.

———. n.d. *Bukka White/Parchman Farm.* Columbia Records LP C 30036 liner notes.

Nelson, David. 1998. "David 'Junior' Kimbrough." *Living Blues,* no. 139 (May/June): 50–52.

Oakley, Giles. 1976. *The Devil's Music: A History of the Blues.* New York: Harcourt Brace Jovanovich.

Obrecht, Jas, ed. 1990. *Blues Guitar: The Men Who Made the Music.* San Francisco: GPI Books.

Odel, Jay Scott. 1984. "Ukelele." In *The New Grove Dictionary of Musical Instruments,* edited by Stanley Sadie. New York: Macmillan.

Odum, Howard W. 1911. "Folk-Song and Folk-Poetry as Found in the Secular Songs of the Southern Negroes," parts 1 and 2. *Journal of American Folklore* 24, no. 93: 255–94; 24, no. 94: 351–96.

Odum, Howard W., and Guy B. Johnson. 1969. *Negro Workaday Songs.* 1926; reprint, New York: Negro Universities Press.

Oliver, Paul. 1965a. *Conversation with the Blues.* New York: Horizon.

———. 1965b. *"The Original" Sonny Boy Williamson.* Arhoolie Records, Blues Classics LP 9 liner notes.

———. 1969. *The Story of the Blues.* Philadelphia: Chilton Book Co.

———. 1970. *Aspects of the Blues Tradition.* New York: Oak Publications. (Originally published in 1968 as *Screening the Blues.*)

———. 1984a. *Blues Off the Record: Thirty Years of Blues Commentary.* New York: Da Capo.

———. 1984b. *Songsters and Saints: Vocal Traditions on Race Records.* Cambridge, Mass.: Cambridge University Press.

———. 1986a. "Blues." In *The New Grove Gospel, Blues, and Jazz,* edited by Paul Oliver. New York: W. W. Norton.

———. 1986b. *The New Grove Gospel, Blues, and Jazz.* New York: W. W. Norton.

———. 1989a. "Songsters and Proto-Blues." In *The Blackwell Guide to Blues Records,* edited by Paul Oliver. Cambridge, Mass.: Basil Blackwell.

———. n.d. *Son Bonds with Sleepy John Estes and Hammie Nixon (1934–1941).* Wolf Records Special Edition 129 liner notes.

———, ed. 1989b. *The Blackwell Guide to Blues Records.* Cambridge, Mass.: Basil Blackwell.

Oliver, Sylvester W., Jr. 1996. "African-American Music Traditions in Northeast Mississippi." Ph.D. diss., University of Memphis.

Olsson, Bengt. 1970. *Memphis Blues and Jug Bands.* London: Studio Vista.

———. 1973. *Cannon's Jug Stompers: The Complete Works in Chronological Order, 1927–1930.* Herwin LP 208 liner notes.

O'Neal, Jim. 1972. "Live Blues." *Living Blues,* no. 9 (summer): 28–31.

———. 1973. "Joe Willie Wilkins." *Living Blues,* no. 11: 13–17.

———. 1978. "Blues for the Tourists at Blues Alley in Memphis." *Living Blues,* no. 41 (November/December): 28–29.

———. 1979. "Gus Cannon." *Living Blues,* no. 44 (autumn): 57.

Oshinsky, David M. 1996. *"Worse Than Slavery": Parchman Farm and the Ordeal of Jim Crow Justice.* New York: Free Press.

Paikos, Mike. 1993. *R&B Covers and Re-Recordings.* Moraga, Calif.: Michael Paikos.

Palmer, Robert. 1981a. *Deep Blues.* New York: Viking Press.

———. 1981b. "Furry Lewis: A Gentle Giant of Blues." *New York Times,* 23 September, sec. 3, p. 26.

Patterson, Neil. 1971. "Walter Horton." In *Nothing but the Blues: An Illustrated Documentary,* edited by Mike Leadbitter. London: Hanover Books.

Pearson, Barry L. 1990. *Virginia Piedmont Blues: The Lives and Art of Two Virginia Bluesmen.* Philadelphia: University of Pennsylvania Press.

Pomposello, Tom. 1990. "Mississippi Fred McDowell." In *Blues Guitar: The Men Who Made the Music.* San Francisco: GPI Books.

Powell, Richard, ed. 1989. *The Blues Aesthetic: Black Culture and Modernism.* Washington, D.C.: Washington Arts Project.

Price, Richard. 1990. *Alabi's World.* Baltimore: Johns Hopkins University Press.

Price, Richard, and Sally Price. 1991. *Two Evenings in Saramaka*. Chicago: University of Chicago Press.

Raichelson, Richard M. 1994. *Beale Street Talks: A Walking Tour Down the Home of the Blues*. Memphis: Arcadia Records.

"The River City Blues Festival." 1973. *River City Review* 3, no. 8: 1.

Roper, James. 1970. *The Founding of Memphis, 1818–1820*. Memphis: Memphis Sesquicentennial.

Rosenbaum, Art. 1983. *Folk Visions and Voices: Traditional Music and Song in North Georgia*. Athens: University of Georgia Press.

———. 1998. *Shout Because You're Free: The African American Ring Shout Tradition in Coastal Georgia*. Athens: University of Georgia Press.

Rowe, Mike. 1973. *Chicago Breakdown*. London: Eddison Press.

Rust, Brian. 1978. *Jazz Records, 1897–1942*, 4th ed. New Rochelle, N.Y.: Arlington House.

Ryan, Marc. 1992. *Trumpet Records: An Illustrated History with Discography*. Milford, N.H.: Big Nickel Publications.

Rye, Howard. 1996. *Laura Smith: Complete Recorded Works in Chronological Order, Vol. 1: 1924–1927*. Document CD 5429 liner notes.

Sacre, Robert, ed. 1987. *The Voice of the Delta: Charley Patton and the Mississippi Blues Traditions, Influences, and Comparisons: An International Symposium*. Liege, Belgium: Presses Universitaires Liege.

———, ed. 1996. *Saints and Sinners: Religion, Blues, and (D)evil in African-American Music and Literature: Proceedings of the Conference held at the Université de Liège (October 1991)*. Liège, Belgium: Société Liègeoise de Musicologie.

Sadie, Stanley, ed. 1984. *The New Grove Dictionary of Musical Instruments*. New York: Macmillan.

Salem, James M. 1999. *The Late Great Johnny Ace and the Transition from R&B to Rock 'n' Roll*. Urbana: University of Illinois Press.

Sampson, Henry T. 1980. *Blacks in Blackface: A Source Book on Early Black Musical Shows*. Metuchen, N.J.: Scarecrow Press.

———. 1988. *The Ghost Walks: A Chronological History of Blacks in Show Business, 1865–1910*. Metuchen, N.J.: Scarecrow Press.

Sapir, Edward. 1949. *Culture, Language, and Personality: Selected Essays*. Edited by David G. Mandelbaum. Berkeley: University of California Press.

Sawyer, Charles. 1980. *The Arrival of B. B. King: The Authorized Biography*. New York: Da Capo.

Schechter, John M. 1984. "Tiple." In *The New Grove Dictionary of Musical Instruments*. New York: Macmillan.

Schrodt, Helen, and Bailey Wilkinson. 1964. "Sam Lindsey and Milton Roby: Memphis Blues Musicians." *Tennessee Folklore Society Bulletin* 30, no. 2: 52–56.

Schuler, Vic, et al. 1951. "The Mystery of the Two Ma Raineys." *Melody Maker* 13 (October): 9.

Sharp, Cecil J. 1932. *English Folk Songs from the Southern Appalachians*, 2nd ed., edited by Maud Karpeles. London: Oxford University Press.

Shemanski, Frances. 1984. *A Guide to Fairs and Festivals in the United States.* Westport, Conn.: Greenwood.

Smith, Francis. 1971. "Hammie Nixon—Sleepy John Estes." In *Nothing but the Blues: An Illustrated Documentary*, edited by Mike Leadbitter. London: Hanover Books.

Sonnier, Austin, Jr. 1994. *A Guide to the Blues: History, Who's Who, Research Sources.* Westport, Conn.: Greenwood.

Spillers, Hortense J. 1985. "Kinship and Resemblances: Women on Women." *Feminist Studies* 11, no. 1 (spring): 111–25.

Springer, Robert. 1977. "I Never Did Like to Imitate Nobody." *Blues Unlimited*, no. 125 (July/August): 19–21.

Stephens, Cal. 1991. "Booker White on Bullet Williams." *78 Quarterly*, no. 6: 83–85.

Strachwitz, Chris. 1965. *Sky Songs.* Arhoolie LP 1019 liner notes.

———. 1994. *Mississippi Fred McDowell: You Gotta Move.* Arhoolie CD 304 liner notes.

Surge, Frank. 1969. *Singers of the Blues.* Minneapolis, Minn.: Lerner Publications.

Talley, Thomas W. 1991. *Negro Folk Rhymes.* 1922; reprint, Knoxville: University of Tennessee Press.

Thomas, William. 1981. "Furry Lewis, 88, Dies in Style of Bluesman." *Memphis Commercial Appeal*, 15 September, sec. 1A, 11A.

Titon, Jeff Todd. 1977. *Early Downhome Blues: A Musical and Cultural Analysis.* Urbana: University of Illinois Press.

Toll, Robert. 1974. *Blacking Up: The Minstrel Show in Nineteenth-Century America.* London: Oxford University Press.

Tremewan, Ed. 1995. "Van Zula Carter Hunt." *Blues and Rhythm: The Gospel Truth*, no. 102 (September): 10.

Trynka, Paul. 1996. *Portrait of the Blues.* New York: Da Capo Press.

Vass, Winifred Kellersberger. 1979. *The Bantu Speaking Heritage of the United States.* Los Angeles: Center for Afro-American Studies, University of California at Los Angeles.

Wardlow, Gayle Dean. 1998. *Chasin' That Devil Music: Searching for the Blues.* Edited by Ed Komara. San Francisco: Miller Freeman.

Welding, Pete. 1971. "Fred McDowell Talking." In *Nothing but the Blues: An Illustrated Documentary*, edited by Mike Leadbitter. London: Hanover Books.

———. n.d. *Shake 'Em On Down.* Fantasy CD 24703-2 liner notes.

West, Carroll Van, ed. 1998. *The Tennessee Encyclopedia of History and Culture.* Nashville: Tennessee Historical Society and Rutledge Hill Press.

Wharton, Vernon Lane. 1947. *The Negro in Mississippi, 1865–1890.* Chapel Hill: University of North Carolina Press.

Whitburn, Joel. 1996. *Top R&B Singles, 1942–1995.* Menomonee Falls, Wis.: Record Research, Inc.

Wilkins, Lane. 1995. *1964: To Profit a Man (Based on the Life and Times of Robert Timothy Wilkins Sr.).* Memphis: Museum Publishing.

Williams, Larry. 1965. "A Banjo in Hand and Tux in 'Yonder.'" Unidentified newspaper clipping, 21 November. In John Quincy Wolf Papers, Lyon College, Batesville, Arkansas.

Wilmer, Valerie. 1966. "Blues People: Fred and Roosevelt." *Jazz Journal,* no. 8 (August): 22–24.

Wolfe, Charles. 1981. "Sam McGee." In *Tom Ashley, Sam McGee, Bukka White: Tennessee Traditional Singers,* edited by Thomas G. Burton. Knoxville: University of Tennessee Press.

———. 1993. "A Lighter Shade of Blue: White Country Blues." In *Nothing but the Blues: The Music and the Musicians,* edited by Lawrence Cohn. New York: Abbeville Press.

Wolfe, Charles, and Kip Lornell. 1992. *The Life and Legend of Leadbelly.* New York: Harper Collins.

Woods, Clyde Adrian. 1998. *Development Arrested: The Blues and Plantation Power in the Mississippi Delta.* New York: Verso.

Worley, William S. 1998. *Beale St.: Crossroads of American Music.* Lenexa, Kansas: Addax Publishing Group.

Yale, Andrew. 1978. "Our Place Was Beale St." *Southern Exposure* 6, no. 3: 26–39.

Index